MRS *Catherine*
GLADSTONE

She was unquestionably a remarkable woman, and very few persons have spent a more unselfish life than she did, in actually striving to do good to others in the kindest possible way. Her first consideration was her husband — how to spare him and how to advise him to spare himself. Her second consideration was the poor and the sick; and her third consideration her friends.

(Sir Edward Hamilton (1847–1908) paid this tribute to Mrs. Gladstone at the time of her death. He was private secretary to Mr. Gladstone from 1880 to 1885 and retained links with the family even after being appointed as Permanent Secretary to the Treasury in 1885–1907. Under the pseudonym 'Nemo', Sir Edward published a diary of political gossip. Sir Edward died in 1908, unmarried.

MRS *Catherine* GLADSTONE

'A woman not quite of her time'

JANET HILDERLEY

THE *Alpha* PRESS

BRIGHTON • PORTLAND • TORONTO

2 4 6 8 10 9 7 5 3 1

First published 2013 in Great Britain in the United Kingdom by
THE ALPHA PRESS
PO Box 139   Eastbourne BN24 9BP

and in the United States of America by
THE ALPHA PRESS
920 NE 58th Ave Suite 300
Portland, Oregon 97213–3786

and in Canada by
THE ALPHA PRESS (CANADA)
8000 Bathurst Street, Unit 1, PO Box 30010, Vaughan, Ontario L4J 0C6

British Library Cataloguing in Publication Data
A CIP catalogue record for this book is available from the British Library.

Library of Congress Cataloguing-in-Publication Data
Hilderley, Janet.
Mrs. Catherine Gladstone : "a woman not quite of her time"/ Janet Hilderley.
p. cm.
Includes bibliographical references and index.
ISBN 978-1-898595-55-7 (pbk. : acid-free paper)
    1. Gladstone, Catherine Glynne, 1812–1900. 2. Gladstone, W. E. (William Ewart), 1809–1898. 3. Great Britain—History—Victoria, 1837–1901.
4. Prime ministers' spouses—Great Britain—Biography. 5. Great Britain—Politics and government—1837–1901. I. Title.
DA563.9.H55 2013
941.08109
[B]   2012029461

Types...   ...bourne.

Contents

CONTENTS

Preface

Working in the voluntary sector, often in old established charities, I came across the name of Mrs. Gladstone. I was intrigued. This was a woman who moved in the highest circles. She was married to one of the most interesting men of the age, produced eight children and yet managed to be a leading figure in the world of Victorian charity.

Catherine came alive for me when I began to read books written by those who knew her — Lord Morley's biography of Gladstone (1903); Mary Drew's life of her mother (1920); and Edwin A. Pratt's, *Catherine Gladstone: Life, Good Works and Political Efforts* (1898), which dealt mainly with her charitable activities. Comparing her experience with my own in the voluntary sector made me realize how much Catherine Gladstone influenced the social and political world around her.

Material taken from diaries and letters have been italicized in the text; quote marks are used to indicate direct quoted speech from these sources, and emphasize the vividness of the occasion or circumstance, such as at the end of Chapter 5 — Mary could be heard calling out, "Lavinia, we are going to Dizzy's party next Wednesday. Oh! It will be such fun!"

My thanks go to Mr. Charles Gladstone for the use of the portrait of Mrs. Gladstone on the front cover of the book, to Peter Francis, the Warden of Gladstone's Library, for answering endless questions and to the Reference Librarians of Guildford Public Library who obtained books for me from the British Library. My personal thanks go to Anne Bowerman for advice and support and to Steve Mitchell of Radstone Computer Services, who brought my script on Mrs. Gladstone into the IT age.

CHAPTER ONE

A Meeting, a Marriage and Rising Power

To 1840

BEGINNINGS

A non proposal

It was already midnight, this 3rd day of January 1839. A youngish man and woman stood close together, closer than politeness demanded. Friends and family tactfully disappeared, leaving the two alone, hidden in the haunting, mysterious shadows of the Coliseum in Rome. Recalling that night, Catherine wrote, *a soft clear light reflected on all around and gave the most beautiful effect.*

Despite all this, Mr. Gladstone did not propose

In such circumstances, a single gentleman should have done so. Gladstone continued addressing the loveliest woman of his age as if she were a public monument. Some said she was the image of George Romney's painting of *Lady Hamilton as Nature*, 1782. Looking across the ruins, he told her that sixty-thousand spectators had watched Christians being martyred — wild animals yowling for blood as creaking lifts brought gladiators up for the slaughter. Amongst all the jollity, slaves scattered sand dyed red, for even the Romans could not stand the sight of so much blood.

Nearly six foot Gladstone might be but Catherine Glynne looked him straight in the eye. He clutched his top hat to him, denting the high crown. Every so often he surreptitiously pulled his shirt collar away from rubbing his high cheek bones. Well brought up to be a lady at all times, Catherine could hardly ignore 'his perfectly proportioned body' of which some went so far as to describe '*as like a Greek god*'. Nevertheless it was covered by a fashionable tight coat and trousers. She wished to cry out, "William, I am tempted to throw my slipper at you!"

Gladstone talked on and on until the leaves on the olive trees began rustling. Through nooks and crannies, light crept menacingly through the old walls. Women came from nowhere, a motley sort, faces powdered with too much hare-foot, colour added to nipples and lips, eyes over bright with laudanum. And men emerging from the gaming clubs looked furtively around them, seeking further depravity. Gladstone, fascinated, placed Catherine's shawl around her shoulders. As a gentleman he did not touch her. A virgin, at twenty-nine, desperately fighting sexual frustration, Gladstone found the evening most unsettling. He wrote in his diary, *female society, whatever its disadvantages may be — has just and manifold uses attendant upon it in turning the mind away from . . . most dangerous and degrading temptations.* But Catherine noticed only the thinness of the women. She longed to gather them up, take them away and give them a good meal.

Miss Glynne

Some weeks later Gladstone explained to a friend, "I did not propose. I feared the romance of the setting might influence Miss Glynne's mind". His friend suspected that Gladstone misjudged his girl. She was an Earl's daughter, *whose beauty showed a profound intelligence.* A wealthy woman, Catherine Glynne lived at Hawarden, in North Wales, managing an estate of eight thousand acres with two castles. On a good day you could see, twenty miles away, the smoke-filled skies of Liverpool, where Gladstone grew up, son of a self-made business man.

The friend must have wondered if Gladstone knew he was one of many admirers, men of such renown: Seymour, Newark, Hill, Vaughan, Egerton, Anson, Lewis, Mordaunt and Harcourt. Catherine swept them all aside and, ignoring her Aunt Neville's advice, "It is not credible or lady-like to be what is called in love", fell passionately for Colonel Francis Harcourt. Society welcomed the engagement as most suitable — Harcourt, a handsome man, with all the right connections and, before him, an outstanding career. Shortly after their engagement, the Colonel met Lady Catherine Jenkinson, a daughter of the third Earl of Liverpool and one of Queen Victoria's ladies in waiting. Younger and prettier than Catherine Glynne, she set her cap at Harcourt. He married her immediately. Henry, her brother, said, "I do not envy him, though of course they are sure to be called the happiest of the happy." Nobody pointed out to Aunt Neville that she had strongly urged her niece to cultivate Lady Catherine's friendship, "I like you to have friends who are not missy or pushing . . . !"

Catherine never mentioned his name again

Jilted, aged nearly twenty-six, Catherine seemed to have no alternative but to remain alone. However, a happily-married friend foretold, *As surely as there is a God in Heaven so surely do I feel sooner or later he will reward you for all you have gone through so unrepiningly. There are blessings yet in store for one who has the blessings of so many on her head.*

Catherine did not believe her friend

On 23rd July 1838, at a breakfast in a house in Tilney Street, Park Lane, a clever hostess placed Catherine next to the brilliant Mr. William Ewart Gladstone, a man with a double-first from Oxford. A Classicist, he could speak Latin, Greek, Italian, French and German. By delivering a powerful speech to the Oxford Union in defence of Church and State, Lord Lincoln, the son of the powerful Duke of Newcastle, offered him a parliamentary seat in the rotten borough of Newark. With his father's support he entered the House of Commons. The great Parliamentarian, Sir Robert Peel, was beginning to notice this young man and Lord Macaulay described him as "the rising hope of the stern, unbending Tories". All looked set for Gladstone to have an illus-

trious career. He noted in his diary, *breakfasted with Miss Glynne.*
Catherine did not mention him in her diary.

Getting to know the Glynnes

On the advice of his doctors, a month later Gladstone set off
for a six-month tour of Southern Europe. His health and eyesight
had been impaired by too much study and reading by candle-
light. In the autumn of 1838, he was invited to join the Glynnes
in Nice. They were relaxing after struggling across half of Europe
in a Berliner, their rickety old coach, which had known better
days. Gladstone was a friend of Catherine's elder brother, Sir
Stephen, who was two years his senior and whom he had got to
know from school and student days. However, he had not met
Lady Glynne, and only one of the two famous *Pussies*, Catherine,
born in 1812, a month before Dickens. He did not know Mary,
two years younger than her sister, or twenty-eight year old Henry
who made up the rest of the family, a somewhat different personality from his brother, Stephen. He was a very masculine little
boy and was delighted at age seven when Mama took him out of
petticoats and put him into trousers. He spent much of his early
childhood with Catherine solemnly inspecting the wheels of the
family carriage.

The Glynnes spoke a private language, 'Glynnesse', amongst
themselves. As he became more involved with the family,
Gladstone struggled with the 'language' but never mastered it. He
met the Glynnes most days and spent Christmas day with them.
Widowed for twenty-one years, Lady Glynne lived a quiet life.
When she was young it was a different story. She was a daughter
of the formidable second Lord Braybrooke and Catherine
Grenville, and sister of the first Marquis of Buckingham. Mary
Neville was a granddaughter of George Grenville, the minister for
American taxation, and first cousin to the Younger Pitt. She was
also a niece of William, Lord Grenville, head of the cabinet of 'All
the Talents,' 1806, and in that year she married Sir Stephen
Glynne (Bart).

Gladstone would boast to his children, "Your Mama is related to five prime ministers: Right Hon. George Grenville, Sir William Wyndham, Lord Chatham, Mr. Pitt, and Lord Grenville." In 1868, he could add his own name to the list.

Lady Glynne — alone

A few years after his marriage, at thirty, Sir Stephen developed tuberculosis. Hoping for a cure, the couple took young Stephen with them and stayed for a time on the Riviera. In 1815, the year of Waterloo, Sir Stephen died in Paris, leaving his wife alone to cope with the traumas of the Hundred Days War. Lady Glynne bought a charger from Napoleon, the same horse that had carried him into the battle of Borodino. Clutching Stephen, the new Master of Hawarden, she rode through Lombardy, Switzerland and Holland back to her parents' home, Audley End, close to Billingham, Essex, and to safety. The horse was put out to grass, dying at Hawarden at a remarkable age.

After such an experience, Lady Glynne decided to remain a widow, dedicating the rest of her life to her four children. She said of Catherine, "At the age of three she is a magnificent specimen, with curly golden hair, a coaxing, passionate little Pussy. Sometimes she pretends to be feminine," saying, "Pussy so frightened." At five, *she reads nicely and begins to write. She knows a little French and geography and showed great pluck over the extraction of a double tooth.* Lady Glynne noted that six-year old Catherine "is much attracted by dress and finery, a beautiful child, but Mary may still grow up to be the prettiest." In January 1818, Lady Glynne wrote in her diary, *Catherine has been in several passions lately, the great punishment — dining by herself on Christmas Day.* Stephen's character his mother found the most interesting and unique. In April 1818, a French governess arrived who taught six-year old Catherine some manners. Mary, at seven, was found to be witty and entertaining. Very much part of village life, Lady Glynne's family accompanied her to the village school. Catherine remembered watching the children dancing the Mulberry dance. When she returned to the Castle she saw that *her peas were very much grown* and told how, "We went to Chester and had our hair cut." Occasionally, Lady Glynne took her children to France. She was described as "a very beautiful woman, possessed of character, activity of mind, with great charm". Lady Mary Glynne was insulted to receive a proposal of marriage. She had a sense of consecration and expected others to understand it.

The Glynne children — growing up

Her two daughters grew into beauties. Mary was the prettier with regular features but Catherine's exquisite colouring made her the beauty of the family. Like many young women of the day did she help to keep her complexion by mixing distilled rose-water and extract of juice of cucumber to 'enliven the skin'? Lady Glynne, clever and cultivated, oversaw her daughters' education. Governesses came and went. Some coped with Pussy's tantrums, others did not. Aunt Wenlock commented, "Catherine as a child was difficult to teach and was recalcitrant in learning any kind of lesson." Nevertheless, Catherine could speak French, Italian, knew Latin and had a remarkable memory for poetry. Above all, Lady Glynne instilled into her children a sense of noblesse oblige — Service to God and Duty above self.

The girls loved horse-riding and rode whenever they could. Catherine rode Fairy. Mary's mount, Dowager, was more sedate. Catherine swam in the sea before breakfast, something which she continued to do even when she was over eighty. She would have agreed with the author of *Sunday Evening, a Book for Girls* (1894), *Don't' be afraid of cold water, A good splash in it will make you all in a glow, and will go some way at least towards putting you in good spirits.* The girls were known for hunting, going to parties, balls, acting in amateur theatricals and being skilled archers, a sport which impressed the gentlemen and could be carried *on from childhood to green old age.* In damp weather, young ladies wore kid boots with cork soles, thus guarding against the harmful effects of standing on damp grass. The Miss Glynnes called on neighbours whom Catherine constantly shocked. Ever in a hurry, she rushed down corridors, often with hardly any clothes on, and, whilst washing, lent out of windows, much to the amusement of men working below. Mary, quieter and more reserved, behaved more circumspectly.

The mail-coach arrives

Four times a week there was excitement — "The mail-coach has arrived." Hawarden lay on the main road from Chester to Holyhead. A coachman recalled, "The village louts flung rubbish at my passengers." Lady Glynne stopped this and closed all the inns except the Glynne Arms. Chaperoned by sensible Henry, Catherine and Mary occasionally escaped from Mama and governesses via the mail-coach to 37 Berkeley Square, the Glynnes' London home. During the season they appeared at Court. As a very old woman, Queen Victoria remembered, *At York '31, I saw the very beautiful Miss Glynnes. I have not forgotten.* Like many aristocrats they continually journeyed from one great house to another such as Stowe, Audley End, and Hagley. The servants went with them. Catherine told of travelling, as a married woman, "seventeen of us in all, not counting the children".

When the girls were sixteen and fifteen respectively they visited Paris, with Mama, where Catherine played the piano under the direction of Franz Liszt, her senior by less than a year. They danced with the 'young bloods', attended the Opera and saw the Duc d'Orleans and the Duchess de Berri.

Catherine — the man of the family

In 1834, life changed dramatically for the Glynnes. Lady Glynne suffered a stroke. It left her a vague and forgetful invalid. Stephen, the heir, was an academic, mostly interested in music (in his lifetime he visited 5,500 churches and his notes remain the definitive study on the subject). As it was obvious he was unlikely to marry and showed no desire to manage the estate, the twenty-two year old Catherine 'became the man of the family'. She still found time to annoy the household as in sweeping leftovers from the table and delivering them to the poor.

Changes to society

The Glynnes followed the pattern of life for their class, a house in London and in the country. They enjoyed the London season. In the summer they escaped to Penmaenmawr, a seaside town in North Wales, twenty-five miles from Hawarden. Scotland beckoned in the autumn for hunting, fishing and shooting. For those comfortably-off folk, unable to face the dreariness of an English winter, the Continent appeared inviting. Like most of the upper-class the Glynnes were aware of strikes and unrest. Perhaps they were like many of the gentry, sympathetic. A man signing himself Captain Swing sent threatening letters to farmers, magistrates, parsons and other such people. *The Times* mentioned him on 21ˢᵗ October 1830. Unlike the Continent, England did not have a peasant class and about six million acres of the common land had become enclosed. Hatred built up against the tithe system, the Poor Law guardians and rich farmers. It was the latter who offered work. Rioting spread throughout the South of England and East Anglia and became known as the 'Swing Riots'. Some of the rioters were young married men who, before the poor harvests of 1829/30, had been stable characters. Machines, such as the new horse-powered threshing machine, threatened livelihoods. They needed fewer hands. The new employers used only casual labour, paid low wages and no longer offered 'living-in'. The workers demanded 2/3d per day in the winter and 2/6d per day during summer.

On 28th August 1830, on a Saturday night in East Kent, the first threshing-machine was destroyed and by October a further one hundred had been demolished. The rioters retaliated against what they saw as their oppressors. They maimed cattle, burned hay-ricks, destroyed machinery, attacked workhouses and even the tithe-barns which stored the produce, which yielded an annual income and of which one-tenth was taxed. If the rioters were caught they faced imprisonment, transportation and execution. One thousand, nine hundred and seventy-six came to trial, of which two hundred and fifty-two met the hangman.

The 1832 Reform Act

As no one day was designated for an election, it took place over a period of time. The 1831 general election was held between 28th April and the 1st of June. Lord Grey swept to power on a landslide victory for electoral reform. In 1832, after visiting Stephen in Oxford, Catherine, returning to Hawarden, found herself caught up among rioters. Earlier, Henry had written from one of the 'Swing' counties, Oxfordshire, *You have no idea of the noise, racket and din which is going on at the minute, what with bands of music, shouts and drunken men.* This was the year the *Representation of the People Act* was passed. It became known as the Great Reform Act. The old 'rotten boroughs', places with few inhabitants, gave way to the new industrial conurbations. Out of a population of fourteen million, one in six of the male population was now entitled to vote.

Railroads

Catherine became aware again of the way society was changing when her friend, Harriet Brooke, wrote to her, *On Tuesday, we prevailed upon Papa to let us have an expedition by railroad and most excellent fun we had. . . . we almost screamed with delight when the first engine came in sight.* They travelled about fifteen miles an hour to Liverpool from Chester. In 1829, the railway company organized a competition to find the most suitable locomotive to steam along their lines. Stephenson's 'Rocket' won. It *chugged-along for seventy miles, at fifteen miles an hour.*

In 1830, a rather shaken Uncle George, returning from the opening of the Liverpool to Manchester railroad, told Catherine that, "as Mr. Hoskisson, the former President of the Board of Trade and cabinet minister, stepped out of the train to greet the Duke of Wellington, tall and clumsy, he was knocked down and killed by a passing train." Catherine did not know then that her future father-in-law was one of the financiers of the project or that Thomas, Gladstone's brother, was sitting in the train as the Dart pulled it in the opposite direction, running over poor Mr. Huskinson in the process.

With Mr. Hoskisson's demise, John Gladstone declined to take his place as one of the M.P.s for Liverpool. Accident or no accident he continued to invest in the new railways and found the excursion trips especially profitable. They took people cheaply and quickly to the most popular form of entertainment — public executions.

Dalmeny House

In September 1837, Catherine, Stephen, Henry and Mary started on a round of visits to Scotland which would result in a useful friend for Catherine. They took the whole of the inside of the mail-coach, four inside, and eight other passengers rode 'atop'. Their luggage was carried in 'boots' at either end of the coach and the mail was piled high on the roof. The first week was spent at Dalmeny House, home of the Jewish Lord and Lady Rosebery. In the evenings, soirées were held. Lady Rosebery played the harp, her son, Bouverie, the cello, and the piano was played by the eldest, rather plain daughter, Louisa. She was to come out the next year. No mention is made of the heir, Archibald Primrose, who became the 5th Earl. He would become a close friend and colleague of Gladstone's, and the master-mind behind the Midlothian Campaign.

When Gladstone finally retired, it was Lord Rosebery who Queen Victoria chose to become Prime Minister. A clever man, in 1878 he married the twenty-seven year old Hannah Rothschild whose father, Meyer, left her Mentmore and a fortune of £2,000,000 in cash. Rosebery treated his wife badly even though he said at the time of his marriage, "She is simple, very unspoilt, very clever, very warm-hearted and very shy . . . I never knew such a beautiful character." Behind fans it was whispered, *"Lord Rosebery has homosexual inclinations and definitely prefers his collection of books to*

his own children." Nevertheless, Catherine's daughter Mary asked
him to be her daughter's godfather.

A 'perilous legacy'

On Thursday, 28th June 1838, when the tour of Scotland had
become something of a memory to the young Glynnes, a young
woman complained of being awoken at 4 o'clock in the morning
by *the guns in the Park, and could not get much sleep afterwards on account
of the noise of the people, bands etc. . . . Got up at 7.* In 1837, her Uncle
William IV had died leaving the young woman 'a perilous legacy'.
At the same time at 37, Berkeley Square, Catherine and Mary were
dressing their hair because, "we must be in the Abbey by eight".
It was Queen Victoria's coronation day. In the evening, in
Devonshire House, at a fancy dress ball, the young Glynnes danced
the night away. Whilst Catherine danced the gavotte under the
chandeliers, the Victorian age began. She did not know then that
she would marry a man who would be a major player in this the
greatest age Britain would ever know.

The moment in 1839 when Mr. Gladstone fell in love with Miss Glynne

Herewith the background of the family which Gladstone joined
in Naples, so very different from his own, a Liverpool boy, the son
of a self-made man. He met the Glynnes nearly every day and they
called him 'Gia'. He spent Christmas Day with them and found
himself acting as escort to the two *Pussies.* Catherine became fascinated by the old buildings, especially the Church of Santa Maria
Maggiore. As she stood before the altar, looking up awestruck at
the gilded and jewel encrusted Madonna, a group of well dressed
people gathered around. A few scruffy children approached, palms
outstretched. Catherine turned to Gladstone, "Do you think we
can be justified in indulging ourselves in all these luxuries?" He
wrote in his diary, *I loved her for this question.*

Besotted as Gladstone was with Catherine he had a book to
revise, *The State in its Relations with the Church.* When it was finally

finished he gave a copy to her. Even Gladstone admitted it was *stern stuff*. She read every single word of it. As in childhood, she copied parts of it, learning passages by heart. For a woman who, in adulthood, rarely opened a newspaper or read a book, it was a remarkable achievement. Sir Robert Peel, the great Tory leader and Gladstone's future boss, asked, "With such a career before him why does he want to write books?"

A proposal

Brought up in a man's world and unused to the ways of women, Gladstone could not bring himself to ask Catherine to marry him. Thinking himself in love twice before, he had proposed to two young women, scaring them half to death, so much so that they rushed into marriage with other men. This time Gladstone considered it wiser to write a letter. On the night of 17th January 1839, he wrote from 62, Piazza di Spagna and, putting his considerable intellect to the fore, he debated the pros and cons of marriage. A hundred years later Prime Minister Attlee came across the letter: "Fancy writing a letter proposing marriage which included a sentence of a hundred and forty words all about the Almighty". When Catherine finally came to the end she read, *I am, Yours, W.E. Gladstone.*

The following day Gladstone received a reply. As an unattached lady should, Catherine stressed she was unaware of Mr. Gladstone's affections. She asked for time to consider his kind offer. However, February was fast approaching and it was imperative Gladstone returned to London for the start of the new parliamentary year. Already, his foot was placed firmly on the bottom rung of the political greasy pole. He was a trusted lieutenant of Sir Robert Peel and served under him in several junior ministerial posts. Also Gladstone knew he had many formidable rivals for the hand of Catherine.

And he would have been startled to learn that his rivals included the young Jew — Benjamin Disraeli

They met at a dinner. In his diary Gladstone mentioned many of the guests but said not a word about the young author of a best-selling 'silver spoon' novel, *Vivian Grey*. Disraeli, in a letter to Sarah, his sister, names 'young Gladstone'. He condemned the dinner as dull and declared that, "a swan very white and tender, stuffed with truffles, was the best company at the table." Gladstone read Disraeli's books but failed to recognize *the spirit of whim in them, the ironic solemnity, the historical paradoxes, the fantastic glitter of dubious gems, the grace of high comedy, all in union with a social vision that often pierced deep below the surface.*

As a young Jew, Disraeli's father had him, at the age of thirteen, baptised. Rising in society, he later changed his name from the family one of d'Israeli to the more Anglo-Saxon sounding, Disraeli. At the time of the dinner Disraeli was recovering from bad investments. He had speculated in South-American mining companies; the bubble burst leaving him deeply in debt which would trouble him into old age. This, together with sympathy for working-class movements, such as the Chartists, and a very public affair, with a mother of four, Lady Henrietta Sykes, made society uneasy about him. Prince Albert considered Disraeli, "not quite a gentleman". As Disraeli enjoyed the favours of Lady Sykes, so did the Tory Lord Chancellor, Lord Lyndhurst, a man of whom Walter Bagehot said, "fewer men have led a laxer life . . . but there was no laxity in his intellectual life".

As the House of Commons was being rebuilt, on the 7th December 1837 Disraeli gave his maiden speech in the Court of Requests on Parliamentary elections in Ireland, a subject about which he knew little. The House was in a restless mood and began baiting him, "Old Clothes sit down," "Take a bite of pork." Gladstone would come to consider Disraeli "one of the greatest parliamentarians of our times". Suddenly, the young Jew raised his right arm aloft. The House surprised, went silent. Disraeli knowing he now had their full attention, bellowed, "Though I sit down now, the time will come when you will listen to me." A fellow M.P. whispered, "I believe we will." As he would do in the future, Disraeli turned on his heel, ignoring them all, and stalked out of the chamber. If Gladstone ever told Catherine about the speech, it is doubtful whether she would have expected Disraeli to become, "William's deadliest rival?"

But the mocking, taunting, and amused Mr. Disraeli, who saw life as a comedy, was way into the future. They were all still young then. In May, Catherine and her family returned to Berkeley Square. 'Gia' was once again welcomed into their inner circle and swept into gaieties, dinner parties, balls and studios, all so loved by Catherine but not so much by Gladstone. Unlike many upper-class women of the day, she wore simple gowns, mostly made by her lady's maid, with little jewellery, usually a single rose clipped onto a sapphire blue dress, matching her eyes exactly. Her maid, who received Mistress's cast-offs, would have preferred something more exotic.

In fact Catherine began to be seen so much in Gladstone's company Stephen was forced to write to him, *it is impossible for me to see the interest you take in my sister's society without feeling deep anxiety* . . . Gladstone replied on 27th May, "What I ask for is next to impossible". Catherine had told him, "I have only half a heart to give to any man."

On 8th June, Gladstone and Catherine attended Lady Shelley's garden party, in the pretty little village of Fulham. The two strolled by the river alone. As they wandered along, Gladstone explained how he longed to be a clergyman in the Church of England. Sadly, his father said, "Not suitable," and Gladstone heard God calling him to enter politics. God explained it, in this way; Gladstone could do HIS will more effectively. Privately, one suspects, Catherine disagreed with God. Her William would have made an outstanding Archbishop of Canterbury. A deeply religious woman, she would have prayed on the matter and, with God's help, settled for Gladstone becoming Prime Minister — four times and the greatest mind of his age.

A deranging incident

Gladstone explained that, during the walk, a deranging incident occurred. Catherine agreed to marry him. Everybody was delighted. On 17th June, the family was surprised again. In the drawing room of the Glynnes' London home, Mary agreed to marry Lord Lyttelton of Hagley Hall near Birmingham. In 1837, he had become the 4th Baron. Gladstone described the twenty-one year old as *a very noble and powerful creature*. He was seized by Gladstone, who was waiting downstairs, and dragged by him down on to his knees, "so together we can give thanks to Almighty God". They had much in common. Both men had been to Eton and Oxbridge. George, too, was a classical scholar. He won the Craven Scholarship and emerged top of the Classical Tripos.

Only a month before, Mary had refused his offer sharply. Four years before she had declined a very prestigious proposal. The Glynnes began to fear marriage was not for Mary. They may have agreed with Queen Victoria who advised her daughter Vicky, "Being married gives one one's position which nothing else can." At the beginning of July, three weeks before the wedding, villagers were startled to see Gladstone and Lyttelton arriving to stay in the same house as their brides at Hawarden Castle. Gladstone travelled part of the journey by train and was annoyed by dust from the engine getting into his eyes. As the two men walked down the village street, Gladstone tall and upright and Lyttelton, short and graceless, a passer-by commented, "It is easy to see which is the Lord." Casual to absurdity, George once climbed in the Highlands in his slippers.

Whilst organizing a double wedding, Gladstone and Catherine distributed two hundred waistcoats and bed gowns for the elderly poor of the Parish. They dithered about having the banns called. The Rector was relieved when they decided not to — this really was for lesser folk. Suddenly, the real world impinged itself on these young people. The weddings were nearly postponed. A mob calling themselves Chartists attacked Hagley, George's Worcestershire home.

The wedding of the two Miss Glynnes

On 25th July 1839, Catherine and Mary, dressed in white, accompanied by bridesmaids wearing peach muslin, stepped into the wedding carriages, followed by twelve other carriages. The band of the Oddfellows led the way as the carriages rumbled through the park, skirting Y Garthddin, the ruined castle, over grass, along the moat, through arches of laurels and flowers and down the village street, flags flying from every cottage. Children strewed flowers in their way while the church bells rang out. The procession halted in front of the little medieval church of St Dieniol's, still standing after nearly a thousand years, on the hillock above the sands of Dee. Finally, drawing up the rear in their own pony cart came Mr. Whittingham, the butler, and Mrs. Hands, the housekeeper, who had known Miss Catherine and Miss Mary all their lives.

Lady Glynne's brother, Uncle George, the Rev. Hon. George Neville Grenville, the former rector of Hawarden and now the Dean of Windsor, married Gladstone and Catherine first. The festivities over, *the nobility and gentry who had honoured the occasion partook of an elegant dejeuner in the Castle. In the evening villagers sat down to dine at the Glynne Arms and toasted the young couples. One hundred and twenty pounds had been raised in order for the orphans and widows to join in the celebrations.* Catherine and Gladstone spent their honeymoon night at Norton Priory, Cheshire, lent to them by an old family friend, Sir Richard Brooke. The Lytteltons journeyed to Hagley. The following morning, Gladstone and Catherine rose early and read the Bible together. They agreed, "the daily practice of which we trust will last as long as our joint lives". Many years later their daughter, Mary Drew, wrote that Gladstone, commenting on his new wife, said "nearly every hour, convinces me of the brightness of my treasure" and often said, throughout their married life, how his Cathie for ever twinkled. A friend had observed, "Gladstone has the nature of a Scotsman but the passion of an Italian."

A fortnight later both couples returned to Hawarden for the

servants' ball. On 13th August, they set out on a tour of Scotland by sea to Greenock, driving through Loch Katrine, Trossachs, Glencoe, Inveraray, Dunkeld, Taymouth, Aberferfeldy and Blairgrove, staying at inns along the way. Henry Reeve, editor of the *Edinburgh Review*, rambling through the wild passes of Inversnaid, was startled to come across two striking young women, mounted on Highland ponies, dressed in the Lennox tartan. *A prettier happier party never crossed the heather.* He guessed they were the Hawarden brides and on returning home told his wife and family all about it, stressing that Sassenachs should not wear the Lennox tartan. Neither party bothered over much about another marriage which took place. In the evening of 28th August 1839, a middle-aged Mrs. Wyndham-Lewis wrote, in her account book, *Dear Dizzy became my husband.* Under the In-hand column she wrote: £300. Outgoings: Gloves 2/6d.

Fasque and honeymoon

Finally, the party arrived at the small village of Fettercairn. The couples made their way up the village street to one of the grand houses at the top of the hill, Fasque, which in Gaelic means 'safety'. On the other side of the road stood Fettercairn House, home of a branch of the Queen Mother's family, the Bowes-Lyons. The Gladstones' carriage rumbled along the avenue of beech trees leading to the eighteenth-century house. The older house on the site had been pulled down fifty years before. In 1829, John Gladstone bought Fasque and its estate for £80,000. He improved and castellated the sandstone building until, with a great deal of effort, it seemed from the outside like a castle. Four years later, in one of the worst winter storms ever remembered, John Gladstone, his wife and daughter Helen moved from living in Seaforth, on the edge of the Mersey, where wild roses still grew, into Fasque. As they did so, many of the huge trees, which had stood for over a hundred years, crashed down.

Shortly after the young couple arrived, Stephen joined them and the group explored the surrounding beauty spots, busy and alive

as only young people can be. They played billiards and chess with
Gladstone's family. Gladstone always won. They tried playing
whist. The Gladstones were experts — none of the non-family
members ever won. Gladstone, who always wished to improve
every moment of every hour read, to Catherine, the latest religious
work, *Anfange der Christlichen Kirche*, the Bishop of London on
education, novels by Sir Walter Scott and Charles Dickens's
Nicholas Nickleby. He observed "Its length will, we fear sink it —
in tone very human — he is most happy in the touches of pathos.
The motives of the book are not those of religion." Gladstone took
Catherine into his book-lined study in one of the turrets. Even
when he was not there, nobody used the room. He showed her
around the village and introduced her to the shop where he ordered
and bought numerous books.

Together they visited the whiskey-making distillery which his
father part-owned. Gladstone asked if she wished to walk to the
railway station. "It is only fifteen miles away. I do it regularly."
Catherine declined. Meanwhile George and Mary had left to stay
for a short time with a distant relative, the Duke of Devonshire, at
Chatsworth. The sisters wrote to each other daily.

Proudly, John Gladstone showed his new daughter-in-law his
treasures. They included the Cantilever staircase, the most magnificent in any of the stately homes of Scotland. He explained that
nearly all the Dutch, Flemish, Italian and British Old Masters
lining the walls and the antiques and objects d'art scattered around
were purchased by William and John Neilson during their grand
tour of 1832. With pride, he showed Catherine a Roman marble
table leg. Slightly embarrassed, John Gladstone told his daughter-
in-law, "I had to rely on my sons making the purchases for me as
I really have little proper education for such things". He explained
to Catherine how he had told his sons his wish, "for my money to
be well invested".

In May 2008, Christie's estimated that the contents of Fasque
were worth at least a million pounds.

When the leaves began to turn and autumn approached, the

Lyttletons felt the pull of home and hurried back to Hagley leaving Catherine, for the first time in her life, without her sister. Alone, she came to terms with her in-laws, a frightening prospect at the best of times.

John Gladstone

Gladstone's father was an awe-inspiring man. Catherine wrote to her mother *The old father becomes awfully cross if anyone is late for prayers.* John Gladstone ran an East India House. His enormous wealth came from trading in corn with the United States and cotton in Brazil. It was said he was worth £502,500. This was a man used to working among belching fires while children crawled under whirling machines, unlike Catherine's world — established, ordered, 'knowing one's place,' the great looking after the weak. It was being threatened by the railway lines crisscrossing the countryside, threatening the hunting, fishing and shooting pastimes of the aristocracy together with a dreadful thought: Would the hoi-polloi soon start strutting their way across 'My Lord's lands?'

John Gladstone's world was a competitive place, 'dog eat dog'. And Catherine knew that places like Birmingham, Manchester and Liverpool encroached daily, bricks stealthily crossing fields, swallowing up villages, changing centuries' old ways of life, everlastingly challenging her sort. She tried to forget that her father-in-law had made money from this new form of wealth. As his power grew, John Gladstone acquired large sugar and coffee plantations in the West Indies, Jamaica, British Guiana and Demerara. In 1807, the slave-trade had been abolished. A man of some compassion, John Gladstone had always refused to ship his slaves from Africa, and instead bred them in-house. In Demerara, during 1823, the slaves rioted. One of Sir John's plantations was right in the centre of it all. Within three days the revolution had been stamped out. Fifty Africans were hanged and many were shot; others were whipped.

In a pamphlet to Sir Robert Peel, John Gladstone explained that

Africans were happier being forced to work and that their labour was essential to the well-being of the colonies. Who was he to question the will of divine Providence which had set the African races under the domination of the white man? They possessed the intelligence of a not over-bright small child and, though in human form, were not *created in the image of God*. He hinted that the British public would be better looking at the conditions of the lower classes than Africans in the colonies. An average price paid for a slave in Demerara was £114.11.51/2d. When emancipation came in 1826, John Gladstone received over seventy-five thousand pounds for 1,609 slaves. Ruthless, as always, when trade with Indian and China opened up, John Gladstone's was the first ship to sail into Calcutta.

John Gladstone, during his fight for power, made sure he made friends with people of influence. He became well-connected. His friends included the Prime Minister, Sir Robert Peel, and the Duke of Newcastle. These gentlemen helped him become M.P. for Lancashire from 1818 until 1827. Gladstone described his father as "an active and effective local politician". Sir John understood this new age, and the growing importance of the media. He had interests in the *Liverpool Courier*, a useful contact for his son. But Westminster was not his world. The North was his battleground. Sir Robert Peel, whose father came from a similar background, created John Gladstone a baronet in 1846. Proudly, the old man enjoyed being known as Sir John. He had mentioned to Sir Robert that, "I differed from you over the injurious consequences of the Corn Laws." Sir Robert replied, "It makes no difference. You are truly worthy of such illustration as an hereditary honour can confer."

John Gladstone knew that when Catherine wrote a letter to the great and the good, the reply came immediately. Catherine's ancestors arrived with the Conqueror. On her family tree she could trace crusaders on both sides of her parentage and one ancestor lay buried under the altar of St Margaret's Church, Westminster. John Gladstone knew that hanging in Windsor Castle was a portrait by

Sir Anthony Van Dyke of Venetia Stanley, Lady Digby, a beauty at the Stuart Court, and a granddaughter of Henry Percy, 8th Earl of Northumberland. The lady died in her bed, in mysterious circumstances, and was Catherine's great-great-great-grandmother. His fourth son had done well, 'marrying her'. In fact Gladstone had married into the *Grand Whiggery* and even gained admittance to Chatsworth and into the presence of the Duke of Devonshire himself.

Catherine and John Gladstone agreed on one point — at all times and in all places they would further William's career

But Catherine could never really appreciate the fight her father-in-law had for his sons to become gentlemen. At twenty-three, John Gladstone journeyed to Liverpool and settled there, discreetly dropping the 's' of his surname. His six children were born in the merchant area of Liverpool at 6 Rodney Street. Gladstone laughingly told her how he had given his maiden speech there. He was three when his father introduced him to the politician, George Canning, one of the greatest orators of his age, *An Irishman born in London*. Until his early death, Canning never forgot the clever little boy who stood on a chair and said solemnly, "Ladies and Gentlemen, I wish to say . . . " Gladstone, commenting on his father, wrote *none but his children know what torrents of tenderness flow from his heart.*

George Canning

Canning may have been amused to learn that the little boy became prime minister four times. As the son of an actress, deserted by her husband, he had little chance of doing so. It was whispered in the corridors of power, "A son of an actress is ipso-facto disqualified from becoming prime minister." He held many senior appointments including that of foreign secretary. Canning was friends with many men of prominence, including the playwright Richard Brinsley Sheridan. He did become Prime Minister but by this time his health had weakened. He died in 1827, in Chiswick, in the same room as James Fox. He was only fifty-seven and had held office for a hundred and nineteen days. But, whenever Gladstone crossed Parliament Square he saw the statue of George Canning, a man who might in different circumstances have become one of the country's greatest prime ministers. He is also remembered for fighting a duel with a rival, Lord Castlereagh, on Putney Heath. George III suggested that both men should leave office! Some years later Castlereagh committed suicide.

John Gladstone's background

John Gladstone's own father had been born in Leith in 1764. He was the second child of Thomas Gladstones, corn merchant, Whig, Elder of the Church of Scotland. The family had come a long way since being the Gleestones, crofters scratching a living from the poor soil of the Borders. John Gladstone remembered selling corn in his father's shop. Only five years after arriving in Liverpool, he married well. She was Jane Hall, the daughter of a Liverpool merchant. After six years she died childless. Two years later John Gladstone married again — this time to Anne Mackenzie Robertson, the straight-laced daughter of the Provost of Dingwall, Rosshire, a man trained as a solicitor, who despised John Gladstone's lack of education but admired his business acumen. Despite being an invalid and lying on a chaise-lounge for most of her life, Anne produced six children in twelve years. She died in the autumn of 1835, aged sixty-three, leaving her children with a deeply ingrained sense of sin. Gladstone wrote at the time of his mother's death, *I looked up at the moon . . . it froze my heart.*

Catherine was to discover it was not only Mrs. Gladstone who was slightly neurotic. In 1802 she gave birth to her first child, Anne, a delicate little girl, pious, gentle, who drifted into becoming a semi-invalid. She was not only Gladstone's protector but his godmother. At twenty-seven Anne departed this world. She left her brother able to talk to his father and completely unable to communicate with his mother or the rest of the family. As a young man, Gladstone's view of women was coloured by his two delicate 'mothers'. On their honeymoon he looked at his resting *Cathie.* He wrote. *She sleeps gently like a babe. May I never disturb her precious peace!*

He did not. Gladstone read *The Taming of the Shrew* before their marriage. Gentle and serene Catherine might be but she was an Earl's daughter, used to her own way. If he needed to, he soon learned to respect her as an individual and her unconscious streak of independence. Catherine noted in her diary, *how every day that passes impresses me with the treasure I am blessed with but also how far I am behind him.*

Thomas

The eldest son was Thomas (Tom), the heir. He, of course, enjoyed most of his father's attention. All his life he resented being sent and made to stay at Eton. The College did not suit his temperament. The Windsor and Slough coaches used to stop under its walls, to watch the boys 'slaughtering each other'. Gladstone fagged for his brother and thoroughly enjoyed his six years there. He left Eton in 1827, complaining "Melancholy that departure is" and went up to Oxford. He upset Tom by achieving a double first and setting out on a great career. Tom became Tory M.P. for Portarlington. In 1833 William joined him in Parliament. In his maiden speech Gladstone spoke for his father, and his kind, opposing the Abolition of Slavery Bill. He received Sir Robert Peel's congratulations. Thomas later complained that, as soon as Gladstone began climbing the greasy pole, he began ignoring his own family. Sir Robert offered Gladstone a junior Lordship in the Treasury. In 1835, he became Under-Secretary for War and the Colonies. Peel had a reputation for being a brilliant administrator but was considered stiff, cold and reserved.

Peel's father, too, was a self-made man. Like John Gladstone's, the family had originally been cotton-weavers. As a factory owner, Peel's father treated the many young children who worked for him with great kindness. However, when they clambered under the machines, he ignored the danger they were in. Robert senior sent his eldest son to Harrow, where Lord Palmerston was a senior boy, together with the young Lord Byron, a year below Peel, who went up to Christchurch, Oxford, and achieved outstanding academic success. While he was there, Peel studied law which helped to make him a powerful adversary. Gladstone enjoyed his 'boss's brain and kindness' which he showed to few men. He also appreciated Sir Robert's ability to say one word when many others would have had to use half a dozen.

Robertson

Robertson, the next son, was a different 'animal' to Gladstone. He was a bear of a man — 6ft 5" tall, weighing 350 pounds. He did not have his father's dominating ways or his elder brother's rigid stubbornness. But John Gladstone saw in his second son sound business sense. He therefore did not waste money paying for an academic education. Instead, he sent Robertson to the practical Glasgow College. John Gladstone was right. Robertson succeeded in business, becoming Lord Mayor of Liverpool. Catherine found Robertson the most obliging of the brothers. He lent her his carriage whenever she wished to go shopping. But she rarely did so for herself, usually only for others. Gladstone, unsuccessful in finding a wife, opposed Tom and Robertson's plans for marriage, until his father told him sharply, "Mind your own business and get on with your own life," which he did.

John Neilson

John Neilson, the third brother, was Catherine's favourite. When he came to stay, she described it as 'a break', 'Glynnese' for pleasurable. She found him agreeable, stable and sensible. Ignoring his father's wishes to send him to Eton, he enlisted in the Royal Navy. At thirteen he joined the Royal Naval College, Portsmouth, and rose to the rank of captain. By the time John Neilson met Catherine, his naval career was over and he farmed successfully in Wiltshire.

It was difficult for John Gladstone to acknowledge that the son who possessed genius was not his heir but his fourth son, William, in some ways a slow developer whom he had always rather overlooked. His other two elder sons also stood for Parliament but lost their seats. However, John Gladstone soon learned that his latest daughter-in-law possessed *a profound intelligence.*

As John Gladstone's business improved, he moved his family, in 1815, to more-up-market Seaforth. He bought a fine mansion built at the mouth of the Mersey. Since the death of his second wife, John Gladstone lived alone in Fasque, except for the company of his youngest child, Helen. A young woman, almost as bright as Gladstone but, as a female, it was not thought necessary to educate her. Gladstone did not act as if he thought women were second-class citizens but "saw no evidence of a struggle in the female mind against the impediments of its condition".

Helen

Helen was attractive, lively and difficult. Her father and brothers longed to see her married and settled down. Tom, too, had suffered in his twenties from depression. The family doctor, Dr. Jepherson of Leamington Spa, advised a rigid routine of cold showers, hot baths, vigorous exercise and a plain, strict diet. This he recommended for all conditions. In 1838, Helen visited Ems, the spa town in Prussia on the River Lahn. The waters were seen as beneficial, especially to women of a nervous and highly strung disposition. While travelling in Europe, with his mind beginning to concentrate on Catherine, Gladstone received a letter. It was from Helen.

She told her brother she had met a Count Leon Sollohub, a member of a wealthy Russian/Polish family, and had become engaged to him. "One of the first things about him that pleased me was he reminded me of you . . . although much fatter." Gladstone sent advice and decided not to become involved. When he learned the Count had served in the Polish Revolution but left when he proved unequal to all its fatigues, he suspected the man was as neurotic as his sister. The Sollohubs demanded Helen came to Russia to live and also to become a member of the Russian Orthodox Church. To the relief of the Count's family, the romance foundered. Helen returned to Fasque, lonely, bored and frustrated. Her father did not allow her to become the mistress of Fasque. Instead he dominated his daughter as if she were a wilful child.

Helen's maid hinted, "Mistress is taking opium." Deeply, unhappy, Helen was forced to face a radiant Catherine who, nevertheless, complained, "I have felt poorly for about six days." She discovered she was suffering from morning sickness. Catherine whispered to Gladstone, "I shall have to let out my sash shortly". She found it helped to take a little bread and milk before retiring. Her back was painful. To relieve it, she "bobbed in and out of a cold hip bath and, sponged her chest, arms and throat in the cold water".

Returning to Hawarden

Christmas was approaching. It was time to leave Fasque and return to Hawarden. On the way they visited several old friends including an old flame of Gladstone's, Lady Milton, née Lady Frances Morton. She was the eldest daughter of the Earl and Countess of Morton. He had met her in her father's town house in Edinburgh. Two years before, Gladstone had proposed to her. Tactlessly, he told Catherine how pleased he was to see how marriage had matured her and improved her looks. Catherine retaliated by telling Gladstone about her numerous conquests. The list went on and on. As Aunt Neville once observed sourly, "Pussy is a sad flirt". Even somebody as innocent as Gladstone must have wondered how far Miss Glynne went with Colonel Harcourt!

On Christmas Eve, Gladstone and Catherine reached Hawarden where they found Mary and Lyttelton to greet them. Lord and Lady Brabazon, who considered themselves to be the young Glynnes' guardians, were also part of the party. Already Ireland was a discussion point. Gladstone talked about Ireland and the Irish Church

and noticed that "Lady Brabazon was the prettiest sight possible.
. . . In short most characteristically feminine." Mary had news as
well. She, too, was pregnant. Together, the young couples
welcomed in 1840. The honeymoon period over, married life
began in earnest. Catherine travelled with Mary and Lyttelton and
stayed with them at Hagley. Gladstone did not go with her. She
cried, "A week's parting stings".

On 27th January Catherine and Gladstone came to London to
stay with John Gladstone at 6 Carlton Gardens. Gladstone looked
for a home and furniture for his wife and new baby. Perhaps the
old man began noticing his youngest son growing away from him.
However, they were too busy to listen to the latest gossip. On 16th
December 1839, the Foreign Secretary, the fifty-five year old
'Cupid' Palmerston, married his mistress of thirty years, the newly
widowed, fifty-two year old Lady Cowper. Society said she was
marrying beneath her. "Was she not a Lady-in-Waiting,
exchanging the rank of countess for that of a mere viscountess?"
Lord Melbourne, Lady Cowper's brother, was the Queen's father-
figure and had her ear. He most certainly disapproved of the
marriage. Palmerston was deeply in debt and a philanderer. "Once,
while staying at Windsor, he had taken a fancy to one of the
Queen's ladies-in-waiting and wandered into her room, in the
middle of the night, just before his wedding, too." He said, "Sorry,
I mixed up the bedrooms." Nobody, of course, believed him except
Prince Albert!

13, Carlton House Terrace

After tough negotiating, Gladstone purchased 13, Carlton
House Terrace in a quiet cul-de-sac close to John Gladstone and
ten minutes walk from the House of Commons. Gladstone undertook the project in a spirit of seriousness, saying "Except the Lord
build the house, their labour is but lost that build it." Society
thought it too grand a home for such a young couple but Lady
Glynne required a London base as did the Lytteltons. Tired and
heavily pregnant Catherine might be but she still had to turn 13,

Carlton House Terrace into a home! On 26th March, she proudly announced the first book-case was in place. Gladstone told everybody, "Beauty is beauty even in furniture," and started collecting ivories and china. He also bought paintings, becoming quite a connoisseur, something which he had in common with Sir Robert, who was considered an expert. John Gladstone had promised, "William when you marry I will provide a house and increase your allowance to £2,000 per annum."

The servants

Without labour-saving devices, numerous servants had to be found. The grapevine remained the best method of doing so. Rosina Harrison, in her book *Rose*, about her years in service, writes, *by now I was well enough known to the staffs of the big houses to be able to put the word round that I was thinking of making a change.* Woe betide any employer who was placed on the servant blacklist. Staff could also be hired via servant registries. These sometimes printed advertisements which listed servants available for work. Disreputable agencies could charge fees up front and later fail to find the person a position or even an interview. It was essential for a potential servant to have good references. All this was time-consuming.

The usual rate of pay was twelve to fifteen pounds a year for a lady's maid and a footman received fifteen to twenty-five pounds a year. Reduced rates, 'board wages', were paid if and when the employers were away. The Disraelis found it difficult to find good staff because they often fled to the Continent to avoid Disraeli's creditors. 'As man does not live by bread alone,' the spiritual and intellectual needs of servants had also to be catered for. Gladstone selected personally the books for the servants' library and joined Catherine in interviewing the staff. She noted in her everyday book, *engaged a cook — after a long talk on religious affairs — between William and her.*

In the case of the Gladstones, if a male servant misbehaved, he was taken for a walk by 'Master'. Mile after mile, he received the attention of Gladstone's tremendous mind telling him, "Jesus is grieved and wounded when we do wrong." Catherine may have wondered if 'the second footman' understood a word Master said. They rarely dismissed a servant and if they did, it was never at the 'fag end' of the season. Staff could be dismissed with either a month's notice or a month's wages. If a servant had committed a serious offence, this would entail instant dismissal. One serious offence was to catch the eye. A boy of ten, working at Windsor, remembered when the quality walked by, "I hid behind a curtain or shrank into the wall, because . . . but the old Queen, she nodded and smiled. They say she rarely laughed. She did you know, quite often, a tinkling, silvery sound. I hear it still."

A great deal of thought went into household rules and regulations. Gladstone and Catherine started the day with prayer. Gladstone then read a passage from the Bible. Later in the morning, master, mistress, guests, servants and children assembled for family prayers. On Sunday evening he wrote a short address for evening prayers. Gladstone taught in St Martin's in the Fields Sunday School. Both Mr. and Mrs. Gladstone were well aware of their parish duties, calling regularly on the sick and the needy and giving meals, in the grounds of their home, to the Sunday school children. Catherine said, somewhat ungrammatically, "I am rather full of getting up a Visiting Lady Society."

'Two Cherries on a Stalk'

In fact, Catherine and Gladstone seemed to be so much as one, Bishop Wilberforce remarked, "They are like two cherries on a stalk." If so, they were very different cherries and both had been used to having their own way. On Monday, at 1 P.M. on 10th February 1840, in the Chapel Royal at Windsor, another young man married a strong-willed woman. The Queen married her Albert. She did not wear silver, the traditional colour for a royal bride but white. The Queen ordered that the lace for the dress should be made in a village close to Honiton, Devon. The cost was over a thousand pounds. A declining industry, it saved the lace-

makers from destitution that winter. When Catherine met the
Prince at a City dinner, she was amazed at how handsome he was.
Gladstone preferred to dine with Catherine but as a young M.P.
he was not grateful for 'the high honour' of being admitted to
Grillion's dining club, Greenwich, "because the rules of the society
oblige me to submit, a thing quite alien to my temperament,
which requires more soothing and domestic appliances after the
feverish and consuming excitements of party life". This June
evening he was dining with the Speaker and reported, "Great
merriment; and an excellent speech from Stanley, good sense and
good nonsense and a modest one from Morpeth. But though we
dined at six, these expeditions do not suit me. I am ashamed of
paying £2.10s for a dinner." However, he remained a loyal member
for the rest of his life.

Accounts and filing

Gladstone, a man trained in business methods from his earliest
years, kept accurate records and accounts. His letters carried the
correct address, date, time and signature. Convoluted his letters
might be but one knew to whom they were sent, where and when.
Correspondence coming in and going out was filed. Such was his
system, Gladstone knew, at a moment's notice, where he could find
a letter or a report, even if written years before. Catherine teased
him, "What a bore you would be if you had married somebody as
tidy as yourself".

Gladstone was shaken to the core when Lady Glynne showed
him her accounts. Catherine's were even worse. She wrote notes on
odd scraps of paper. Her handwriting was often undecipherable
and letters were frequently written around the edges of other
letters and sometimes on papers which had contained sandwiches.
However confidential, once read they were dropped on the floor.
Servants picked them up. Stamps lay scattered around. Gladstone,
on the other hand, kept a record of the way he spent every fifteen
minutes of his day. Occasionally, however, he had to make a confession. On 21st January 1844, he wrote to Catherine, *I have carelessly*

*left at the Board of Trade your other letters on which I wished to have
something to say . . .*

As a new wife, she was disappointed when alone with
Gladstone. No cuddles, no kisses, instead he took out his little
pocket Homer and disappeared into it — forgetting her. She, on
the other hand, never kept him waiting. The carriage was at the
door precisely when he wanted it. If *The Times* published an article
critical of Gladstone, it was destroyed. Catherine never used two
words when one would do. Her family wondered if she should join
the Preservation of Breath Society!

Society demanded ladies lived serenely. Impossible for
Catherine, ever going into perpetual motion, she ran more than she
walked. She lived a hundred years in a moment, rarely reading a
book or opening a newspaper. Mrs. Gladstone remained unpunc-
tual, scatterbrained and, worse, pinned notes to her husband's
speeches. Gladstone would rise. The Chamber hushed. If he were
not careful he might read out, "Darling, out of marmalade. Buy
from Fortnum and Mason".

He could forgive Catherine her faults

He forgave Catherine her eccentricities, saying, "My dear wife
has a habit of getting into scrapes. It is remarkable to me how she
manages to get out of them". Early in their married life Gladstone
gave Catherine the choice of knowing all his political secrets or
none of them. She chose to know everything. Towards the end of
their lives he said, "My wife has known every political secret I have
ever had, and has never betrayed my confidence." She nearly did
once. When she was a young wife Catherine dropped a word in the
presence of some of his colleagues, which implied that she knew
some matter of confidential importance. Immediately realizing
that she had made a slip, she left the room and wrote an apologetic
note, which she sent to Gladstone. His reply came back, *Dearest C.
Don't blame yourself. I don't blame you. It is the only little mistake you
ever made.* A colleague of Gladstone's said, "Mrs. Gladstone's
discretion as to public secrets of which she knew was remarkable".

Colleagues watched Catherine being 'pumped'. Her smile was childlike and bland. "What is Mr. Gladstone going to do about ... ?" "Well I wonder. Don't you?" "What do you think he ought to do?"

Every evening Gladstone wrote up his diary and, when apart from Catherine, he gave her an account of his day. For a woman uninterested in politics she made sensible comment. On 22nd February 1850, he started his letter to her with a typical reply, *Indeed you do rise to very daring flights to-day, and suggest many things that flow from your own deep affection which, perhaps, disguises from you some things that are nevertheless real.*

Growing Up, 1841–1851

Sir Robert Peel

In return society forgave them for their insults. Mr. and Mrs. Gladstone were kind and courteous but were considered arrogant. Society functioned by strict guidelines. Ladies called and gave cards. The principle was unbreakable. Catherine rarely left cards or returned them. She was brought up in a charmed circle of influential people which included Prime Ministers, Archbishops, and distinguished people. She saw no reason to bother with bores, toadies or people she disliked. There were occasions she could not ignore.

She recalls a City dinner to meet the Prince Consort. *Peel spoke well, and the Prince was evidently affected by his allusion to the dear ties which bound him to England. Elizabeth Fry sat between the Prince and Prime Minister Peel.* She did like the Duke of Wellington. She first met the Duke at the Duke of Northumberland's house and exclaimed with delight, "He went out of his way to speak to William." Catherine was flattered on another occasion when she attended a party at Lady Jersey's. The Prime Minister, Sir Robert

Peel and Gladstone's 'boss', asked "Would you introduce me to Mrs. Gladstone?"

Catherine looked into blue eyes. They were remarkably alert. But first she saw a country man and then noticed his prominent curved nose. She observed a fine pair of legs and the whitest of white waistcoats, stretching across a comfortable stomach. All this was topped by a mass of fiery, auburn hair. Sir Robert Peel bowed low and, with a nervous smile, that *was unlike a silver plate on a coffin*, began talking to her. Seeing she was of a sympathetic nature, the normally reserved Sir Robert told Catherine, "I require little sleep and can get little rest when my mind is 'occupied'." He continued, "I regret the power the 'Old Duke' still has." He told Catherine a few funny jokes, but not his usual bawdy tales; these were kept for 'over the port'. When Sir Robert moved away, she saw he walked with a limp.

Catherine, busy with her family and charity work, tried whenever Gladstone addressed the House to find time to climb the eighty-six steps into the 'tiny cupboard' of the Ladies Gallery. On 14th February 1842, she observed, "This has been a happy chance which fixed my night at the House of Commons for his speech. I found myself nearly upon Lady John Russell's lap". The Parliamentary day started at 4.30 in the afternoon. The House adjourned for dinner between 7.00 and 7.30 and major debates often ended at around 2 o'clock in the early hours of the morning. However, there were some consolations. When she gave her occasional *little singing soirées*, Gladstone's fine baritone voice resounded around the drawing room. Catherine helped to keep his voice in fine 'feckle'. During a speech, Gladstone would put to his lips a stout-necked, ungainly, glass bottle, draw from it and carefully replace the cork and restore the bottle to a safe place in front of him, ready to be used again. Each time he would pause and start again like a giant refreshed. The contents were a mystery to M.P.s and newspaper men alike. Eventually, they found out that the bottle contained eggs beaten up in sherry. The magic ingredient was love, for Catherine mixed the concoction herself.

A 'Golden Couple'

Busy with his career, Gladstone had little time to respond to invitations to dine. Catherine often dined out alone, "which I detest". There were, however, compensations. Catherine and Mary attended a fancy dress ball at Buckingham Palace. Mary dressed as Henrietta Maria and Catherine as the wife of Francis I. She wore a deep crimson petticoat and cap and the dress had large flowing sleeves of tissue. It was all very striking, especially the royal procession. Catherine may not have been over-interested in fashion but she told Mary, "I find it difficult to resist the lure of the London shops." John Nash's elegant streets, Regent Street, and Cavendish Square were filled with fine carriages. Elegant ladies paraded through Burlington Arcade and Catherine looked forward to taking tea at Fortnum and Mason's. She was one of the few people who found it not amazing that two 'mere footmen' could start up such a store to be enjoyed by the most genteel of society.

When Gladstone entertained, Catherine placed their guests together whether they had anything in common or not or even liked each other. Despite it all, people flocked to them, including The Duke of Wellington, The Archbishop of York, The Duke and Duchess of Cambridge and Marie, Marchioness of Aylesbury of whom Catherine coolly observed, "Ugh, her hairstyle does not suit her." Attending a Buckingham Palace garden party, she told her friends how impressed she had been with the twenty-year old Queen's grace and dignity. Asked to describe the gown of one of the ladies, a lady of dubious repute, she gave an outline and then said sharply, "As to the body — well — I can only describe it as a 'look at me' body". Always observant, she said of a newly engaged couple, "To be sure they did sit side by side upon the couch, but they looked like a coachman and footman, sitting on the box, so stiff and upright, you could see the light between them" and, of Lady M.'s magnificent jewels, "I think perhaps, paste."

Now Madam was married, Catherine's maid hoped she would wear gowns which, when she cast them off, were suitable for a maid to wear on her day off without embarrassment. Catherine did not.

She continued to annoy her maid. The girl told of the occasion when, "Madam, unable to find the bodice of her gown, late as usual, flung a shawl around her shoulders, rushed up the stairs to the grandest of receptions . . . anyone who was anyone saw it. The bodice of Madame's gown was pinned neatly to the back of her skirts."

Entertaining

It took the young couple time to settle into 13, Carlton House Gardens but, in the autumn, Gladstone continued his Thursday 10'clock breakfasts, which he began as a bachelor living in The Albany. They were always his favourite form of entertaining. The meal ended about midday and became very much part of the London scene, lasting well into Gladstone's old age. Invitations were sent out a week in advance. Catherine often forgot who she had invited, calling to Cook, "It's twelve not eight to sit down". Sometimes invitations were found sometime later, slipped down a couch.

Guests were served an excellent red wine and meat dishes as well as some more usual breakfast fare. *Habits of Good Society* stresses food should be ready in silver dishes on a side table. Enough should be served to last people until dinner. Hungry guests waited, while a footman scuttled down the road, carrying a large shopping basket. When they did sit down, Gladstone, short-sighted, sometimes thought he was talking to a quite different person! Nevertheless, people still continued to gather around Mr. and Mrs. Gladstone, even though smoking was not encouraged. When Tennyson and his son Hallam came to stay at Hawarden in 1876, the poet said, "I will only come if I am allowed to indulge in my beloved pipe in the security of my bedroom." Presumably, Catherine did not bother to read *The Habits of Good Society* when it was published in 1864. It told people, new to society, the manners and etiquette expected of them.

Beginning of family life

At this time John Gladstone disposed of his West Indies Properties. He divided the monies amongst his sons, asking Robertson to manage the affair. Gladstone told his father, "It was a beautiful act" and complained, "This increased wealth, so much beyond my needs with its attendant responsibility, is very burden-some". It left Catherine and Gladstone with a problem of how to use the money most effectively — in Victoria's England, there were so many in desperate need.

They did not have time to consider things for long. Catherine's baby was due in early summer. Like many an expectant mother, she worried about "bringing into the world a being whose happiness here and hereafter may mainly depend upon one". Gladstone spoke of "that dark spot of peril for your precious life which hangs in the sky". He maintained the suffering endured by women, during childbirth, gave them a greater understanding of the agonies suffered by Christ on the cross, bringing the mother closer to God.

THE FIRST FOUR BABIES

William Henry, 1840

On 3rd June 1840, Catherine gave birth to William Henry. Catherine's labour lasted for over twenty hours from the early hours in the morning until a quarter past eleven at night. The pain was especially severe for the last four hours and was *awful*. Catherine would, of course, have had no chloroform or any form of pain-relieving drugs. The birth took place in London with the Queen's obstetrician, Dr. Locock, in charge. Although Mrs. Smith, the midwife, would have had no formal training, she probably learned her craft well from her own mother and knew how and when to dose the mother with laudanum or opium. Society was shocked to learn that Gladstone remained with his wife throughout her ordeal. Aunt Wenlock and Aunt Braybrooke added support, encouraging Catherine to "Forget you are a lady, scream!" After such an experience, even Gladstone must have wondered if his view were right about the purpose of the pain in childbirth. But when he saw Catherine, radiant, cuddling her baby, he understood the nature of things.

Society was shaken again. Mrs. Gladstone insisted on feeding baby herself, like any peasant woman. It was difficult at times. Gladstone and Mrs. Smith muttered about, "Much rubbing required, however, it seems to keep the right organ from getting into an obstinate state." One of Willy's godfathers was the Reverend Henry Manning whose 'darkening prospect' of joining Rome would cause Catherine and Gladstone such distress. Two years later she gave birth to a delightful little girl, Agnes. When the tussle of feeding the child became too much, Catherine bought a donkey, asses' milk being the closest thing to human milk.

Stately Homes found themselves opening their doors to welcome Mr. and Mrs. Gladstone, servants, children and a donkey

Regardless of having a minor heart defect, Catherine gave birth to six more children: Stephen, 1844, Catherine Jessy, 1845, Mary, 1847, Helen, 1849, Henry, 1852 and Herbert in 1854 — eight children in thirteen years. Each birth was *awful*. Each child was blessed. As each year passed, its parents loved each child more deeply.

Despite all these children, Catherine had a husband who needed to be cared for. Within a year of their marriage Gladstone was Vice-President of the Board of Trade and Master of the Mint, working at least fourteen hours a day. He remained much of the time in London. Catherine loved Hawarden and was needed there but she longed for Mary's company and stayed often with her. Aunt Wenlock observed, "Hagley is a Palladium Palace, as fine as Stowe or Holkham, with an atmosphere of such high breeding. In such a setting nobody could wish for modern furniture." Catherine found the Park so well managed that when she wandered with Mary, not a single rabbit appeared. The children could hunt for wild violets, watch the cows being milked and drink their milk immediately. They even helped the baby calves with their next meal. Catherine and her children spent from early July into August at Hagley.

Catherine disliked London, describing it as 'grubous', the 'Glynnese' word for dirty and dingy. The constant noise of the clatter of horses' hooves, the smells and the stinking closeness of unwashed bodies, were not to Catherine's taste. For most days a pall hung over the City and, during winter, a thick, yellow fog enveloped it. Following a stay in London, Catherine usually took her children to the seaside where she carried-out a schedule of brisk walks, 'dips' and a regular opening of the lungs 'to partake of the fresh air'. Brighton was her favourite destination. Often away from each other, Catherine told Gladstone, "William, you are 'My Oak and I am your Ivy.' I dream of you most of the night while looking sorrowfully at your empty place. When I lay myself down, I am so lonely without you." She sent him violets from Hawarden. He replied, "Your violets are nice, but your letters are all violets."

Tough on the outside Gladstone might be but only Catherine knew he was sensitive, highly-strung and not over robust. Despite her feeding his rude appetite and insisting, when they were together, that her husband took seven to eight hours sleep every night, she told Mary, "He can go down quickly with minor illnesses." A great believer, even for a City-dweller like Gladstone, in fresh air and exercise, Catherine tried to persuade her husband to buy a horse of his own. "One ride a week is better than nothing."

Teaching the children

It is said parenting skills are passed from one generation to another. John Gladstone taught his children to discuss and debate, thus helping Gladstone to become the greatest orator of his age. Playing whist from his earliest years helped, too. From his mother Gladstone learned to pray. Mary's baby, Meriel, born shortly after

Willy, delighted his aunt and mother "when she played very pret-
tily with Willy". "At eighteen months, when told, the babies knelt
down, and put their little hands together saying, "Papa, Mama.
Amen."

It was not Nanny or Governess who gave the Gladstone children instruction in scripture, Latin and Greek. It was their father.
They sat on his knee, climbed on his back. He even went on all-
fours for them, making funny noises and helped build snowmen.
He hugged them, he kissed them and, however busy he was, he
threw his arms open to welcome them. Until quite grown-up, the
Gladstone children were unaware that Father was somebody
special. It was a different upbringing from the one Gladstone had
received, from loving but rigid parents. Catherine and Gladstone
obeyed the Latin poet Juvenal's maxim, *Maxima debetur puero rever-
ential (the greatest reverence is due to the child).* The Jury is out on
whether he demanded that his children chew their food thirty-two
times.

Catherine, on the other hand, was surrounded by love. A
mother's girl, she said "Nuffink too good for Mama". When they
were old enough, Lady Glynne sent her boys away to Eton. In April
1820, she employed a French governess for the girls. Catherine
immediately lost her tomboyish manners. By 1822, she spoke
excellent French, good Italian and constructed Latin verbs nicely.
She recited poetry well and acted in plays. If the audience enjoyed
the performance, the actors received cold custard and a glass of
milk flavoured with nutmeg. Aunt Wenlock left on record, "as a
child it was difficult to teach her and she was recalcitrant in
learning any kind of lessons". Mary, however, was less of a
problem. She was witty and more serious than her elder sister.

In child care, Catherine followed her mother's example. She
taught her children herself, dosing them with every kind of physic
and emetic for example: cordial water for gripe in babies, *take an
ounce of aniseed, one pint pure water, two tablespoons of treacle and three
drams of tincture of opium and mix well* or for the itch, *heat lard and
melt into some brimstone,* for piles, *roast snails in their shells, pick out the*

meat, beat into powder of pepper then take the dried roots of pilewort in
powder and apply it as hot as can borne. At bedtime Catherine read
aloud to them, often Scott's novels, and discussed with Gladstone
every childish ailment, characteristic, development, comings and
goings and sayings and doings.

The couple suffered agonies if one of the children needed a
smack. Presumably the nursery was full of toys that Victorian children played with: rocking-chairs, dolls-houses, toy theatres, magic
lanterns, jig-saw puzzles, dioramas and stereoscopes. The boys
went to Eton and the girls had governesses, under the tight control
of Catherine. Mr. and Mrs. Gladstone prayed nightly that the children would find their place in the world and love God. They were
relieved when they received an invitation for Catherine's four to
play with the Queen's four. They felt they must be doing something right.

Catherine must have done for in 1883 she was invited to write
the introduction for a re-issue of a little book on child-care, entitled, *'Early Influences.' How valuable would such a book have been to me*
in the happy years of the past! The old memories awoke, and the thought
of the mother's responsibilities from the moment of the baby's first cry to the
riper years of her children's life. The subject of early training had ever been
to me most interesting. It is the step-by-step training — the learning of a
child's disposition by means of hourly watchfulness-which is too often
neglected . . . And now let me turn aside for a moment and consider the
way in which children are over-noticed and over-petted, and considered in
every conceivable way . . . One word as to religious teaching. How many
parents neglect this, or leave it to others? Why are the children of the rich
often worse instructed than the children of the poor? . . . In my opinion this
little work has not undeservedly been called "a book of gold" and I very
earnestly recommend it.

On 4th January 1846 Willy, Agnes, Stephy and Jessy joined the
Royal family. Victoria gave the children a huge white fluffy toy
lamb to play with. Sturdy little Agnes caused the Queen "to fall
into fits of unrestrained laughter". Before they left, she asked
Catherine, "If my children were always so good, nice and kind?"

That night Catherine noted in her diary, *the royal children had fat white necks, Prince Alfred very pretty, Princess Royal was not exactly a pretty child but like the Queen. Princess Alice was a nice fat baby, the Prince of Wales, very small and the head not striking me as very shaped. His long trousers tied below the ankle, rather full and very unbecoming, especially with his height. He looked quite a quiz.*

The Queen and Prince Albert found the Dowager Lady Lyttleton, a lady-in-waiting to the Queen, "so agreeable and sensible" that, in April 1842, they appointed her governess to the Royal children. She was assisted by Mrs. Sly, the head-nurse, nursery-maids and a footman. Like Catherine, Lady Lyttleton considered the royal children over-dressed. The little Princess Royal was 'donned-out' in blue velvet, Brussels lace, white shoes, diamonds and pearls. 'Laddle' persuaded her parents to dress the child in Holland cotton and, in the summer sun, allow her to wear a straw bonnet. When, eight years later Lady Lyttleton resigned, Catherine and Gladstone lost an 'insider', a woman at the very centre of Victoria's court. Until the day she died Lady Lyttleton was called by 'her charges,' 'dearest Laddle'.

Gladstone's accident

In September 1842, they faced a disaster. Catherine and Gladstone were enjoying being together at Hawarden. In the morning Gladstone left early to join the guns. When the luncheon had been cleared away, shooting started again. At 2 P.M. Gladstone loaded his gun. It was a difficult twin-barrel muzzle loader. Unlike most of the other men he was not used to guns. The keepers were too busy to help him. Suddenly, the gun went off, blowing away the first finger of his left hand. At 3 P.M. Catherine stepped into the Irish carriage to meet the shooting-party. She saw Henry, one of the keepers, who told her, "Mr. Gladstone has had an accident".

Mr. Phillimore, the surgeon, was called from Chester. It took him time to arrive. Heavily pregnant, Catherine wished to remain with her husband. The surgeon saw the state Gladstone was in and refused to allow his wife to stay in the room. Without anesthetics, he removed the finger and then found he had not cut off enough. He removed a second piece. The 'removals' were preserved in a jam-jar. The surgeon told Catherine "the remarkable composure of Mr. Gladstone would be a lesson to me for the rest of my life".

While he recovered, Catherine had Gladstone all to herself. She said, "We play at Chess most nights and are very snug and quiet". On 18th October 1842 she wrote in her diary, *my little girl* (Agnes) *was born at 8 P.M., a fine healthy baby with pretty features.* By this time Gladstone was back at work and she would return to complaining to Mary, "Here I am and William gone off at eight o'clock, just having swallowed his dinner. I now seldom get any sort of talk and even at breakfast he is reading the newspaper." Throughout his long political career Gladstone used a fingerstall. No cartoonist ever made 'mock of' his disability.

Illness — Agnes

For those times, the Gladstone children seemed remarkably healthy but, in the autumn of 1847, while they relaxed at Fasque, five-year old Agnes contacted erysipelas, or St Anthony's Fire, an infection which had been especially prevalent in the Middle Ages caused by an inflammation of the skin; it was sometimes deadly. It killed Gladstone's mother. Privies at the bottom of gardens, chamber pots under beds, open sewers — these were the root of nineteenth-century infections and no penicillin existed to kill virulent germs such as streptococcus. Of course, Catherine, with Gladstone's help, cared for her daughter. Nursing skills were expected of women of her time. Miss Nightingale had not yet trained her 'girls'. The fever raged. Prayers were said in the Parish Church and then slowly the delirium abated. Willy, walking with his father, observed, "Lucky it was a Saint's day, for you see Agnes is not grand enough to have a service all for herself and if she had not been prayed for she might have died." Gladstone could not think of a suitable reply. The illness overcame him, too. For a short time both his arms were crippled.

Jessy

On 4th April 1844 Stephen Edward quietly entered the world.
Fifteen months later Catherine's fourth baby, Catherine Jessy, was
born on 27th July 1845. Gladstone and Catherine debated whether
to stop at four children. Unnaturally, for a small child, Jessy,
watching Agnes struggle, seemed to understand the nature of
death. She was quicker, eager and more loving than her brothers
and sisters. A strange, quiet child, 'a mummy's girl', Catherine
called her *My Dormouse*. Gradually, a cloud settled over the little
girl. Her eyes grew round, larger, more serious. She seemed to be
drawing away from them, becoming drowsy. Three years after the
worry of Agnes, the doctors said "This child has meningitis".
Again, Catherine became a nurse. Gladstone took his turn too. *He
was particularly fond of small children.* Racked with pain, Jessy called
out, "I want Mummy." Such a cry no parent ever forgets. The
struggle lasted for two weeks and then, on 9th April 1850,
Gladstone wrote in his diary, *the blessed child was released at 2 o'clock
this morning.* He lost control, giving way to such a grief that he
terrified Catherine, his children, his servants and all those around
him. Alone, Gladstone took Jessy to Fasque and buried her in the
family vault. From that moment, Catherine hardly mentioned
Jessy again or placed her photograph on show. In a sense she had
been lucky. One-fifth of the children born at that time died before
their first birthday of scarlet fever, diarrhoea, smallpox, measles or
gastroenteritis. Little Mary berated Gladstone, "Naughty Papa for
taking Detty away."

CHAPTER TWO

Death of a Daughter, Ladies of the Night and Financial Disaster

The 1840s

THE WOMEN IN THEIR LIVES

Alone with Jessy

Gladstone placed Jessy's coffin on his knees, just as she had sat on his knee as a little girl. The carriage and pair rattled across London, fighting its way along the Euston Road. With a final thrust the coachman took his horses through the new seventy feet high Euston Arch and into the hubbub of Mr. Cubitt's railway station. Distraught as Gladstone was, he managed to find the platform easily. In fact, there were only two: one for trains coming in and the other for going out. The engine driver pressed the horn. The train gathered steam, escaping from beneath the station's great iron roof, past lines of terraced cottages and on into the green of the countryside. Wishing to be alone with Jessy, Gladstone pulled down the shutters, grateful that, with modern means of travel, his journey would be in hours not days. He arrived at Laurenkirk Station. Still holding Jessy's coffin, he saw his father's carriage waiting for him. It took him to Fettercairn and up the hill into the grounds of Fasque.

Weary and sad, Gladstone entered his father's house, having to adjust to the gloom as 'old man Gladstone' did not waste money on candles. Emerging from out of the shadows came a figure,

wringing its hands, worthy of Lady Macbeth. Glittering gold
crosses dangled from ears, wrists and around its waist. Slowly, it
approached him. Looking down at Jessy's coffin Helen enquired,
"As a Roman, may I attend the funeral?" Gladstone, overwrought,
wrote to Catherine, "May she attend?" Her answer was impossible
to understand.

Helen

By the time of Jessy's death, Helen had been a 'Roman' for
almost ten years. A few years later, her family, along with many
other people, were frightened out of their senses by a document
from the Vatican dividing England into dioceses bearing territo-
rial titles and appointing Cardinal Wiseman as Archbishop of
Westminster. The Gladstones, like many other families, would
have viewed the Pope with alarm. Lord John Russell spoke for the
majority of people when he said that, "the great mass of the nation
looked with contempt upon the mummeries of superstition".
However comforting Helen found her faith she obviously had little
consideration for her family. She continued taking laudanum, a
drug so popular it was available from any apothecary. Gladstone
told Catherine, "She is full of horrible apprehensions. She sees
people coming in through the walls, little people covering her
drawers."

Helen was beyond Catherine's understanding. On one occasion,
when she was staying by herself at Fasque, Catherine heard a
commotion. On enquiry, she found Helen was 'enjoying' a fit. She
wrote to Mary, *As you will say, Helen's enjoying it does not make it any
better.* Often, furiously angry with Helen's behaviour, Catherine
and Gladstone sent her to Coventry. In return, Helen refused to
talk to them directly but through the servants, to their amusement. Shortly before her conversion to Rome, Helen's behaviour
became even more bizarre.

A source of much pleasure and inspiration to Gladstone was his
collection of books by eminent Anglican theologians. He dipped
into them often — in fact, nearly every day. However, he began to

become confused. Pages were missing. On enquiry, he was told "Miss Helen has strung the missing pages across her 'cabinet'. She uses them for lavatory paper."

Gladstone, once more in pursuit of Helen

During the summer of 1845, Sir John's concern for his daughter's health grew. People recommended a visit to the hot springs of Baden-Baden. Sir John sent Helen, with a suitable doctor/companion, to take the waters there. He knew she would enjoy meeting the famous people who flocked to the summer capital of Europe. Sir John gave strict instructions, "Helen's flirtations and drug taking must be controlled." His orders were obeyed to the letter. However, Helen found the discipline unacceptable. She dismissed the man. Angrily, the family wrote to Helen demanding an explanation. She did not reply. Catherine agreed with them. Gladstone must go immediately and bring Helen home, "before she does any more damage to our reputation". Gladstone again journeyed across Europe. He could not find Helen. When he did he was shocked. Every day Helen dosed herself with three hundred drops of laudanum, forcing her doctors to pin her down so leeches could be applied.

Two years later Helen asked for permission to enter a Roman Catholic convent in Leamington. The family agreed. Tom took her. She languished there for a while and then, to her family's dismay, returned home. Helen continued being a constant source of worry. Eventually, her histrionics became too much. The family agreed she must be restrained under the Lunacy Act. Sir John snapped, "You are behaving with over-refinement, scrupulosity and uncharitableness, and if you continue to do so, I will not see you," with the hint he would leave his children out of his will.

Helen became paralytic, her hands clenched, her jaw locked. Sir John, concerned his daughter would die, sent her to see Dr. Miller, the famous Edinburgh nerve specialist. Before the consultant discussed treatment, he demanded, "You ladies, down on your knees surrounding my patient, remove yourselves now." When they had departed, much put out, he began to discuss Helen's treatment, in the middle of which, Dr. Wiseman, Helen's spiritual advisor, arrived, clutching a knuckle bone of some female saint. Helen touched the bone and was instantly cured.

Dr. Miller, said hysteria; Dr. Wiseman said, miracle

As a reward for good behaviour, Gladstone and Catherine invited Helen to stay with them. They named their new baby daughter after her. The little girl did not follow in her aunt's footsteps but instead followed an academic career.

Lady Susan

Gladstone actually liked women. Catherine probably did not realize this was unusual for a strongly-sexed Victorian male. As Disraeli pointed out, "especially if they are young and pretty". Lady Susan Douglas was both. She was the only daughter of the 10th Duke of Hamilton. Her father believed he was the rightful heir to the throne of Scotland. A dandy, he wore rings on every finger and craved being the centre of attention. The Duke insisted that, on his death, his body should be mummified. His family did so, burying him in a coffin which they believed once housed a royal person from ancient Egypt. Two hundred years later, historians told the family, "Very sorry, the coffin belonged to the court jester."

In 1832, Lady Susan married Lord Lincoln, a trusted friend and colleague of Gladstone's from his Eton and Oxford days. He was the eldest son of the Duke of Newcastle, who had been John Gladstone's political patron and friend. The Duke lost his wife early and tried to bring up his family on his own. He loved them dearly but was stern, unbending and dominating. His heir grew up to be an introverted, serious-minded and deeply religious man living in the shadow of his powerful father — a prig, hardly the ideal husband for a sparkling, fun-loving girl.

Lord Lincoln took Suzy into the wild countryside of Nottinghamshire, to the Newcastles' country seat, Clumber.

Marble staircases, magnificent halls, statues, everything was created from marble. Even when Lady Susan wandered into the garden, she could not escape. Marble surrounded her on all sides. Water swirled from and around a fountain created from a fifty-ton block.

In the middle of the lake a miniature frigate pointed its guns straight at her

In these surroundings, the future Duchess bore five children and remained 'not at ease' with her in-laws. In the evenings they sat round the fire 'in a stiff, horse-shoe semi-circle'. Ten years after her marriage, she 'bolted'. In 1847, 'Suzy' left her family again and took to laudanum. Catherine and Gladstone, remembering Helen, told Lord Lincoln, "We know laudanum. It destroys responsibility and unfits people for punishment." Two years later Susan 'bolted' again to the Continent with Lord Horatio Walpole. This time she went for good. Lord Lincoln begged Catherine to take care of his children. When Suzy's four-year old daughter looked up into Catherine's eyes and said, "Mama," all Catherine could do was hug the little girl and say, "Oh! William. What a melancholy sight!"

Gladstone now in pursuit of Lady Susan

Catherine, who was fond of 'poor Suzy', asked Gladstone to go to Europe to rescue her. John Gladstone said, "The idea is ridiculous." Once again, Gladstone set out for Europe with Catherine praying Suzy was not pregnant. She gave Gladstone a letter for her friend, *Follow his advice and listen seriously to what he says. He has no motive but your good: it is that, believe me dear, which actuates him to follow you.* Catherine, heavily pregnant herself, ended the letter, *Had it been possible for me to have gone with him, how quickly I would have done so.*

Gladstone journeyed through Naples, Rome and Milan, searching for the couple to no avail. On a Saturday afternoon Lord Lincoln wrote to Catherine, *I assure you my own grief does not make me forget all the trouble and annoyance my dear friend is undergoing for me*. Eventually, Gladstone traced Suzy to a villa on the shores of Lake Como. He left a note for 'Mrs. Laurence'. Suzy did not answer it. When darkness fell, Gladstone, in disguise, crept into the grounds and hid. He watched a heavily-veiled woman and a man enter a carriage. The blinds came down. Whether they knew Gladstone was there or not, is not known. Sharply, the coachman cracked the whip. The horses went into a gallop. The carriage and four drove straight past Gladstone, nearly running him over, landing him in the bushes.

The next day he made enquiries. The carriage was taking Walpole and 'Suzy' to Verona. When Gladstone arrived in the town he tried to speak to Lady Lincoln. She ignored him. However, he saw 'she was with child'. He wrote to Catherine, *The same post which carries this carries also the dagger to Lincoln.* Gladstone returned home. As Sir John pointed out, "You have travelled for twenty-seven days, covered nearly three thousand miles, at what cost — only to tell Lord Lincoln his wife was pregnant by another man." Sir Robert Peel, on the other hand, told Gladstone, "my sincere admiration for truly virtuous and generous conduct". On 31ˢᵗ January 1853, Lord Lincoln wrote to Catherine from Clumber, *Your kindness to me and my children is really very great . . . I really do not know what I should have done if it had not been for the way in which you have adopted them.*

Lord Lincoln divorced Suzy in 1850 — something only the rich could do. He found the process tedious. It required a private Act of Parliament. Seven years later, the Matrimonial Causes Act allowed a man to divorce his wife for adultery, alone. The wife had to prove her husband had committed an additional offence such as desertion, physical cruelty, incest, sodomy, bigamy, or just bestiality! Of course, Walpole did not marry Lady Lincoln but did inherit a title and became 4ᵗʰ Earl of Oxford. Suzy would have paid a high price for her love affair. The 1839 Custody of Infants Act refused an adulteress access to, or custody over, her children. Lord Lincoln did not marry again. He became a sound politician visiting the Crimea to see conditions for himself. In 1860, Suzy married a

Belgian. She outlived her first husband who died at fifty-three years of age in 1864. Suzy died in 1889, aged seventy-five. Her daughter, Susan, became one of the Prince of Wales's favourite mistresses. Some years later Suzy asked a fellow guest, "Do you know Mrs. Gladstone? Will you give her a message from me, a terrible one! When she is happy with her children let her think of me." When she was told, Catherine whispered, "Poor creature, oh the poor, poor creature."

THE HUNGRY FORTIES

Starvation and Financial Crisis

These dramas took place against the background of an insidiously developing financial crisis. During 1829/30, 1838/41 and May 1845 the rains came down. They were the wettest anybody could remember. The hungry demanded "Abolish the Corn Laws". Vested interests knew that cheap corn coming into the country would keep the price low of home-grown wheat and barley. Tenants would not be able to pay their rents. The Sussex-born countryman who understood the landed aristocracy, Richard Cobden, together with a son of a Rochdale mill-owner, John Bright, explained, "Wages are not related to the price of bread." Others said, "Cheaper bread will allow your employers to pay you even lower wages." Cobden and Bright considered that "reducing duties on corn imports should be carried along with reducing duties on many things".

But for many poor, the potato was the staple diet especially in the Scottish Highlands and Ireland. In Ireland alone a million people died of starvation. The feminist reformer, Josephine Butler, said of her childhood in Ireland, "I recollect when walking through the lanes and villages, the strange, morbid, famine smell in the air, the sign of approaching death, even in those who were still dragging out a wretched existence." A large number fled to America and the Colonies, hoping against hope to find better lives for themselves. Lord Palmerston, like many of the well-to-do, remembered the French Revolution and feared the overturn of British society. Catherine's relative, Lady Dorothy Neville, declared, "In the eighteen-forties, a good many of the wealthy had no more heart than a stoned peach on a lodging house chimney piece!"

Gladstone becomes Vice-President of the Board of Trade

The year 1841 saw Gladstone rise to become Vice-President of the Board of Trade, Master of the Mint and Peel's right-hand man, dealing with the complicated area of fiscal reform, an experience which Peel felt would benefit his protégé in the future. Gladstone is remembered for tariff revision and the removal of hundreds of restrictions. In the course of a few years he freed 371 commodities from taxation. Mary Drew, his daughter, wrote, *Thus he put into the power of the people to buy food and many other necessities that up to then had been beyond them.*

On 6ᵗʰ January, 1842, Catherine wrote in her diary, *I am thirty today — terrible thought!* A month later, she wrote, on 13ᵗʰ February 1842, *a note from Sir Robert Peel desiring William to follow Lord John Russell in the House on Monday, on the Corn Laws. He made no preparation today.* On 14ᵗʰ February, Gladstone gave his first great speech on the Corn Laws. Catherine reported, "Peel was evidently delighted and, from all I gather, this speech has made a great sensation." Lord Morley, Gladstone's colleague and biographer, refers to the speech as, *the first invasion of the Old Tory Corn Law of 1827.* On 20ᵗʰ February, Catherine complains again in her diary. *I have had very little of William this week, and have felt unduly vexed. I fear, he must get ill from this excessive labour. We went to church together on Wednesday. I have great comfort in my darling boy.*

Two Nations

A year later, in 1842, the Chartist editor of the *Northern Counties Illuminator* was brought to trial by the Government for, amongst other things, speaking out against the reduction of wages. The Chartists wished for political reform and for males to have the vote — in short, an elementary form of democracy. Throughout the North, especially in Yorkshire and Lancashire, men rioted. The cotton workers removed the factories' boiler plugs and caused production to stop. Wellington demanded that Peel send out the troops. Gladstone, in London, was concerned for Catherine's safety at Hawarden but, thankfully, he was able to write to her, *You do not seem much troubled by the neighbour-hood of this turnout.*

However, he observed, "This is the time when we may reflect on the rottenness of the system which gathers together huge masses of the population which have no tie to the class above them." In 1845, Disraeli published *Sybil or Two Nations*. The principal character, Egremont, declaims, *'say what you like, our Queen reigns over the greatest nation that ever existed.' 'Which nation?' asked the stranger, 'for she reigns over two'* . . . *two nations, between whom there is no intercourse and no sympathy* . . . *THE RICH AND THE POOR.'*

President of the Board of Trade, 1843

On 13th May 1843, Peel further promoted Gladstone as President of the Board of Trade, together with a seat in the Cabinet. Before accepting the post Gladstone walked in Kensington Gardens with Catherine, begging her to pray for him. She wrote in her diary, *How thankful I am to be joined to one whose mind is purity and integrity itself.* Catherine was no longer married to an up and coming man. He was travelling up the 'greasy pole' fast. During this period Gladstone received numerous deputations, including one from the young John Bright. Gladstone noticed the Quaker clothing together with a fashionable monocle. In 1843, Bright joined the House of Commons and, with his colleague, Richard Cobden, stumped up and down the country speaking against the Corn Laws.

Through his work, Gladstone was becoming increasingly aware of those who did not know how society worked, such as the coal whippers. These men worked in the London docks, 'whipping' coal

into baskets from the ships moored along-side. Jobs came via
public houses. The more a whipper drank the greater his chance of
the publican recommending him for work. In 1843, Gladstone
passed the Coal Vendors Act. It set up a central office for employment. In Gladstone's old age he wrote, *In principle, perhaps, my
Coalwhippers Act of 1843 was the most socialistic measure of the last half-
century.*

Like many a young wife married to a brilliant and ambitious
man, Catherine complained, "William works fourteen hours a day.
Even when he is at home, he works so hard and it is a little dreary
sometimes." He said of himself, "there is no man, however near
me, with whom I am fit to live with when hard-worked". In admiration, colleagues exclaimed "What Gladstone does in four hours
would take any other man sixteen." He told Lord Morley, "I usually
work fourteen hours a day." Peel's Government was coping with a
slump in world trade, a deficit of seven and a half-million pounds,
collapsing banks and a loss of business confidence. It was during
this period of intense activity that Gladstone suffered his shooting
accident.

However, much of his attention was taken up with his health.
Sporadically, Gladstone suffered from St. Anthony's Fire
(erysipelas) and other ailments. Well cared for by Catherine he
might be, but he spent much of his time in London, away from his
wife, and communication in those days was tiresomely difficult.
The City's filthy conditions proved ideal breeding grounds for the
cause of infection and the growth of the streptococcus virus.
Catherine enjoyed robust health herself but had to cope with not
only pregnancy but neurotic governesses. They were often difficult
women, rejected by a suitor, not attractive enough or rich enough
to attract a man, so were forced to earn a living, making them
neither 'beast nor fowl'. A cynical butler observed, "There are very
few young ladies who get husbands except they are very handsome
or got a large fortune."

Immersed in the Condition of England question, Gladstone
received a note from Catherine, *Please speak severely to Miss Brown,*

if not for the sake of the children but for her own sake, I feel she is worth moulding. I know, my own, you will do so. Shortly afterwards Gladstone received another letter, *I am so sorry to have bothered you and Free Trade so on, all overwhelming you.*

Maynooth Grant

Ireland again proved to be troublesome. Peel, with his experience of being Secretary of State for Ireland, tried to bring about conciliation. The Roman Catholic Church, to which most of the population belonged, was poor, the Anglican Church wealthy. Maynooth College, Dublin, trained Roman Catholic clergy. Parliament wished to increase their annual grant from £9,000 to £26,000 and to make the grant permanent and also incorporate the College.

In the *Church in its Relations with the State*, Gladstone, a high-church man, condemned the original grant. He addressed the House for an hour on the subject, managing to mystify both Peel and Disraeli at the same time. Gladstone told Catherine. "If I go, I shall go on the ground of what is required by my personal character, and not because my mind is made up on the course that they propose can be avoided, far less." On 12th July 1844, Gladstone sent his resignation as President of the Board of Trade and member of the Cabinet to Peel, who received it with astonishment. Gladstone told Catherine, "Peel told me that no one could have acted more candidly or considerately and was very kind and open in his manner towards me." Peel confessed to a friend, "I really have great difficulty sometimes in exactly comprehending what he means." Disraeli said with glee, "Mr. Gladstone's career is over."

The year 1844 was to be distressing on 'many fronts' for Catherine and Gladstone. Their 'dear friend Newman' entered into the Catholic Church and Gladstone asked Peel to send him to Rome as a diplomat to the Vatican. In later years he said resigning was the silliest action of his life. One journalist observed, "A lady's footman jumped off the Great Western train, going forty miles an hour, merely to pick up his hat. Pretty much like this act, so disproportional to the occasion, is Mr. Gladstone's leap out of the ministry to follow his book." A rather confused Catherine commented, on 29th January 1845, "William has virtually resigned his seat in the Cabinet, on the burning subject of Irish education (the Maynooth Grant) and, though he cannot be one of the originators of the government scheme, it would not true to say that under existing circumstances, he disapproves of their measures."

A few days after Catherine's letter, in January 1845, Gladstone went to Windsor to resign. He wrote to Catherine about having dinner in the evening. *Lady Lyttleton was suddenly invited and it fell to my lot to hand in and sit by, which was pleasant. I am, as you know, a shockingly bad witness to looks, but she appeared to me, I confess, a little worn and aged. She ought to have at least two months holiday every year. After dinner the Queen inquired as usual about you. . . . Then we went to cards, and played commerce; fortunately I was never the worst hand, and so was not called upon to pay for I had locked up my purse before going to dinner but I found I had won 2s 2d at the end, 8d of which was paid by the Prince. . . . I had a rather a nice conversation with him about the international copyright convention with Prussia.*

Whitehall, 11th January, I came back from Windsor this morning, very kindly used. The Queen mentioned particularly that you were not asked on account presumably of inconvenience. When Gladstone said good-bye to the Queen, he told Catherine that when she brought the little people to the corridor, *they behaved very well.*

The Corn Laws: The final chapter, 1846

In May, 1841, Mary Anne Disraeli wrote to Sir Robert Peel begging him for a place for her husband in his new government, an act which no gentleman would countenance. Peel had continually promoted Gladstone but overlooked Disraeli. He felt, as did the Prince Consort, "Mr. Disraeli is not quite a gentleman." In Peel's view he was not reliable and 'too sharp by half'. Long before, when Disraeli was a young man, he had annoyed Sir Robert by flirting with pretty Lady Peel. He told Mary Anne, "When I asked him to lend me some of his private papers for my next book he was quite unpleasant, burying his chin in his neck-cloth. You could tell he is not a gentleman by the manner in which he attacked his turbot with a knife." Of course a man of Peel's standing would not consciously carry a grudge but . . .

Mary Anne ended her letter, *Be pleased not to answer this, as I do not wish any human being to know I have written to you this humble petition.* Peel did not reply. Five years later on an evening in May 1846, Disraeli entered the House of Commons. For a time he sat quite still and then, like the incredible actor he was, stood up and, for three hours, baited Peel. Suddenly the 'great presence' of 'Butcher Gladstone' rose, demanding "If Mr. Disraeli has so much contempt for Sir Robert Peel why did he ask for a post in his government?" The Chamber gasped. Disraeli froze. "I assure the House nothing of the kind ever occurred."

Peel lifted up his carpet bag and began taking out an envelope. Suddenly he paused, as if thinking. Disraeli, 'with a fury second to none', went into the attack. Disraeli turned on his heel and left, leaving Peel who loved the House, standing with tears rolling down his cheeks. An observer exclaimed, "Disraeli must have taken a vow of hatred to Sir Robert Peel. No ordinary condition of mind would lead to such ferocity." Peel and his government fell and Disraeli began his climb up 'the greasy pole.' On his return to Grosvenor Gate, Mary Anne told her husband that, "Henrietta died this morning." Mounting the stairs, Disraeli turned to her, "Oh the terrible catastrophe of Henrietta, she nearly ruined my career." One of the most beautiful women of her age, Lady Henrietta Sykes, was the great love of Disraeli's life. Her rejection caused him to have a break-down. Mary Anne knew she could never compete with her ghost. Catherine was fortunate she did not live with a man haunted by what might have been. Catherine knew the story. Normally, a sympathetic woman, she always referred to Disraeli as *that beast, d'Israeli,* even in writing she wrote *d'Israeli,* thus emphasising his Jewishness. She knew Disraeli had anglicized his name to conform to society.

'Little Johnny Russell'

On 29th June 1846, Peel resigned. The Whig and Liberal, Lord John Russell, became Prime Minister. As the younger son of the 6th Duke of Bedford, 'little Johnny Russell's title was an honorary one and so he was entitled to sit in the House of Commons. Russell was in favour of the repeal of the Corn Laws, but his life was made difficult by his party's in-fighting and conflict with the boisterous Regency Buck of a man, Lord Palmerston, who clung to being Foreign Secretary. Gladstone continued to serve, but the 'convulsions' of the Corn Laws and receiving a ministerial salary forced him to resign from Newark which remained under the control of the Duke of Newcastle. As he fought for foreign corn to come into the country, duty free, it brought him into conflict with his father and the Duke of Newcastle, both protectionist men. Gladstone told Lord Lyttelton, "My father is so very keen in his protective opinions, and I am so decidedly of the other way of thinking, that I look forward with some reluctance and regret to what must, when it happens, place me in marked and public contrast with him." In 1847, Gladstone was elected M.P. for the University of Oxford (representing the M.A. graduates) and became Colonial Secretary, without a seat in the Cabinet. Catherine described Russell's time in office as "that flat and miserable sham government" and told Gladstone, "I wish you had a nice party assembled around you." Neither Catherine nor Gladstone had time or inclination to pay attention to Oak Farm, Sir Stephen's business venture, until, in 1847, they faced bankruptcy and the loss of Hawarden.

Facing bankruptcy

At the time of Catherine and Mary's joint wedding, part of the marriage settlement had been, for each couple, a tenth share of Sir Stephen's prosperous iron works which he owned on the Staffordshire/Worcester border. At that time Oak Farm was a valuable business concern. Underneath its hundred acres ran seams of coal and iron. Catherine's father had also dabbled in iron. In 1835, Sir Stephen rejected an offer of £35,000 for the property. In 1840, he sold the land for £55,000 to invest the money in the ironworks. Encouraged by the Hawarden Estate Manager, Mr. Boydell, Sir Stephen formed 'The Oak Farm Company'. Sir John advised, 'Keep a watch on Boydell'. His warning seemed unfounded but John Gladstone knew only too well that life is a game of cards with a joker in the pack. Share prices rose and links were made with the Grand Union Canal Company. Machinery was installed. Sir John pointed out, "unwise".

However, in 1844 Gladstone wrote to his father: *It is an indifferent business* and, against his better judgment, John Gladstone stood credit. Nobody controlled Boydell. John Gladstone sensed danger. He told Gladstone, "At almost whatever sacrifice may be required — get out." Money was needed. Sir Stephen mortgaged Hawarden to the hilt.

They all began feeling uneasy about Oak Farm

In 1847 the market crashed. The railways' boom collapsed and a bank crisis loomed. The debts on Oak Farm amounted to £395,000. It was the time before unlimited liability. Gladstone, George and Sir Stephen bought out the liquidators for £1,000. Even Catherine's £30,000 dowry had to be used. Now Sir John cried, 'Sell.' A quiet, artistic man, Sir Stephen did not know how to cope with the situation. He continued enjoying being Lord Lieutenant of Flintshire until somebody told him, "As a bankrupt you will have to resign." Sir Stephen watched horrified as the catastrophe of Oak Farm unfolded. He saw his income of £10,000 a year disappearing and more importantly, his mother's comfortable allowance of £2,500 a year at risk. In London, during the difficult days of 1839, four thousand people were arrested for debt. Suddenly, Sir Stephen saw the debtors' prison, 'The Clink', looming up before him.

In order to cope, Gladstone considered resigning his seat in the House but decided to continue and try to limit the damage. Catherine wrote, *It is melancholy to see the miserable way everything has been carried out without system or judgement . . . in fact it is chaos . . .*

and now here again is a fresh and important subject which his good old
head and wits are hard at work upon.

Hawarden at risk

Suddenly Catherine realized Hawarden itself was at risk. She
attacked Sir Stephen." How could you? Why were you so stupid?"
She continued, over and over again. Gladstone, angry in his turn,
told his wife, "If you keep on at Stephen you will addle his brain."
Knowing his brother-in-law would be of no use, he sent him to
Constantinople where he happily collected antiquities.
Meanwhile, Gladstone wrote 140 letters to Freshfields, the
Glynnes' bankers. A meeting was held. Oak Farm was found to be
hopelessly insolvent, and it was determined to wind up the
company. The bankruptcy court agreed with Sir John, 'Sell.' In
April 1849, at Birmingham, Gladstone purchased the concern on
behalf of himself and his two brothers-in-law, subject to certain
existing interests. In May, Sir Stephen resumed legal possession of
the wreck of Oak Farm. The burden on Hawarden was over
£250,000, leaving its owner with no margin to live upon.
Gladstone sold £200,000 worth of land. With the help of Sir John
and Lord Spencer, one part was taken by Lord Lyttelton and two
by Gladstone.

However, the full burden fell on Gladstone's shoulders. He
called a family conference and suggested the most business-like
place for them to meet was the library of 13, Carlton House
Terrace. He opened the discussion by reminding the Glynnes he
had recently had the embarrassment of appearing not only before
the Bankruptcy Court in Birmingham but reading 'in *The Times*'
on 3rd December 1847, an account of the creditors' meeting held
in Birmingham. Gladstone produced the following formula to get
them out of the crisis. It satisfied the bankruptcy court and Oak
Farm's creditors. He told the family: (a) Hawarden and its estate
must be let and (b) Sir Stephen's income must be reduced to £700
a year, and carriages and horses must go. Sir Stephen generously
offered to forego his valet but continued to accept the responsi-

bility of supporting the Hawarden Parish schools. Had he sold he would have come out with £120,000, free of all encumbrances, but the jointure.

Lady Glynne offered to forgo nothing. On learning her annual income was to be reduced, she muttered about "having come to this" and slid into depression. Catherine scolded her mother, "Mama, you may have less money but you do not have a household to run. I have had to dismiss my second footman." Miffed, Lady Glynne decided to spend most of her time with Mary at Hagley, who was more sympathetic.

Meanwhile, Gladstone, not to be outdone, sighed, "I am the poorest man living in Carlton House Terrace." The house was put up for sale. There were no buyers and Gladstone closed up the house. Eventually, he sold 13, Carlton House Terrace to Lord Grey, the former Prime Minister, for a 'wretched price'. If that was not enough, Catherine announced, "I have to let my sash out again." Three months into her pregnancy, wearing old slippers and carrying fifteen-month old Mary, she fell down stairs. Fortunately, Catherine was only cut and badly bruised. Nine days before giving birth, Gladstone waved goodbye to her from Euston Station. The express train took five hours before it reached Chester Station. As he saw the train vanishing, he must have prayed for his wife but the thought must have passed through his mind, "What will I do if my Cathie dies? With all those children, I will have to marry again. Who would have me?" However, Helen was born, safely, in August 1849. Her father said, "not the less dear and acceptable because she happens to be the fifteenth Miss Gladstone, amongst my father's grandchildren". The little girl found herself staying with Grandpa, at 6 Carlton Gardens. Her Mama was often distressed because Papa was busy raising money by selling his collection of books, paintings and ceramics.

A learning experience
Gladstone gave the disaster deep thought. Nothing happened without it being God's will. He considered the matter. On 20th

January 1849, he told Catherine, "The catastrophe has come about by the ordinance of God. In due course His purposes will be made clear." They were. Gladstone believed the experience of juggling the debt of Oak Farm, which eventually amounted to £395,000, helped him to become one of the most successful Chancellors of the Exchequer of all time. It brought him into contact with the material interests of the country which was new to him. He had been bred in the atmosphere of commerce. At the Board of Trade, in the reform of the tariff, in connection with the Bank Act and in the growth of the railway system, he had been well trained in high economics. *Now, he came to serve an arduous apprenticeship in the motions and machinery of industrial life.*

Catherine made no comment but continued trying to curb her disorderly nature. She checked bills, kept tight accounts, noting: *1/- for sandwiches, 3/- bun and biscuits, 3d for milk for baby.* If she needed to attend a grand occasion, she borrowed flowers and feathers from her sister. She reduced expenditure on food. Gladstone thought they ate too much anyway. She employed fewer servants but refused to dismiss them at the 'fag end' of the season. She fought the temptation to fritter money away in the London shops and took to making her clothes herself. A gentleman allocated at least £500 a year to his wife for dress; Catherine would have said, "far, too, much."

The coming out of the Misses Gladstones

Some of the consequences of Oak Farm were born by Catherine's daughters. As they grew up they were forced to wear clothes described by Society 'as moon frocks'. The girls found it hard to forgive 'Mama'. In the highly competitive marriage market they needed to look their best, "Mama, you would look marvellous dressed in a sack." In order to find a suitable husband, a girl from an upper-class background of marriageable age was dependent on her mother who, *The Illustrated News* described, *as farther into life's summer and wears the rose of beauty in its fullest blowing and its deepest blush* . . . Parliament sat from Easter to August, the same time as the London Season. Prior to the commencement of the season, an application was made to the Lord Chamberlain by 'Mama', or a woman of blameless virtue, for a young lady or with her sisters, to be presented at Court and thus 'come-out'. It was followed by a constant round of visits to the Court dressmaker and hairdresser.

The presentations took place in the afternoon. The debutante wore a delicate, white evening dress indicating virginity, and a necklace of pearls encircled her neck, usually family jewels. Her hands were covered by long white gloves. She waited in the family coach, stuck in The Mall, in a queue for an hour or more with the blinds pulled up. *Noblesse oblige* was not only expected of those in High Society but to entertain the hoi-polloi with spectacle as well. On the young lady's head ostrich feathers tossed around, hopefully holding a veil in place. When she finally arrived at Buckingham Palace she found herself placed in one of the four drawing rooms, clutching a train of three or four yards, where she joined an 'endless' queue waiting to enter the Throne Room. Cold and tired she might be but curtsy to the Queen she must. The young lady then left the 'presence' walking backwards, trying not to trip over the train. It was 'a rite of passage', marking a young girl's transition into Womanhood, Society and Motherhood.

Before settling down to marriage and motherhood, she could enjoy the social whirl of Ascot, picnics, dances and balls. The hunt for a husband was intense. Society did not accept a Cinderella — any man was better than none! The Gladstone girls were more independently minded. Agnes and Mary married late, Helen never did!

As a postscript to Catherine's lack of fashion-sense, years after the Oak Farm fiasco, in June 1872, Catherine and Gladstone paid a visit to Birmingham. The ladies of the City put on their finest. They complained that Mrs. Gladstone's style did not fit in with such a lady of quality. "Her bonnet looks thrown together and as for her dress!!! Mr. Gladstone must indeed be a mean man to clothe his wife so poorly." If they had known it, Mr. Gladstone was not in the habit of noticing what his wife wore. Catherine did not care a fig for their good opinion. She considered fashion was for house-maids and, what's more, she probably made the dress herself and borrowed the bonnet.

After Oak Farm

Following 'Oak Farm' Mr. and Mrs. Gladstone possessed only one carriage. This was used by 'Master'. Catherine took to travel-ling by public transport, usually in a horse-drawn omnibus. In the early 1860s she was excited to discover trams. In 1860, an American called George Francis Train began operating a horse-drawn tram along Victoria Street in London's Westminster. In 1870, an Act of Parliament authorized that a two-horse tram could draw a carriage containing sixty people. Now Catherine could travel all over London for one penny a mile. Many a person was shaken to receive a cheque from the Chancellor of the Exchequer. "My wife tells me she forgot her purse . . ." Trams became Mrs. Gladstone's favourite means of getting from one place to another. She so enjoyed "rubbing shoulders, dear, with people, one would not meet in the usual course of one's life".

As Catherine and Gladstone struggled to economize, the castle remained empty. 'To Let' signs swung from the trees around Hawarden. Catherine and Gladstone looked at their children and knew they were homeless, hopefully just temporarily. The family had to stay with relatives. Catherine continued to find London 'uncongenial with its turmoil, its clack, its fog and its cold.' She insisted that when she was in London the children, "drive into the country, and play in the fields; they need not go many miles, indeed, only just beyond Regents' Park." Sir John continued to say, "Sell," ignoring the many times he was told, "Father, if you are an aristocrat you are a custodian only. Hawarden is not ours to sell. It is our duty is to pass it on to our heirs." Sir John snapped. "It is a pity you did not think of that beforehand" but Lawyer Barker and Mr. Burnett, the land-agent, sympathized.

By 1852 there was a slight improvement in the situation. The house was re-opened and Sir Stephen's income doubled. In 1865

Gladstone paid £57,000 for the bulk of the property, subject to debts not exceeding £150,000. Even, on 3rd October 1885, Gladstone was writing to Willy from Hawarden, *Since the revision came in, I have, as you know, forwarded that process; but it has been retarded by agricultural depression and by the disastrous condition through so many years of coal-mining; so that there still remains considerable work to be done before the end can be attained.*

Gladstone concluded the letter, *When I concurred in the decision to struggle for the retention of Hawarden, I had not the least idea that my children would have an interest in the succession. In 1847, your uncle Stephen was only forty; your uncle Henry, at thirty-seven, was married, and had a child almost every year. It was not until 1865, that I had any title to look forward to your becoming at a future time the proprietor.*

Henry, the Rector of St. Deiniol's Church, Hawarden, was Catherine's youngest brother and married to Lavinia', George's sister. They lived next to the church in the beautiful eighteenth-century rectory whose red bricks and sash windows dominated the High Street. Every year Lavinia produced a rather weak baby. Following the Oak Farm catastrophe Catherine pointed out, "The Rectory is still large enough to accommodate us and all of our children." Her seventh child, Henry, was born in the Rectory. The Gladstones also lodged with Mary and George at Hagley. Catherine forgot herself enough to lecture her hosts on ways they should economize. She went so far as to say, "If only George would exert himself, the financial problems of Hagley would soon be over." He responded by writing to Catherine, *It is not fair to accuse us of extravagance in our general style of living.* He was not a careerist or politician. He had held only one senior political appointment. In 1846 he joined Peel's administration as Under Secretary for War and the Colonies. He enjoyed meeting his fellow peers in the House of Lords and being Lord Lieutenant of Worcestershire. Kindly, George refrained from mentioning that he and Mary had not been forced to impose themselves on relatives. He spent much of his time with his Classical studies and compiling the Glynnese Glossary. This much impressed Catherine. Gladstone made little comment. He barely bothered to use the 'language'. Catherine and George remained friends. On 30th January 1849, Catherine wrote to Gladstone, *Conceive your old wife going a regular buck to Exeter Hall with George last night. I certainly now feel I heard Jenny Lind. We sat in the gallery places looking down on our grander friends!*

Sir John dies

On 7th December 1851, Sir John died at Fasque. Tom, as the heir, became Sir Thomas Gladstone, Bt., of Fasque and Balfour, and owner of his father's estate. Gladstone, who loved Fasque, asked if he could buy the property. Sir Thomas refused. Gladstone removed most of his books from his study and visited Fasque far less. Sir John's will gave Helen the interest on £50,000 of which she could only will £15,000. It is here that Miss Gladstone leaves the stage to live in Germany. Gladstone received a legacy of £151,000 which improved his financial situation considerably, helping Catherine and him to move away from the fiasco of Oak Farm. However, the OF remained a shadowy presence for the rest of their lives.

In 1852, Sir Stephen returned to Hawarden. All through the crisis he had remained the Lord Lieutenant of Flintshire. Now, feeling in reduced circumstances, he managed to live on his income of £2,000 a year. Catherine and Gladstone had offered him a joint occupancy of Hawarden. The result: Sir Stephen sat at the head of the table, with Catherine and Gladstone sitting either side, treating him with the deference due to his position. He, in his turn, referred to them as 'the great people'. Lady Glynne managed to overcome her depression enough to assist with expenses.

A house of charity

Ever since their marriage charitable activities had been a part of Catherine and Gladstone's marriage. Beneath the stability of much of England's middle-class life lay fear of poverty and starvation. Men searched in the gutter for snails to eat, others swept dog dung off the streets to sell to the tanners and, here and there, amongst the chaos and degradation that was Victoria's London, a country girl could be heard singing out, *Sweet Primroses, two bunches a penny. Buy my Sweet Primroses*.

In 1842 Gladstone started on the course of 'rescue work' which was to enthral him into old age. First he worked within the context of a lay Tractarian brotherhood of fifteen members. They had links with the Oxford Movement. This was based at the Church of All Saints, Margaret Street, London, and was mostly concerned with liturgy but had twelve rules. The first and most important was to undertake regular charity work. Gladstone decided to help with both male and female homeless, and Catherine joined him in his work for the House of Charity for Distressed Persons. This was a former workhouse at 9 Rose Street, Soho. It gave assistance to superior persons, that is, to ordinary vagrants who had fallen on hard times, often through illness, and were fast drifting into abject poverty. Too proud to apply to the Poor Law they slipped further and further down the social scale. No charity existed to help this group of people until in 1846, Dr. Henry Moore, with other distinguished people, established the House of Charity. It accommodated fifty to sixty persons and children. They were lodged comfortably and offered proper clothing so that they could accept suitable employment, which was found for them by the warden.

Only one thing was asked of the inhabitants, that they possessed an unblemished character. Those helped included: clergymen, dissenting ministers, solicitors, schoolmasters, farmers, merchants, artisans, orphans, widows and immigrants — anyone who was friendless and destitute. In 1848 Dr. Moore became physician in charge to Bethlehem Hospital (Bedlam). In 1863 the House of Charity moved to 1 Greek Street, Soho, where it still remains. The House of Mercy was in many ways Catherine's introduction to the world of charity.

Other ventures
In 1848 Gladstone, together with Bishop 'Soapy Sam'

Wilberforce and the Bishop of London, Bishop Blomfield, founded the Church Penitentiary Association for the Reclamation of Fallen Women. Another venture was the Clewer Home of Mercy. While in Naples Catherine and Gladstone met a Mrs. Monsell and with her started a charity, in connection with the Church of England, under the control of the Community of St. John the Baptist, an Anglican Order. It was housed in a beautiful group of buildings at Clewer near Oxford and had links with the House of Charity. A typical inmate was Rebecca Ayscough, who came from the Millbank Penitentiary, repented of her past life and wished to reform. After a suitable time she went to work for Catherine and Gladstone's friend, the celibate Revd. Henry Manning. The experience was too much for both of them and Rebecca returned to her original ways.

From 1849 to 1901, 2,501 girls passed through the Home of Mercy. The numbers may have been increased when the Home moved to Old Windsor, a garrison town. Some of the girls said, "We had a good home until [our] mother died." In other cases their father had remarried and the stepmother did not want a constant memory of the first wife 'hanging around'. Many were labourers' daughters with no real education. A few of the girls went out to work at ten years of age. Some were feeble-minded, alcoholic, "tramps, or thieves and could not be reclaimed but Clewer gave them a respite for a while." Just after the Millennium, the sisters moved away and the buildings were converted into up-market flats.

Mary Drew, in her biography of her mother, wrote, in 1863, *they held a meeting at Carlton Terrace to start the Mary Magdalen Rescue Home, which later on moved to Paddington. The chief object of this Home was to shelter the babies as well as the girl mothers. This was, at the time, quite a new departure. They held strongly to the opinion that it was the most natural as well as the most wholesome course and often a means of regeneration to the mother. In the streets of London they worked with tireless energy. She shrank from nothing.* It is believed that the Rescue Home was moved to Paddington in 1852. Canals and the Great

Western Railway meant the area changed from that of pleasant market and nursery gardens surrounded by tiled cottages to the grimy buildings of the Harrow Road. Once celebrities such as the actress Sarah Siddons or the poet Leigh Hunt (author of *What is Poetry?*) had a place there; even Queen Adelaide resided in the neighbourhood. Celebrities could be found living in the elegant houses of Little Venice, lining the edge of Regent's Canal.

During the 1860s several charities were founded for the genteel poor such as the then Royal United Kingdom Beneficent Association (RUKBA). Six clergymen became alarmed at the prospects facing destitute gentlewomen. Such women were befriended and offered an annuity. If the individual's circumstances did not change, it was for life.

Rescue work

At one point in his life, Sir Stephen had been nearly sued for homosexual behaviour, which up to 1861 was a hanging offence. It was Gladstone's intervention which saved Sir Stephen. Female prostitution held a fascination for Gladstone. In August 1828, as a young man considering going up to Oxford, during an evening stroll he met in the town a 'lady of the night'. They talked for a long time. The following evening he met 'the poor creature' again. Once more, he *only* talked to her. The girl must have wondered about her appeal. Gladstone was eighteen.

In nineteenth-century England a surplus of over 500,000 women searched for a marriageable man. Little respectable work was available to lone women and even when it was, it was poorly paid. In London, out of a population of a million, eighty thousand prostitutes nightly roamed the East End, Strand, Leicester Square, Soho and Seven Dials. As they came out of Covent Garden visitors to the opera tripped over 'women of the streets'. Returning to Carlton House Gardens, Gladstone could not avoid them, so 'close to home'. They 'showed themselves' off along Haymarket and Piccadilly, even posing on the Duke of York Steps, gaudily dressed, gowns cut so low their breasts hung out, with nipples rouged. Black patches covered smallpox and other scars. Around them urchins chanted, "Red Hat, No drawz."

Later generations considered that some of the blame lay with wives, namely that they were brought up to be prudes. *They did not all lay back and think of England.* Ineffective contraception, painful childbirth and venereal diseases made many women turn against their husbands. Some men, in their turn, turned to prostitutes. A young wife is reported complaining about her husband's performance, "I think men have not been properly trained." If not, why not? Brothels existed from London's Argyll Rooms in the Strand to houses in the back streets in any market town.

Three categories of prostitutes

The sociologist (and journalist) Henry Mayhew observed that there were three types of prostitutes: Up-market kept women, girls working in brothels and street walkers. It could be argued that all women, without financial and emotional support of a family were at risk. If such wayward girls as Helen and Lady Suzy had not come from wealthy families, they may well have become one of the pretty, little horse-breakers, riding along Rotten Row. Catherine Walters, 'Skittles', came from a poor family. She attracted numerous wealthy lovers, including the Marquis of Hartington, later the 8th Duke of Devonshire, but she was called a courtesan not a prostitute. 'Skittles' was discreet as well as 'sexy'. She died a rich woman, living in Mayfair's South Street, next door to Florence Nightingale.

A madam of a brothel would be interested in a pretty girl like Elizabeth Roberts. She was one of Catherine's Carlton House Terrace maids. She stole and tried pawning some of her mistress's jewellery. Roberts was lucky, when she appeared at Bow Street Magistrates Court Mr. and Mrs. Gladstone spoke up for her. Catherine described it as "quite a new scene to find myself there. I felt very shy." Roberts was given hard labour — meaningless work, crushing stones or unpicking rags, in the Penitentiary at Millbank.

The prison was founded in 1816, close to Vauxhall Bridge, on 'humanitarian' lines. Males and females were segregated. They were forced to work and received moral and religious instruction. The inmates were fed so poorly their health suffered. Dysentery was prevalent throughout Millbank. Many faced transportation to Australia. Once out of prison, with no references, Roberts would not have found work. On leaving the Penitentiary, instead of a madam she found Catherine and Gladstone waiting for her. Gladstone sat on the committee of management. They took her under their wing and prayed God would reveal His purpose for her. It was certainly not prostitution! One of Mrs. Disraeli's maids stole from a neighbour in Grosvenor Gate. The girl went to prison and Mary Anne sacked the husband, a faithful servant and coachman. Sarah, Disraeli's sister, asked "What will become of them?"

In 1890, Millbank closed. It had cost over £16,000 a year to run and during 1890, a year of government restraint, the Home Secretary announced, "Too much. Cuts must be made." If Roberts, in her old age, ever strolled along the river bank at Vauxhall, she would have passed a bollard: *Near this spot stood Millbank Penitentiary. It marks the place where prisoners were deported.* In any year at least four thousand men or women found a 'new home' in Australia.

Life for a working girl

By 1848, Gladstone said he had found working in the House of Charity too time-consuming. True, he was involved in other ventures but like many Victorian men he was preoccupied with the taboo subject of the time — sex. As a young man he would have been lectured about self-harm causing madness or blindness, or both! Men must suppress their desires. Only an unnatural woman had any! So Gladstone began battling against the 'great social evil' of prostitution, which was especially prevalent in the 1840s. He left the House of Commons after midnight and wandered the streets. Armed only with a strong stick he talked to the girls and *trod the path of danger.* Sometimes, *Our Old Glad Eye* accompanied them into their homes, to take tea. He wrote their names and details in his diary. If very beautiful, he noted the fact in Italian. In 1852, he described the prostitute Elizabeth Collins as *beautiful beyond measure.* Another, Marion Summerhayes, he describes as *full in the highest degree both of interest and beauty.* Gladstone never mentioned the 'rent boy' hidden in a doorway, which lifted his shirt for a gentleman, sometimes to raise funds to buy his 'Sweet Jenny' a home. However, he did record coming across young girls of twelve or thirteen walking the streets. They were no longer 'profitable'. It was a commonly held myth in Victoria's times that intercourse with a young virgin cured venereal disease. Once used, the child was no longer 'fit for purpose'.

Gladstone offered a street-walker an escape from her 'mackerel', the man who controlled her life. Gladstone made sure she received three square meals a day, medical attention, new clothes and the possibility of a new life, perhaps emigration or even marriage to a respectable man. Those who slid back into life on the streets did not receive a lecture from him. A 'rescued' prostitute, Jane Bywater, wrote to Catherine in 1854, *I have no doubt you wished to do me service but I did not fancy shut up in your House of Mercy for perhaps twelve months. I should have committed suicide.* A parlour-maid could expect to work from 6.30 A.M. until the company had finished dinner and then she had to clear the dessert things away. If it was acceptable to Mistress, she had one day off a week and must be in by 10 P.M. Marriage would be difficult for her, "no callers allowed". And while she worked she must 'dust' in the way Madam commanded. If the girl 'got herself into trouble', her mother would shut the door. It was never the fault of the young master of the house or sometimes the old one! It was better that baby went to Coram Hospital for Foundlings (now the Foundling Museum) than being dragged up by a single 'Mum'.

If a girl climbed-out of service and became a shop assistant, she still worked long hours for little pay and remained at risk. A shop walker stood at the entrance of an emporium or shop enticing customers. Once caught, he would conduct the potential customer to a chair and call, "forward if you please", to a waiting shop assistant. The girl would then serve the customer. The purchase completed the lady would leave the premises. If Madam noticed a girl was pretty or slightly misbehaved, she had her dismissed.

Did Gladstone know of the practice of the young men about town to 'pick-up' a prostitute, ply her with alcohol until she was drunk and, then for the amusement of the company, make her swallow a concoction of vinegar, mustard and pepper. Hopefully she would go into convulsions or if she became insensible, the young gentlemen could practice all sorts of obscenities upon her. Some who were bored with this orgy enjoyed thinking-up even more ingenious methods of degrading girls.

It is not reported if Gladstone knew of these 'goings on', but he punished himself for harbouring impure thoughts. In the margins of his diary appears the sign of a whip. Some men even scourged themselves with a thong bedded with nails. What did the servants feel or his children when they heard him abusing himself? Gladstone knew suffering was in the Christian tradition. He observed, "For all we know Cranmer may have had the joy in the burning of his hand more than the pain of it." Did Catherine think *Le vice anglais* was normal, something English gentlemen did? 'After all William has been to Eton.' Did she call up the stairs, "William, do stop whipping yourself. You are upsetting the servants?"

We will never know but it is highly probable that he brought the girls he met on the street back to Catherine. There is the story of a young man who saw Gladstone pick up a prostitute and asked him "Sir, what will your wife think?" Astonished, Gladstone replied. "But it is to my wife that I am taking her." He knew Catherine would sympathize. In 1850, a working-girl told Catherine, "I have a son to support and, working very hard with my needle, I may reach 6s a week. I send my boy to school for 6d a week and pay 5s for my lodgings." Did all this activity lead Mr. and Mrs. Hampton, butler and housekeeper, to the Gladstones, to confess to their employers, "We had sexual relations before marriage, and thoroughly enjoyed it?"

Gladstone's interest in prostitution leaves a query over Catherine. She was certainly not an *'Angel in the House'*, a woman who lived only for her husband and family. For the first thirteen years of her marriage Catherine was often pregnant. A gentleman would never sleep with his wife 'in such a condition'. Gladstone spent much of his time working in London, and Catherine disliked politics almost as much as she disliked the capital. She loved Hawarden and spent as much time as possible there or went away to Mary at Hagley for weeks at a time. Even when she was at Carlton House Terrace, Catherine did not play the supportive political wife, *called on Mrs. Egerton and loved her momentarily for being out.* In London, a society lady was expected to make calls between three o'clock to six o'clock in the afternoon. Calls were expected to be returned the next day. Catherine may have kept her cards in a case and even had illustrations of Hawarden Castle on the lid. Such illustrations were popular, ever since Albert and Victoria bought Balmoral. Catherine's case probably wore well!

Alone, as Gladstone often was, he did not resort to keeping a lady — a common enough pastime for Victorian husbands. The *Punch* cartoonist Linley Sambourne enjoyed taking photographs of a nude girl riding a bicycle. Mrs. Sambourne was shaken to discover her husband had started a second family with one of the 'ladies'. The cookery book author Mrs. Beeton died of syphilis given to her by her husband. Venereal disease hid in every nook and cranny of Victorian life. Did Catherine never worry about her husband? There were so many dangers surrounding his 'rescue work'. Did she know of his passion for soft-core pornography? He studied the medieval Giovannni Boccaccio, read *Satyricon* by the Roman Petronius and the French *fabliaux*, the bawdy poetry of the twelfth and thirteenth centuries. On one occasion Catherine did enquire about, "your own peculiar night work".

In May 1853 Gladstone, the then Chancellor of the Exchequer, was returning to Carlton Gardens with a friend late one night. He was accosted by a young woman. When she left Gladstone, a man, who was a clerk in the General Post Office, tried to blackmail him. Gladstone turned him over to the police. On 15th June 1853 the man was sentenced to twelve months hard labour. He wrote to Gladstone begging for forgiveness. Due to Gladstone's intervention he was released after serving only half of his sentence. It was then that the general public learned that Gladstone, with Catherine's help, had been involved in rescue work for some years.

On 20th May 1898, following Gladstone's death, an old friend, M.M. published a story in the *Daily Chronicle*. He ended the article, *the fact is, Mr. Gladstone was a man of singularly unsuspicious character. Knowing the purity of his own motives it would not have occurred to him that anybody would misconstrue his conduct.* On another occasion, on a beautiful June evening in 1878, Gladstone dined at Rutland Gate and walked home with a fellow guest. Opposite Knightsbridge Barracks they were accosted by a young woman. Gladstone asked his companion, "Do you always repel the advances of such women? Perhaps you are right. But I never like to. I have come across terrible tragedies in that way and perhaps been able to do a little good. I believe that as a rule they are more sinned against than sinning."

Disraeli said, "Mrs. Gladstone is the most beautiful woman I ever saw." When Gladstone became infatuated with the great courtesans of the day, Laura Thistlewayte, Lily Langtry, 'Skittles' and one of Disraeli's paramours, Lady Loudon, did she feel so secure of her husband that she brushed his interest in these women on one side? Did she feel no other woman could compete with her? Even into her old age society remarked, 'Mrs. Gladstone **is** beautiful,' not 'Mrs. Gladstone is still beautiful.' Was Catherine like the Victorian wife who wrote, *Love: the highest devotion is based upon it, a very beautiful thing, I am glad nature gave it to us?* It is true she was a Lady Hamilton 'look-alike'. Did she know Gladstone would never stray, because she too understood the arts of the bedroom? Or was she blinkered? She referred to Mrs. Disraeli 'as that ridiculous old woman'. Catherine never knew her husband called on Mrs.

Disraeli and bowing over a bowl of strawberries, gazed into her eyes, muttering, "Dear lady, sweet from the sweet." Mary Anne told Disraeli, "You know Dizzy; with a little encouragement Mr. Gladstone can be most charming." Disraeli replied, "Don't, dearest, don't."

Even though Gladstone was to carry on 'his rescue work' into old age, in January 1854 he recorded in his diary, *I have spoken to eighty to ninety girls, "Among these there is but one of whom I know who has abandoned her miserable life and can only fairly join that fact with influence from me."* Another girl told a commentator, "Sir, why should I not marry well? Am I not pretty? I dress well. I know how to handle my affairs. I know what men want. Pray Sir why should I not marry well?" It is not known the answer Gladstone would have given her. A strong, sensible girl could retire, buying a shop or seaside boarding house and thereafter be known as a most respectable widow.

Divorce

Marriage for the Victorian middle and working classes could be a prison, with no release date. A man with a frigid wife was trapped and had little alternative but to find a more congenial sexual partner. To Catherine and Gladstone, divorce was an immense evil. It was possible for the wealthy to do so through a Private Act of Parliament. In July 1857, the Divorce Law was introduced. Gladstone hurried to Westminster. He remembered the terrible time when he had been summoned to the House of Lords to give evidence in Lord Lincoln's 'wretched divorce, a most tedious process' and an excessively expensive one. Lord Morley recounts the story of how Gladstone travelling to London to discuss the Divorce Bill, told Catherine of how a stranger travelling with him, "in the railway carriage, more genial than congenial, offered me his *Times*, and then brandy. This was followed by a proposal to smoke, so that he had disabled me from objecting on personal grounds. Tobacco, brandy at odd hours, and the newspaper made a triple abomination in a single dose." Over-strung, Gladstone told his wife, "As you know, none of the three was ever a favourite article of mine."

Gladstone, recovering from his unfortunate experiences, spoke against the Bill especially on its inequality for women. "It is the special and peculiar doctrines of the Gospel respecting the personal relations of every Christian, whether man or woman, to the person of Christ that form the firm, the broad indestructible basis of the equality of the sexes under Christian law." He held the view that, "In the vast majority of cases where a woman falls into sin, she does so from motives less impure and ignoble than those of the man." The discussion of the Divorce Bill occupied eighteen sittings before it became law but Gladstone managed to incorporate into it, 'that no clergyman should be requested to marry divorced persons.'

Gladstone allocated £2,000 a year to 'his rescue work'. By the time he died he had spent £94,000. During the next decade Catherine would face a terrible loss while Gladstone continued to advance his political career.

CHAPTER THREE

Journey to Naples, King of an Island and Goodbye to a Sister

The 1850s

DEPARTURES

Sir Robert dies

Saturday, 29th June 1850, was a particularly beautiful day. Sir Robert Peel left his house, enjoying the sunshine. He resented having to be indoors by eleven o'clock for a meeting to discuss the Great Exhibition. It was a project dear to his heart. In the afternoon the sun still shone, and against the advice of his coachman he decided to try out a difficult new horse. Sir Robert rode the animal up Constitution Hill. Within sight of St George's Hospital the horse met a skittish young horse. Sir Robert's mount plunged and reared. The animal tossed its rider over its head. Three days later Sir Robert died, in agony. He was only sixty-two years of age. Gladstone had lost his political father-figure and Catherine a dear friend. Nine years before she had dined with Sir Robert. The subject turned to children and education. He said, "I like my girls to travel with me, it enlarges their minds." Catherine observed, "It shows that amidst his great cares the domestic element is deep in his heart." In 1842, on another June day, Sir Robert had written to Catherine about Gladstone, one of his young, junior ministers. She especially valued the appraisal of such a man: *At no time in the annals of Parliament has there been exhibited a more admirable combination of ability, extensive knowledge, temper and discretion — your feeling must be gratified in the highest degree by the success which has naturally and justly followed his intellectual exertions, and that the capacity to make such exertions is combined, in his case, with such purity of heart and integrity of spirit.*

Slowly during 1850, the nightmare of Oak Farm came to an end. On 28th August, Gladstone announced, "I am now at the bottom of these difficulties which, although lessened, are still frightful." The news cheered the Glynnes. They could relax but Sir Stephen had shown little real concern. With remarkable delicacy, he ignored his brother-in-law's struggles to keep the roof over the family's head. He continued collecting antiquities and visiting churches with gay abandon. Henry offered little practical support either. He did, however, pray for a good outcome. Sir John wearied by it all made, No. 6. Carlton Gardens over to Gladstone who by 1856 felt comfortably off enough to purchase the lease of 11, Carlton House Terrace. It was next door to No.13 where he and Catherine had begun their married life.

Lavinia

On 15th September, two weeks after Gladstone had told his family, "All is well," Lavinia gave birth to a little girl. This was her fourth baby. At the time of the birth Catherine and Gladstone were enduring their annual three-week break at Fasque. When they returned to Hawarden Henry reported that "the birth has been difficult. Our baby survives and is strong but Lavinia is weak". Shortly afterwards his wife died. As usual, Catherine took control of the situation. Living as she did in the shadow of the hurly-burly world of politics, often alone, she had appreciated the gentle, kindness of Lavinia. Catherine longed for the support of her 'Oak' but he was in London and his Masters could not spare him. When Gladstone arrived to attend Lavinia's funeral, he found it was 'his Cathie' who *was the prop and centre for all the rest.*

Naples

As so often happens after you lose somebody close to you the world seemed to Catherine a much colder and quieter place. With

Sir Robert's death it appeared even more so. As the leaves began blowing around the hill and through the walls of the old fortress-castle, autumn arrived, heralding a bitter winter. Gladstone looked particularly hard at Catherine. Not usually an observant man, he assumed his wife always 'twinkled', but now he noticed a lowness of spirits. Catherine's fortieth birthday approached and she showed signs of yet another pregnancy. He said "Catherine, 1850 has been a year of anxiety. Let us spend the winter in Naples." He knew the town would restore her. Was it not in the Church of Santa Maria Maggiore that 'Mr. Gladstone had really fallen in love with Miss Glynne?' On 18th October 1850, Gladstone, Catherine, Agnes and Mary started out on the journey to Naples. It would restore them all.

Henry's children were left in charge of the Dowager Lady Lyttelton. She wondered if Gladstone appreciated the sacrifice she had made. He did. She was at the centre of the Court and knew all that was going on. The position of lady-in-waiting and 'Nanny' to the Queen's children was not one to be given up lightly. However, they all joined together with a fond memory, the day that Lavinia made her 'agreeable match' which so pleased her Mama and Papa. Henry, overjoyed with his 'treasure', presented his fiancée with a red rose. Lavinia placed it between the pages of her prayer book. Mary Drew wrote that, *it is nearly a century since she passed away; the rose still lies in the book, treasured by her surviving daughter.* Lavinia's youngest daughter, Gertrude, the one she died for, became mistress of Penrhyn Castle, Bangor. She died in 1940. Lady Penrhyn spent her life in a mock, nineteenth-century fortress. Like Sir John, the Pennants, the family to whom she married into, owed their fortune to Jamaican plantations worked by slaves. The family too showed compassion. They did not ship in new slaves from Africa but built-up on those already working on the plantations. It was these monies which helped to found the Welsh slate industry. Penrhyn Castle houses a bed in which Queen Victoria refused to sleep in. It is made from a ton of Welsh slate.

The family became respected for their charity. One wonders if Lady Penrhyn followed in her Aunt Catherine's footsteps.

Who should inherit Hawarden?

Even after Lavinia's death, Henry continued to lead a comfortable life. The benefice of Hawarden was worth £4,000 a year. This allowed for the keeping of a carriage and pair, the enjoyment of a good port, an excellent table and the company of convivial friends. Every Sunday Henry climbed into the pulpit to deliver a respectable sermon. During weekdays he visited his parishioners. In fact, as a Rector, he did exactly what was expected of him. Only as Sir Stephen's heir did he disappoint Catherine.

He, too, took little interest in the Hawarden Estate. As the bells rang out, announcing the birth of Lavinia's first baby — an heir for Hawarden — the little boy was discovered dead amongst the clothes on his mother's bed; he was not even an hour old. Four girls followed, who, on the death of Lavinia, gave Catherine and Gladstone a problem. The estate could not pass to a girl. After Henry, who should inherit Hawarden?

The journey to Naples

On 18th October 1850, Agnes's, eighth birthday, Mr. and Mrs. Gladstone with Agnes and Mary began their journey to Naples. Gladstone was weary, Catherine pregnant (yet again), Agnes was recovering from St. Andrew's Fire (which had nearly killed her), and Mary's eyesight was failing. In the excitement of travel they soon forgot Oak Farm and all its problems. The little group boarded the Continental-boat at London Bridge. Agnes celebrating her birthday received her first kiss from a 'non-family-man'. The ship's captain wished her "A happy birthday." Gladstone was shocked! Agnes said, "Don't be Papa, I enjoyed it!"

When they left the boat they boarded a train and rode third-class to Naples, in a carriage, which they had bought to fit in into a railway-coach. The quality, even those travelling third class, did not wish to rub shoulders with the hoi-polloi. Gladstone noted that the European rate was dearer than in England. The complete journey took them nearly a month. He estimated they covered nearly two hundred miles by rail and it cost him £10 3s 0d.

When the party arrived in Naples, Catherine found that Gladstone had not booked them into a hotel-suite, in fact, not even in to a hotel. He had rented an apartment. He told Catherine, "I knew you would prefer it." When she complained he reminded her that the Oak Farm fiasco had reduced his income to £5,100 per annum and that most of his Carlton Gardens neighbours enjoyed an income of £20,000 per annum. Had he not been forced to write to her? *I am thankful for your letters and will continue to have them on any terms but I suggest you stop your habit of sending them unpaid which is now so frequent.* Catherine replied sharply, "William, I have travelled three nights, in a carriage, with no opportunity to remove my clothes."

Mary hoped that being in Naples would restore her eyesight. Agnes just loved the place. Gladstone, as a private person, wished to pursue his interest in Italian art uninterrupted, and Catherine shook Gladstone by telling him with some glee, "The men say I am like a Spanish woman, not a bit like an English woman!" Busy he might be in wishing to study the art of Naples but in London he had heard disturbing reports of the way political prisoners were kept in Italian jails. He felt it was his duty to inspect the prisons. The reports were true. The men were housed in appalling conditions. He saw political prisoners chained two by two in double irons to common felons. He watched sick prisoners, men with death etched on their faces, toiling upstairs to see doctors. The lower regions were too foul for professional men to enter. *One grows wild at being able to do nothing,* Gladstone wrote to London colleagues. Some say it was this experience which turned him into a Liberal.

As Gladstone struggled with Italian politics, Catherine's health deteriorated further. Late in November, in the early hours of the morning, she miscarried. Four weeks later she suffered a severe haemorrhage. Unusually for Catherine, she was in a highly nervous state. She even began taking laudanum to calm her down. Meanwhile, in London, Prime Minister Russell resigned and the Whigs fell. The House demanded Gladstone's return. Lord Canning and Lord Richard Cavendish begged him to do so. He ignored them. On 18th February 1851, he reluctantly travelled back to London, leaving Catherine alone, vulnerable and unwell. She wrote to her husband, *I hope you make the world (who is interested) take in that you left me the very soonest you could.*

Catherine was not alone for long. With trepidation, she learned Sir Stephen was coming out to care for her. Once, she had written, *I sometimes feel inclined to laugh as I ask him to do something, the very simplest thing such as shutting a window or paying a cab fare; the one he shuts 'to', perhaps without attempting to bolt it and open it flies, the other he pays according to my order but is sure to rush after me to know what is to be done, the man perhaps after him, or, what it ends in, after me.*

Sir Stephen arrived with a manservant. He could not, of course, make such a journey alone. Despite or because of Sir Stephen's best endeavours, Catherine recovered. The three months spent in Naples also restored Agnes' health and Mary's eyesight. From then on Mary was nicknamed 'Naples Mary'. Gladstone met them in a Paris showing signs of spring. He chaperoned his wife and daughters back to England. On his return, Gladstone immediately set to work, writing to the new Prime Minister, Lord Aberdeen. He called for the Government to intervene in the condition of political prisoners. The influential newspapers published Gladstone's letter. The anger of the public forced the Government to take action.

Homecoming

They spent little time in London. Catherine longed to return to her children and to Hawarden, even though Gladstone had described the estate as, 'not in the first class but quite at the top of the second class'. As they approached the Castle a row of colourful dressing gowns fluttered from windows, the Gladstone children's customary welcome home. When Catherine's maid had finally unpacked, her mistress came down to the drawing room where her children were waiting for her. Into old age, they remembered their mother throwing her arms out to them, her dark hair sliding down her back. "Hello, my darlings. We are back together again." She stood on the hearthrug, a shade too close to the fire and as the coals fell, flung her arms around Gladstone's shoulders and they began chanting:

A ragamuffin husband and a rantipoling wife
We'll fiddle it and scrape it through the ups and downs of life

The children knew the song and the servants did as well. They all joined in, including Gladstone. Catherine would pause and begin kissing her children over and over again, "Oh, my darling ones." Did she ever glance around her looking into the shadows of the room for Jessy? We shall never know, but we do know that she mourned not seeing Lavinia running out of the Rectory to greet her. For a long time Catherine whispered to herself, "Oh, how one loves one's mourning so." Mourn she might, but she had Lavinia's four little girls to care for. Soon, Catherine herself would be pregnant again and within the next three years produce two little boys, 'My Sugar Plums'. She did not know then that before the decade was over she would be responsible for twelve more children, 'George's Cricket Team'. Under a carefully hidden watchful eye, Catherine allowed her children to 'roam free'. They borrowed planks from the timber yard, straw from the stables, fruit from the kitchen-garden, candle-ends from the pantry, and anything they could persuade cook to give them. They were as 'wild as hawks'.

The Great Exhibition

After the excitement of Naples came *The Great Exhibition of the Works of Industry of All Nations*. Gladstone agreed with the instigator, Prince Albert, *The Exhibition of 1851 is to give a true test and a living picture of the point of development at which the whole of mankind has arrived in this great task of applied science and a new starting point from which all nations will be able to direct their further exertions*. Lord Russell cheered Gladstone's heart by stating that, "a large fund requisite for this purpose ought to be provided by the voluntary contributions of individuals, rather than from the public revenue".

Catherine tried not to be too joyful. The Exhibition was built across the road from No. 1 Grosvenor Gate, where Mr. and Mrs. Disraeli lived. When Mary Anne looked out of her windows, she saw, glittering at her, 1,073 square feet of glass, with 203,655 panels, together with 1,245 roof girders and 3,000 columns, dwarfing the two great elms, which she so loved. Indeed, it was a Palace of Crystal, designed by the Duke of Devonshire's gardener, Joseph Paxton.

The idea came to him when his little girl stood in the middle of the lake at Chatsworth, balancing on *Victoria regia*, the giant water-lily.

Messrs Fox & Henderson, contractors, were appointed and on 4th December 1850 the ribs of the transept were hauled up. In the New Year 2,112 workmen arrived. On the morning of 1st May 1851, the Queen with the Prince Consort opened the Exhibition, with little Princess Victoria and the Prince of Wales watching opened-mouthed. The Queen wore a diamond diadem with a little crown at the back and two feathers, a pink and silver dress with a full skirt and a lace *fichu* draped over her bust — pink particularly became her.

The Royal couple were obviously moved when the organ and six hundred voices thundered out the Hallelujah chorus. They visited the fourteen thousand exhibits from all over the world. Apart from Victoria and Albert, six million people visited the Great Exhibition. Londoners became used to mingling with foreigners of all colours and persuasions. Mr. Thomas Cooke and Mr. W.H. Smith were delighted with the profits they made. The cost of extra policing amounted to £5,043.19s 6d. A senior police officer reported that, "not a flower was picked, not a picture smashed". The money taken by the Exhibition was £186,000, 93 per cent above the guaranteed sum.

A Mr. Thomas Masters, confectioner, paid £5,500 for the right to sell refreshments: 6d for a cup of tea or coffee, lemonade, orangeade and ginger beer were obtainable, at 6d a bottle but no beer (which had been banned by Prince Albert). Strawberries, ices, fresh pineapple, savoury pies, patties and sandwiches were also available.

On 15ᵗʰ October 1851 the Exhibition closed. It had been instrumental in making the British people aware of their status as the greatest trading nation on earth and the most powerful country in the world. Public taste improved, gummed envelopes could be purchased (already to lick), and 827,000 people, of all classes, used the public lavatories. The Trustees managed to find and buy land in South Kensington.

They built on the Estate: The Imperial College of Science, Royal College of Art Organists and Music, the City and Guilds College of Engineering, The Natural History Museum and The Victoria and Albert Museum. In 1874, the Physical Society of London found a home on the South Kensington estate. The first President was a chemist called John Gladstone. He did not claim any relationship to Mr. William Ewart Gladstone!

The Exhibition was a fantastic success, Prince Albert's greatest achievement. But Lady Lyttelton observed, "I believe it is quite universally sneered at by the beau monde, and will only increase the contempt for the Prince among fine folk. But so would anything he does."

The Prince of Wales wrote to Baron Stockmar, his father's former tutor, *I am much excited by some waxworks models of murderous Indian thugs.* The Baron reminded him, *Sir, you are born a Christian and live in an enlightened age in which such atrocious acts are not even dreamt of.* Catherine conveyed the feeling of the opening ceremony to Gladstone, who could not be there. *It would be absurd to describe the sight, one's very idea of Arabian nights and fairy scenes, and as glittering and lovely as anything of the kind could be. The Queen looked her very best and the two children played particularly 'nice'.*

Catherine and Gladstone were saddened in 1851 when Willy's

godfather, the Revd. Henry Manning, joined Rome. Catherine and
Gladstone had always valued his advice. They could no longer do
so. Subsequently, he became Archbishop of Westminster and in
1875, a Cardinal and Lord Archbishop of Westminster. The
friendship never quite recovered.

The elegant Aberdeen and friends

While people flocked to the Great Exhibition, politics
continued. On 3rd December 1851 the Foreign Secretary, Lord
Palmerston, had secretly supported the coup d'état of Louis
Napoleon Bonaparte. The Second Republic had been overthrown
by a coup led by its own president who was now Napoleon III.
Against his better judgement, in 1852 Disraeli became Chancellor
of the Exchequer, under Lord Derby. On 3rd December, Disraeli
introduced his first budget. Sick, Disraeli appeared drunk.
Gladstone noticed the bottle of restorative brandy in front of the
Chancellor and called Disraeli and the budget, "disgusting and
repulsive". Figures spoke to him. Obviously they did not to
Disraeli, deeply in debt. The 1852 budget was an attempt to
compensate major interests such as agriculture, shipping and sugar
at the expense of the small taxpayer. The budget of 1851 was badly
received.

On 16th December Disraeli replied to his critics. Gladstone
answered him. In the evening he wrote to Catherine, *I have never
gone through so exciting a passage of parliamentary life. I came home at
7, dined, read for a quarter of an hour, and actually contrived to sleep for
another quarter of an hour. Disraeli rose at 10.20 and from that moment
I was on tenter hooks, except when his superlative acting and brilliant
oratory absorbed me and made me quite forget that I had to follow him.
He spoke till 1.A.M. His speech on the whole was grand. The House has
not, I think, been so excited for years.* Gladstone ended his letter. *I am
told Disraeli is much stung by what I said. I am very sorry it fell on me
to say it. God knows I have no wish to give him pain; and really with the
deep sense of his gifts, I would only pray they might be used well.*

The budget was rejected by 305 votes to 186. The Tories,

Disraeli's party, fell. At about this time Mary was playing with another little girl. "Is your Papa a Whig or a Tory?" "I don't know," replied Mary, "but Dizzy is a beast."

Chancellor of the Exchequer, 1852

Mary Drew says, *The blow to protection and all its work resulted in the defeat of the Government, and Mr. Gladstone became Chancellor of the Exchequer. This appears to have been the only occasion that Mrs. Gladstone was absent from her husband at a time of great crisis in the history of our times. In a letter written to her a few days later, Mr. Gladstone comments on the unexpected loss of temper shown by Lord Derby on his resignation of the Premiership; he contrasts with what took place in the House of Commons.* "Nothing," he wrote, "could be better in temper, feeling and judgement than Disraeli's farewell.

Shortly afterwards Gladstone again wrote to Catherine giving her details of the Chancellor of the Exchequer's official residence: 11, Downing Street. He had been *agreeably surprised with its goodness both as to accommodation and stated that the number and airiness of the bedrooms was satisfactory,* (important to Catherine, a great believer in fresh air) *the servants quarters varied and good, and there were stables closer to the house than they were at Carlton Gardens.* On 3rd February, the Gladstones moved in. On 7th February they celebrated with a party. Catherine's Sugar Plums complained "It is so dirty and we can't climb any trees."

However, Catherine and Gladstone did not celebrate when Disraeli refused to pass on the Chancellor's robes. Disraeli had paid his predecessor £787 12 6d for the furniture of the house and had received a refund from the Office of Works of £479 16s. He asked Gladstone for £307 16 6d to make up the shortfall. There was a disagreement about who should pay. Discussion continued further. Letters were exchanged. Finally, Gladstone wrote to Disraeli, *It is highly unpleasant to Mr. W.E. Gladstone to address Mr. Disraeli without the usual terms of courtesy, but he abstains from them only because he perceives that they are unwelcome.* Disraeli kept the robes. To annoy Gladstone, he wore them during his terms of office. They remain at Hughenden, proudly on display, with a notice, *Pitt the Younger's Chancellors Robes as worn by the Rt. Hon. Benjamin Disraeli M.P. when Chancellor of the Exchequer,*

During 1852, George Hamilton Gordon, 4th Earl of Aberdeen, had become leader of the Peelites. After much horse-trading, the Queen invited him to form a government. He brought together a coalition of Free Traders, Peelites and Whigs with Gladstone as Chancellor of the Exchequer, Lord Russell as Foreign Secretary and Lord Palmerston as Home Secretary. Disraeli coolly observed "England does not love coalitions." Aberdeen and Palmerston were both Harrow men and gossiped about the exploits of Aberdeen's cousin, Lord Byron, whom they both disliked. Both men were suspicious of Disraeli. Neither man knew that Lord Byron had been the young Disraeli's role model.

Aberdeen's inspiration had been Pitt the Younger. Orphaned early, Pitt the Younger became the young aristocrat's guardian, mentor and best friend. Aberdeen said of Pitt, "He had embraced every school of politics which had been of any distinction for more than half a century." Disraeli was also a great admirer of Pitt the Younger. He commented on Aberdeen, "His manner, his education, his prejudices are all of the Kremlin school . . . not a night passes that his language or his demeanour does not shock and jar upon the frank and genial spirit of our British parliament."

However, Mr. and Mrs. Gladstone were very fond of Lord Aberdeen. Gladstone arrived at Hawarden during a blizzard on Christmas Day to tell Catherine the good news. "Aberdeen has made me Chancellor of the Exchequer." When Catherine and Gladstone no longer possessed a London base, Aberdeen's successor, the 7th Earl, placed at their disposal his estate in Dollis Hill, *The most fervent words of gratitude to Lord and Lady Aberdeen could never adequately express the blessing and refreshment of that perfect haven.* They used Dollis Hill for fifteen years. The ties were close. Lord and Lady Aberdeen came to stay at Hawarden and Catherine and Gladstone, travelling to Fasque, sometimes cut the journey by staying at Haddo House, enjoying its homeliness. It was not a

Scottish Castle but an Adam-style house. On display in the National Portrait Gallery is a portrait, *Dinner at Haddo House, 1884*. Gladstone is in the forefront of the picture.

The House had a private theatre which many of the aristocracy possessed. Leading actors and actresses would be invited to give a private performance, something which Catherine and Gladstone would have appreciated. Aberdeen married twice. His first wife, Lady Catherine, daughter of 1st Marquis of Abercorn, died of tuberculosis. He subsequently married Harriet, his sister-in-law, and described her as "the most stupid person I ever met with". The couple created five children. Despite that, Lord Aberdeen told friends, "We do not have a happy marriage!"

Crimean War

The background to the Crimean War is a complicated one. The conflict started in 1853 and concluded with the Treaty of Paris in 1856. In 1844, a meeting was held in London at which Sir Robert Peel, Prime Minister, Lord Aberdeen, Foreign Secretary, the Duke of Wellington and the Tsar of Russia were present. The minutes showed that the meeting was pro-Russian and anti-French. On leaving the Tsar declared, "Europe has a sick man on its hands — Turkey." The British saw the Russian Empire as malevolent, stretching across Europe, expanding into Asia and controlling parts of North America. In February 1852, Lord Russell fell. Lord Derby became Prime Minister and was alarmed when he learned of Russia's ambitions. France and Britain joined together to balance the 'Russian menace' making Russia nervous. The new Foreign Secretary, Lord Malmesbury, was a personal friend of Louis Napoleon Bonaparte. 'Uncle Leopold' wrote to his niece Victoria, *How the Emperor could get himself and everybody else into this infernal scrape is quiet in comprehensible* (sic). The Emperor was anxious, even at the cost of war with Russia, to cement an alliance with Great Britain.

Lord Malmesby's grandfather had been Lord Palmerston's guardian. Palmerston offered to call on Malmesbury privately and give him a sketch of the *status quo* of *Europe*. He advised, "Keep in with France."

The collapsing Ottoman Empire controlled the Holy sites in Palestine. 'A series of churchwarden quarrels' broke out between the Greek Orthodox monks and Roman Catholic monks, with the support of the French Emperor. Eastern Europe and the Middle East seemed to be in a power vacuum. So much was the confusion that Members of Parliament had little time to enjoy Sir Charles Barry's re-built House of Lords and House of Commons. (It would be another thirty years before the whole project was completed.)

In October 1853 Russia and Turkey declared war. The Prince Consort was sucked into the debate, as it was believed he had pro-Russian sympathies. On 16th January 1854, Gladstone wrote an article which appeared in the *Morning Chronicle*, defending the Prince. In February the newspapers were full of how Lord Aberdeen, by nature a peaceful man, was trying to preserve the peace. On 22nd February 1854 he asked Gladstone's view as "to whether I should resign before War is declared". Gladstone responded, "Great Britain has a duty to defend Christians placed under Turkish misrule in the Balkans. It is both a right and a duty, which derives from the public rule of Europe. It was perverted and abused when Russia took it into her own hands in pursuit of selfish ends." Gladstone was prepared to engage in war "until the public law of Europe had been vindicated, and not for a day longer".

In 1854 Wellington's protégé, the one-armed Lord Raglan, was sent out to command the British forces. It was the first time he had led troops in the field. Raglan was instructed to lay siege to Sebastopol. Disaster followed disaster. On 25th October, the Russians made an attempt on Balaclava which eclipsed the Light Brigade. Tennyson read the account in *The Times* and wrote his poem *The Charge of the Light Brigade* within minutes. Every schoolboy is able to recite, "Into the valley of death rode the six hundred . . . "

On 6ᵗʰ March 1854 Gladstone raised income tax from seven pence to one shilling and two pence. In his speech to the House of Commons he said, "The expenses of warfare are a moral check, which, it has pleased the Almighty to impose upon the ambition and lust of conquest that are inherent in so many nations." On 28ᵗʰ March 1854, Britain and France finally declared war on Russia. Gladstone told Catherine, "War! War! War! I fear it will swallow up everything good and useful." He told her later, "We do not know the real meaning of the word." In his emergency budget on 8ᵗʰ May, he was forced to borrow money on Exchequer Bonds. He tried to meet the costs of the war by taxes rather than by loans.

It was the first war which actively engaged the public on a daily basis. Photographs of the realities of war appeared in the newspapers. Two young journalists, Roger Fenton and William Russell, made their names, by reporting to *The Times*. Catherine, caught up in it all, visited Fortnum and Masons to buy gifts for 'our boys'. Twelve-year old Agnes made shirts for the soldiers and Cousin Lucy collected small change, learning the art of fundraising. She was told by Aunt Pussy, "Never mind, Locket, every penny counts."

Catherine, who enjoyed being so much at the centre of great events, longed to take a more active part in the war. In 1854, while preparing for Christmas at Hawarden, she wrote, *It feels very odd here, so quiet. I don't think I like it for in London one could feel to be of some use in the war troubles, whilst it seems unnatural to hear the twaddle remarks and croaking of country friends with no reliable information and no hope of details.*

However, the Queen did receive full details and told Lord Aberdeen she was startled to be asked, within two months of the outbreak of war, for a Day of National Humiliation. The suggestion infuriated the Queen. She commanded, "Let there be a day of prayer." As the war dragged on Her Majesty presented medals, "From the highest prince of the Blood to the lowest private, all must receive the same distinction. The Queen's heart bleeds for them as if for our nearest and dearest."

On 25th January 1855, Aberdeen resigned. Lord Palmerston became Prime Minister. After only a fortnight Gladstone resigned. He could not tolerate the criticism of Lord Aberdeen's policies, especially as he had been one of his most active supporters. After two years of conflict, Palmerston brought the Crimean War to a satisfactory end. Catherine lost two cousins, sons of Uncle Braybrooke. Henry Neville died in battle and Grey Neville in a hospital in Scutari. Henry wrote home describing how *awful it all is waiting to have your head blown-off.* On 30th March 1856, the peace treaty was signed.

Mrs. Disraeli declared, "London has gone mad with fêtes and festivities every night, and we have received an invitation to the palace, where we shall have the honour of dining." Though out the War, the Prince Consort had continually complained about the lack of organisation and munitions. He insisted that men should shoot each other with rifles, instead of the traditional musket. Disraeli recommended that the Ministers responsible for the fiasco of the War should be impeached.

On the evening of 28th June 1855, Lord Ragland died. He had been forced to state, "I have served under the greatest man of the age more than half my life, have enjoyed his confidence, and have, I am proud to say, been ever regarded by him as a man of truth and some judgement as to the qualifications of officers, and yet, having been placed in the most difficult position in which an officer was ever called upon to serve, and having successful carried out different operations, with the entire approbation of the Queen, which is now my only solace, I am charged with every species of neglect . . ." The war transformed Europe. The old order would never return. It laid the groundwork for the military advances of the Great War and, improbable as it would seem, France became Britain's chief ally.

The Family Growing Up

Willy

Each of Catherine's children possessed a very different character. Catherine was too fair ever to acknowledge, even to herself, that she had favourites. However, Willy was her first-born. He was a dark, sensitive boy. Catherine told Gladstone, against all the evidence, that Willy had inherited his father's drive and intelligence. When he was ten she wrote, *He goes daily to William for his Latin lessons. His father tells me his choice of language is remarkable.* On her return from Naples she had written, *the dear boy goes to school next month. May God keep him safe?*

Catherine rose before dawn to see her 'little boy' off to school. For the first time he put on a peak cap and a short jacket. Clutching a portmanteau he joined his father, who would take him south to Birmingham and on to his preparatory school at Geddington. Here he would, in particular, study classical Latin and Greek, ready for his University years. Willy struggled through his entrance examination for Eton.

He was unhappy all the time he was at school. Catherine wrote, *I do miss Willy sadly, even more than I expected really. I feel as if I had lost part of myself.* Gladstone possessed more understanding of his children and wrote to comfort and to amuse his son:

At which I now my pen employ,
In writing to my darling boy.

The relationship between Willy and Gladstone was close. As a small boy he was taken to see Gladstone at work. He thought he was seeing 'Papa' at his lessons.' In 1844, when he was four, his father resigned from the Board of Trade over the Irish question. The little boy read out the words on the door, 'Board of Trade'. When he visited Gladstone for the last time, Catherine told him, "Willy, you will remember this visit for the rest of your life." As a small boy, the fashionable artist, George Richmond, painted Willy's portrait, he found the boy difficult. Richmond was a friend of Willy's parent's. In 1849 he painted the delightful watercolour of Catherine Gladstone which appears on the cover of this book.

In 1855, Willy gratefully left Eton and went up to Christ Church, Oxford. It was a time of religious and scientific controversy and Gladstone knew, from his own experiences as a young man at university, that Willy would come into contact with many influences which conflicted with those in which he had been brought up. Concerned, Gladstone wrote a letter to his son reminding him that, *the purpose of a Christian's life is the recovery of the image of God, as shown unto us in our Lord, Jesus Christ.*

Willy was not an academic so he was not overcome by the theological or philosophical problems of the day. In fact, his career at Oxford could not be called brilliant. He obtained a 2nd in Greats and a 3rd class degree in law and history. What Willy lacked in intellect he made up for in 'niceness'. Whilst at university Willy made many sound and lasting friendships. One friendship especially delighted Catherine and Gladstone. Willy entered into the Prince of Wales' set. In August 1857, the Queen chose Willy to accompany the Prince on his first tour abroad. Catherine wrote to Gladstone, *I keep the details regarding the Prince of Wales (of course) to myself.* They were, however, less delighted when the Prince became involved in a 'squalid debauch' with an actress.

Gladstone wrote to Catherine that, in his view, the Prince had *not been educated to his position . . . kept in childhood beyond his time, he is allowed to make that childhood what it should never be in a Prince, namely wanton.* On the other hand, Willy did behave well, being suitable to become, if necessary, the heir to Hawarden.

Agnes
Catherine's second child, Agnes, was born a month after Gladstone's shooting accident. She was a beautiful baby who grew into a lovely, placid woman with none of her parents' toughness, only her father's tendency to suffer from St. Anthony's Fire. Agnes

was Sir John's favourite among his many granddaughters. This may have made up for the fact that Catherine unconsciously over-looked her daughter in favour of Willy.

Stephen

In 1844, Catherine had a third baby. Stephen proved to be a withdrawn little boy. In January 1849 Catherine wrote, *Stephy at five and a half is a curious child. I feel there is much to come out of him and he will not be commonplace. Feelings warm, kindness and what he may think unkindness sink very deep. There is much in him for good or evil.* Gladstone, on the other hand, thought Stephen showed 'an outright earnestness of purpose'. At nearly twelve years of age the little boy told his father he wished 'to become a clergyman if he could manage the sermons'. He followed Willy to Eton. Unlike his elder brother, Stephen enjoyed Eton and his parents were pleased with his academic progress. However, his poor sight caused his teachers to observe, "Stephen is able to keep up in Latin transla-tion but lettering in ordinary maps is quite beyond his strength of sight and it will be quite a puzzle to convey to his mind a clear idea of what it all means."

Mary

On 23rd November 1847, while Gladstone continued to cope with the Oak Farm crisis, Catherine gave birth to Mary. She was probably the most interesting of the Gladstone children. When Catherine was away nursing her sister, Mary, she left the girls in charge of Mrs. Talbot, a family friend. Rich and widowed she found 'Naples Mary' 'wanting'. Gladstone noticed, early in her life, *Mary's extraordinary responsiveness to music.* She never developed a musical career but became her mother's official biographer and her father's unofficial secretary. Like Gladstone, she loved Fasque. As a young woman, barely out of childhood, she fell in love with one of Sir John's neighbours, Lord Lorne of Inverary castle, heir to the Duke of Argyll. The romance never took off. In 1871, Lorne, a cultivated and intelligent man, married one of Queen's daughters, the beautiful Princess Louise, who produced the sculpture of Queen Victoria in her coronation robes. It stands in the grounds of the 'Aunties' Palace', Kensington Palace. A refined woman, a plaque placed on an old bank in Guildford High Street reads, *this building was altered and extended in 1899. The old front was retained, by special request of HRH the Princess Louise, Marchioness of Lorne.* Her marriage was deeply unhappy. No children arrived and society questioned Lorne's sexuality. Behind fans it was whispered, "a streak of homosexuality lurks in the family".

Mary enjoyed a dalliance with Arthur Balfour, John Ruskin and Lord Tennyson who stared hard into her eyes and stroked her nose, while muttering, "un petit nez retroussé." *Very odd*, Mary wrote in her diary.

Helen

In 1849 Catherine produced another little girl, a very different character from either of her sisters. Helen was overdue. This was the baby that Catherine was carrying when she slipped down the stairs. Helen grew into a blue-stocking. Mary worked hard to persuade Catherine to allow 'Lena' to go to Newnham College, Cambridge, where Arthur Balfour's sister was Principal. Catherine, unlike Victorian women in so many ways, expected her girls to be satisfied with an establishment, marriage and the bringing up of children. 'Lena' did none of these things. Attractive, it was true, but she preferred to study history, literature and political economy to a conventional life. Disliking domesticity and dreading becoming the supportive, spinster daughter, she told Harry, "Mary is the only one of us who really does help Mama and, moreover she does it constantly and lovingly." Lena's' obvious intellectual ability even impressed Catherine. She became her father's occasional, unofficial secretary and Catherine asked, "Will you allow Helen to study the Cypher? I think it very wholesome for her to feel herself useful and to master a thing."

Helen, of course, did not obtain a degree. These were not awarded to young ladies until 1921. However, she became Vice-

Principal of Newnham. After her parents' death, Helen joined the University Settlement at Southwark as Warden. In the grounds of Newnham stands a magnificent oak. Gladstone planted it as a gift for his daughter.

The Sugar Plums

Catherine bore two more babies. On 2nd April 1852, Henry Neville came into the world and in 1854, her final baby, Herbert, was born. Willy was the baby of an up and coming young couple. Thirteen years later, Herbert saw the light of day in 11, Downing Street. He was the son of a middle-aged couple — the Chancellor of the Exchequer and his wife. As this would be her last baby, Herbert remained especially precious to Catherine.

Early influences

All the children learned early in life there were three grave misdemeanours: 'never disturb Mama or Papa, tell untruths, or go to bed at night without feeling you have done some little act of kindness or selflessness.' Really bad behaviour was reported to Mama who, with tears in her eyes, raised her Japanese fan and smacked little bottoms. Catherine, in the preface to *Early Influences* had commented that, *Children are often over-noticed and over-petted and considered in every way conceivable.*

Unlike many other Victorian gentlewomen Catherine continued her activities even when heavily pregnant or feeding her babies herself. She would have snapped at dowagers, "It is a perfectly natural condition, Madam, given to us by God."

Throughout their long lives, Catherine and Gladstone continued to love their children but, as her 'Sugar Plums' prepared to go away to preparatory school, she wrote to Gladstone, *It is trying, the going away of the youngest pair, and the first launching of them into the new world. You do understand and will not think me very weak if I own I am crying at the thought.*

Catherine's two little boys were also in tears. Henry wrote to his brother Willy, *I hope you like Naples better than we like school. I do not like Mr. Church. I can't help telling you he gets into such a dreadful passion and is cross directly we arrive.* The headmaster complained that, "Herbert was a canny little thing who told direct falsehoods, while Harry could talk himself into lies by too much talk and so must be restricted to yes/no answers."

Henry was to inherit Sir John's commercial shrewdness and trained for a business career. Herbert worried his parents, his poor health reminding them of Jessy. Herbert appeared to plod through Oxford, disappointing his Father. However, he obtained a First Class Honours degree in History. Catherine wrote to Herbert, *I know the pleasure you have given your father is one of your chief delights — you should see his countenance all lighted up!*

A middle-aged Catherine became so immersed in her charitable work that she left her girls in the care of governesses. Mary and 'Lena' complained 'they were not up to standard'. Mary said they crushed her inner confidence, telling her she 'possessed no talent, not even in music'.

Convalescence for the children
However, the old Catherine returned when her children were unwell. She swept them off to Brighton, Folkestone or Bournemouth for the beneficial effects of sea-bathing and fresh air. They watched Punch & Judy shows, built sandcastles with wooden pails and spades, rode donkeys and paddled in the sea. The children rarely swam in the sea. Into her eighties, Catherine did so, even though she could afford a bathing-suit; she usually dived into the water, with little or nothing on, often when others found it too cold to do so. One birthday, Herbert and Henry gave their mother a carpet for her bedroom. She would not accept it. "You will not be hurt, but I adhere to having my floor scrubbed constantly with soap. Carpets, like curtains, exhaust the air."

Family life
As she grew older, Catherine might at times, seem to forget her children but the love she really felt for them returned at Christmas,

making it a special time. School children, farmers, tenants, villagers and servants were all invited to Hawarden. A huge Christmas tree glittered in the library, high tea was served in the drawing room and in the servants' hall they drank ale, raising their glasses to toast 'Mrs. Gladstone'. Her children did likewise to their 'Dear Mama' — in spite of her faults.

The family may have felt concern when Gladstone, too busy with affairs of state, allowed Catherine to organize the family holidays. The Gladstones always travelled by public transport. Gladstone wrote many times to his wife, "Which train am I catching? What time? Where do I change? Where are we going?" For example, in mid-August 1853 Gladstone met Catherine, with their six children, on a platform at Stafford Station. He found her clutching numerous pieces of scruffy paper on which she had written: *a night here, a week there, don't forget the boat, venues and times.* They were travelling to Fasque via the Duke of Argyll's at Taymouth, Lord Aberdeen's at Haddo and the Duke of Sutherland's at Dunrobin. Amazingly, Mr. and Mrs. Gladstone, with all their children, arrived safely. On another occasion, two years later, Gladstone wrote complaining, "*C and Co arrived very late after all sorts of miscarriages.*"

In his rare leisure time, Gladstone rode with his children and took them for walks. On one occasion Gladstone and Willy walked from Barmouth to Dongellau. While Disraeli planted trees, Gladstone cut them down, but only when they were dead or diseased. He even engaged in tree-felling with his sons. Accident-prone he wrote, *today a tree we were cutting fell with Harry (fifteen year old Henry) in it. He showed perfect courage and with God's help was not hurt.* Gladstone was proud of his ability to cut a tree down smoothly to ground level and annoyed when he saw a cartoon that showed him leaving a tree-stump two feet above the earth.

It was Gladstone, however busy he was, who gave the children their scripture lessons. Even when he was Chancellor of the Exchequer Catherine wrote to remind him that *Mary and Lena need a scripture lesson.* He often opened his study door to find his children waiting, 'like little dogs', just outside it. It was said that Mr. Gladstone was *always of a playful mind* and, while he instructed them, he presented his children with teaspoons of black coffee and small gifts. He opened desk drawers, saying, "What shall we find?" They made all sorts of discoveries, bits of string, stamp edgings, half sheets of notepaper which he called 'orts'. Sometimes Gladstone would go on all fours. The children would cling on to his back while he crawled around singing *Ride a Cock-horse to Banbury Cross*. Sometimes he sang them comic songs, played 'Commerce' and was a successful batsman in 'Cricket round the Hat'.

Sir John had encouraged his children to debate, catching him out whenever they could. Gladstone followed his example. Visitors were shaken to hear a chorus of small voices shouting, "A lie, a lie, Sir, a lie!" Even quiet Agnes had to be refrained from addressing her father as 'Bill'! Catherine and Gladstone encouraged their children to perform, not to be self-conscious but they were never as bubbly as George and Mary's children.

In the New Year of 1857, the Gladstones descended *en-bloc* on George and Mary. In the elegant interior of Hagley, printed play-bills appeared, pinned-up on every possible spare-space announcing: *At the Royal Lilliputian Theatre, on Wednesday, 7ᵗʰ January, 1857, there will be performed, for the first time on any stage, the highly attractive melodrama entitled Marina or the Truant Heart.*

All the children took part, from sixteen-year old Willy to three-year old Herbert. Lucy breathlessly announced that, "it is all becoming dangerous and boundless". Catherine supervised rehearsals with help from a tired-looking Mary. In fact the whole household became involved, despite cook and the kitchen-maid taking to their beds, with suspected smallpox. The audience of friends and neighbours sat enraptured, exclaiming, "Oh what talented children!"

In the professional theatre, encouraged by children's writers such as Lewis Carroll and the readings of Charles Dickens, child actors strutted across the stage, becoming celebrities and in constant danger of exploitation by adults. Tucked away up in the nursery, a successful West End production could once more come to life in Mr. Pollock's Toy Theatre. Paper cut-outs: 1d plain or 2d coloured of Mr. Kean as Iago or Mr. Macready as Rob Roy Macgregor, declaimed against a background of printed scenery, thus making an additional income for jobbing printers.

Gladstone loved the theatre but disliked falseness in real life. A tolerant man, untruthfulness was abhorrent to him. On one occasion, Henry and Herbert lit tapers and made a bonfire in their bedroom. Gladstone discovered them, asking, "What are you doing?" "Nothing", the little boys replied. The next morning Gladstone pointed out, "Sirs, your lie was obvious and cowardly."

Mary Drew wrote, *It was a cause of wonder to me when those who came to the house, specially our cousins, treated him with awe and reverence. Indeed we treated him with scant courtesy, arguing across him while he was talking, contradicted him. Both our parents were extremely simple and never seemed conscious of occupying an exceptional plane.*

Katherine Lyttelton, one of Mary's daughters, remembered her Aunt Pussy. *Children felt, especially in times of anxiety or distress, that somebody had arrived who was going to help, to solve difficulties, to light up the road, and, incidentally, to make fun for all concerned. "Well, darlings!" I can hear her now, the gay voice at the door . . . see her come in with arms outstretched into which we all tumbled . . . and she would sit amongst us and laugh and joke . . .*

A dreadful disaster

After the birth of Mary's eleventh child in July, the doctors told her, 'No more.' She knew George, a keen cricketer, hoped for twelve children. Unfortunately, the doctors did not tell George.

In the autumn of 1856 Catherine had written to Gladstone, *Alas there is a secret at Hagley which has come upon me quite a blow; what think you of number twelve being on the way?* On 7th February Mary gave birth to a little boy. Catherine cried out with relief, "The baby is born."

George took Mary to Brighton to convalesce. Catherine joined them, sending an invitation to Gladstone: *Lord and Lady Lyttelton and Mrs. Gladstone request the honour of the company of the Chancellor of the Exchequer, at dinner on Saturday and Sunday, to remain two nights, plain fare but excellent Southdown mutton, fish and claret.*

Lady Mary Lytellton

Mary recovered enough to borrow Gladstone's horse, Budget, and to ride a little but, later in July, she greatly weakened. She faced the doctors unflinchingly as they told her, "You are dying." Touching her fluttering heart, she asked, "Why are you so silly?" As there were no professional nurses in the 1850s Catherine looked after her sister. Urgent affairs of State kept Gladstone in London, leaving Catherine to meet the greatest sorrow she would ever face — alone. On 16th August 1857, Gladstone escaped from his duties and came to Hagley, to say goodbye to Mary. She managed to whisper to Gladstone, "Take special care of her. It will make a great change for her and after a time she will feel it more and more."

Mourning

The next day Mary died quietly in her sister's arms. Catherine's twinkle left her, never fully to return. She once said, "There are moments which open the heart." Mary's death was Catherine's own Gethsemane. Gladstone had liked Mary. Shortly after her death he told his friend Arthur Gordon, "She seemed to be one of those rare spirits who do not need affliction to draw them to their Lord and from first to last there was scarce a shade of it in her life."

As always, Catherine took charge. Now, she had a further twelve children to care for. "I must keep my promise and do what I can for her darlings. It is a sacred duty." Gladstone who needed peace and order must have found the new arrangements very difficult to cope with. In April 1859, Catherine wrote thanking him for his patience, *Your unselfishness makes me wish that I could see my way without putting it upon you, but I feel an additional duty is thrown upon me now and you poor dear, must share some of it. I am not as we were when we married. I must keep my promise.*

It was at this time Gladstone began building his Temple of Peace, his new library and study at Hawarden. In 1859, Catherine planned to bring out Agnes. With Mary's death she decided her sister's two eldest daughters, Meriel and Lucy, should also be introduced to society. The three girls came out together. For the Queen's Ball they wore silk stockings, 'tartalatane' dresses trimmed with three skirts with wire ruches, twined round with pink trimmings. On their feet they had white satin shoes. When Catherine escorted her girls to be presented she wore a train trimmed with lace, a white satin petticoat trimmed with flounces of Brussels lace, a bodice of blue velvet, and a diamond tiara and necklace.

At a ball a young unmarried lady could not of course waltz. However, she could enjoy square dances, quadrilles and reels. She must not dance more than three dances with the same partner or sit-out a dance with a young man. Victorian society was full of balls and soirées but as death was so common a youngish woman could find herself out of society for a couple of years at a time. The widowed Mrs. Wyndham Lewis, Disraeli's future wife, regretted she could not enjoy the festivities at the time of the Queen's Coronation, as she was still in mourning for her husband, over eighteen months after his death. A year following Mary's death, Catherine told Meriel, "You might have black lace put upon your thick black scarf." Catherine would have worn full mourning for six months, three in crêpe and three in black.

Meriel's coming out was seen as a success. In 1860, she married her childhood sweetheart, Edward Stuart Talbot, who became the first warden of Keble College, Oxford and subsequently, Bishops of Rochester and Southwark. When Talbot became Bishop of Winchester, the couple moved to Farnham, the traditional home of the Bishop of Winchester. In 1878 they founded Lady Margaret Hall, Oxford, the first hall for women. This meant that Lucy, the second girl, at just eighteen, found herself the chatelaine of Hagley. 'Dearest Locket' grew up to become Catherine's closest confidante and friend, dearer to her than her own daughters.

'Old Pam' resigns, 1858

In 1858, Catherine, overstrained, became out of sorts. She went to Brighton to recuperate. Gladstone wrote to her telling her of Palmerston's resignation. He reminded her that 'Old Pam' had taken over from Lord Aberdeen. Catherine wrote, *You dear old thing, I was especially thinking of you when I went to bed on Friday night* and finished her letter with, *Poor Pam I am sorry for him, for he is hit in every way. Surely he cannot do otherwise than resign.*

Gladstone remained an M.P. However, he took no position in the new, somewhat languid Government of Edward Stanley, 14th Earl of Derby. Disraeli was Chancellor of the Exchequer and, with Lord Derby in the House of Lords, acted as Leader of the Commons. It was a minority government and fell in less than a year.

Catherine continued to be unwell. At the beginning of October, while they were on a visit to Lord Aberdeen at Haddo, Gladstone was amazed to receive a letter from the Secretary of State for the Colonies, Sir Edward Bulwer Lytton, the author of *The Last Days of Pompeii* and other romances, and a great friend of Disraeli's. As young men they visited the 'naughty houses' together. He offered Gladstone the position of Lord High Commissionaire-Extraordinary of the Ionian Islands. The Government knew Gladstone had just completed his first study of Homer. Bulwer Lytton suggested, "This would be to render to the crown a service that no other could do so well, and that might not inharmoniously blend with your general fame as scholar and statesman. To reconcile a race that speaks the Greek language to the science of practical liberty seems to me a task that might be noble episode in your career." Gladstone took time to consider. Catherine advised against the move. She suspected, 'Out of sight, out of mind.' "I shall be glad if you do not take the mission. You must take care not to let the poetry of it mislead you." She also reminded that she still felt, "so unhinged as to wish to see Dr. Griffiths. I cannot at all account for these odd unearthly feelings."

Corfu

Gladstone was out of office. He needed something definite to do and took the position. A deciding factor was that his wife was still unwell. With Catherine and Agnes he reached Corfu on 24th November 1858. Before his arrival a secret despatch from Sir George Young, the Lord High Commissioner of the Ionian Islands, was stolen from a pigeon hole in the Colonial Office. Much to Sir George's dismay, a morning paper printed his recommendation for the transfer of the smaller islands to Greece and the outright annexation of Corfu to the British Crown.

However, Sir George had changed his mind and wished to keep to the *status quo*, but the damage was done. Austria became uneasy, France perturbed, Russia irritated and the Islanders excited. Gladstone's mission was seen as the first step towards Sir George's recommendations. His task was impossible but always 'terrible on the rebound' he began his journey to Corfu on 21st November 1858, with Catherine and Agnes on the warship *Terrible*. They travelled via Dresden, Vienna and Trieste. Gladstone prepared himself all the way for the task which lay ahead of him. Mr. and Mrs. Gladstone found themselves busy. They received. They talked. And even met ancient archbishops. All the time Gladstone complained, "The islanders are completely and utterly idle." He tried his best 'with the utmost gravity' to cope with the complex challenges facing a Protectorate of about two hundred and fifty thousand people.

Catherine loved the Islands' beauty and climate. She met the Queen of Greece and tried to answer her endless questions about Queen Victoria and her family. While she did so Gladstone received 'a blow'. He learned he was incapable of being elected in Britain until he had ceased to hold office abroad. At home whispers behind fans said, "He stays away to avoid discussing the Reform Bill. Even Lord Aberdeen considered, "he is too headstrong, and if possible too simple and honest".

If during February 1859 an enemy had chosen to move for the vacant seat at Oxford, the election would have taken place too early for the completion of the business at Corfu, thus making Gladstone ineligible for re-election. Palmerston exploded, "Send him elsewhere and he will run wild." Disraeli suggested quietly, "that Mr. Gladstone should be crowned King of the Ionian Islands".

In mid-February 1859, Gladstone returned to London, with Catherine now restored to health and with Agnes. The generally held view was that his reputation would never recover from his stay in Corfu. His enemies whispered, "Gladstone must have a serious lack of judgement to accept such a fifth-rate job." He was, however, re-elected unopposed to Oxford on 13th February and 19th February 1859. The Islands are seen today as the place where in 1921 Prince Philip was born, Gerald Durrell wrote *My Family and Other Animals* and the site of the film and best-selling novel, *Captain Corelli's Mandolin.* The Islanders remember the British for improving education, communication, the justice system and introducing cricket.

Chancellor of the Exchequer — again

In 1859 Lord Palmerston formed a new 'mixed' government with Radicals included and Gladstone as Chancellor of the Exchequer. He inherited a deficit of five million pounds. Income tax stood at five-pence in the pound. Gladstone argued, "In time of peace nothing but dire necessity should induce us to borrow." He therefore increased the income tax to nine-pence in the pound. On 14th January 1860, Gladstone explained his thinking to Catherine, "I am certain, from experience, of the immense advantage of strict account-keeping in early life, it is like learning grammar then, which when once learned need not be referred to afterwards."

In December 1861 there occurred an event which Gladstone could not foresee or its consequences. Meanwhile, Catherine would find she possessed 'a genius for Charity'. It all began with Miss Nightingale.

CHAPTER FOUR

Upsetting Miss Nightingale and Fighting for Poor Suffering Humanity

Victorian Poverty

Miss Nightingale

Catherine wished to become more involved in the War but, when her two cousins were killed, she became aware of its horrors. In the middle of it all, Catherine crossed swords with Florence Nightingale. She was overjoyed when a chance arrived to become actively engaged. The Secretary of State for War, Sidney Herbert, lived with his wife, Liz, in Carlton House Terrace. They were not only near neighbours but close friends. Liz became involved with a Miss Mary Stanley, and introduced her to Catherine. She proved to be jealous of 'Dear Flo's' popularity and prestige but, nevertheless, tried to become part of her circle. Mary Stanley was a friend of Revd. Manning and, encouraged by him, trembled on the brink of becoming a Roman Catholic. Her problems were many. The celibate Manning had not forgotten that Mr. and Mrs. Gladstone encouraged him to take on a 'rescue girl' as a maid. The results were disastrous. Also, Miss Stanley's family connections made conversion difficult for her. She was the Bishop of Norwich's daughter and sister to a man who was shortly to become the Dean of Westminster.

Miss Stanley considered herself to be a nurse but, as an evangelist, she knew a man's soul was more important than his body. In 1854, she published *Hospitals and Sisterhoods*. In it she complains

of the shortage of priests and chaplains and the lack of opportuni-
ties for spiritual regeneration. This was the woman who joined
Catherine and Liz Herbert to find and interview 'nurses'. These
women had to work amongst men dying in the disgusting conditions of the Crimea. Miss Stanley sought 'ladies' not working
women, whatever experience they possessed.

Late in 1854, Miss Stanley, a nun, Mother Frances Bridgeman
of Kinsalie, a Jesuit Chaplain, twenty-four professional nurses and
nine ladies attended a church service to prepare them for the long
journey to the Crimea. Catherine presented each woman with a
shawl. After numerous trials and tribulations the party arrived on
Miss Nightingale's doorstep. Thin, exhausted, working twenty-
four hours a day, she had neither the time nor need for them. Miss
Nightingale was startled when Mary Stanley went down on her
knees and, ignoring the state of the wards, began to pray that the
men would repent of their wicked ways and come to Jesus.

As a young woman Florence Nightingale taught herself to
nurse. Her horror on her arrival in the Crimea contrasted with
Mary Stanley's behaviour. As a 'man of action', Miss Nightingale
set out to cope with overworked medical staff, official indifference,
rampant infection, lack of medical supplies and no proper hygiene.
She did not even possess the necessary equipment to process the
indifferent food. Miss Nightingale found some twelve thousand
men dead or dying around her from typhus, typhoid, cholera and
dysentery; in fact more would die in the hospital wards than were
killed on the battlefields. Florence Nightingale described the war
as, "calamity unparalleled in the history of calamity." Even the
horses which took part in the Charge of the Light Brigade had
starved to death.

These were the conditions she had to face. From her earliest
years Miss Nightingale had known only graciousness. Even her
name Florence came from being born in that most beautiful of
cities. As a young woman she had horrified her mother by refusing
a proposal of marriage from Richard Monkton Milnes, 1st Baronet
Houghton. She had forfeited status, home and children to live

faraway in a foreign land, spending her days amongst rough men dying in appalling conditions. Her explanation was, "God called me in the morning to do good!" Mary Stanley was hardly the person to appeal to the over-busy, sharp-tongued Miss Nightingale who like Catherine had little time for other women. Somebody such as Mary Stanley was unlikely to understand a woman like Florence. Bemused, she wrote to Catherine, *I came out loving and admiring Flo and I was loath to believe she was not as great as I had believed her to be.* Some of the 'ladies' too were bewildered and wrote to Catherine for help and advice. In the end, Miss Nightingale was forced to write a long letter of explanation to Catherine who, embarrassed, wrote to her sister, *After all the trouble and all the care here it seems Miss N had managed the doctors with enormous tact and had got over their jealousy but she had been promised no more nurses should be sent. Forty-three arrived and her breath was taken away!!!*

Most of the women returned to England. Catherine wrote a letter of apology to Miss Nightingale. As a peace offering she sent the lady a warm, woolly dressing gown. Presumably, it joined the other '99' thrown in a corner. Miss Nightingale received endless such items from admirers. It is known she walked the wards late at night, carrying a lamp but she did not do so in dressing gown and slippers. After a short time, Mary Stanley decided her health was not up to the task. She retired to England where she continued her good works, complaining all the time, "I am not appreciated." Mary Stanley died at sixty-six, Florence Nightingale at ninety.

After the Crimean War Miss Nightingale came to live in Mayfair. A semi-invalid, she spent much of her time trying to ignore the callers knocking on 'Skittles' front door. The courtesan lived in the next house to Miss Nightingale. Nevertheless, it is due to Florence Nightingale's efforts that nursing is now one of the most honourable of professions. The Crimea never deserted her. In old age she wrote, *When I am no longer even a memory, just a name, I hope my voice, may perpetuate the great work of my life. God bless my dear old comrades of Balaclava and bring them safe to shore.*

Did Catherine ever read Miss Nightingale's *Notes on Nursing* which she wrote in 1859 (Glasgow/London: Blackie & Son). Miss Nightingale explained, "These notes are meant simply to give hints for thought to women who have personal charge of the health of others . . . It is recognised as the knowledge which every one ought to have — distinct from medical knowledge, which only a professional can have . . . I do not pretend to teach her how, I ask her to teach herself, and for this purpose I venture to give her some hints." The table of contents includes: Ventilation and Warming, Noise, Cleanliness of Rooms and Walls, Chattering, Hopes and Advice and Conclusion. After reading *Notes on Nursing, What it is, and what it is not*, was Catherine moved to appoint a professional nurse to take care of the tenants and villagers of Hawarden?

The Newport Refuge

Ever since their marriage Gladstone had encouraged Catherine to pursue her charitable activities. She was a woman 'not quite of her time' who climbed her own 'greasy pole' with a professional intensity, unusual in an upper-class Victorian woman. Gladstone did not behave true-to-type either. Later generations may see him as a 'Denis' to Catherine's 'Mrs. Thatcher,' a view which would have shocked her.

Mrs. Gladstone may not have known the cause of why the poor suffered so. One reason was that during the mid-nineteenth century the great towns were adrift with the spill-out from the industrialization taking place. Notices appeared on workhouse gates, 'TAKE NOTE THE CASUAL WARDS ARE FULL'. People drifted away to sleep on the streets, starve or drown themselves in the Thames. The Newport Refuge grew out of Catherine's experience with the House of Charity and her friendship with Revd. John Williams who had been saddened by the inadequate provision made for the destitute by the Poor Law. He hired a room where eight or nine unsuccessful applicants for workhouse relief could lie down with a shelter over their heads. Of course, this did little to relieve the situation. Mr. Williams appealed to the public for help.

Catherine formed a committee, asked advice from police and others relevant organizations.

Some members of her committee, wishing to know more, visited the workhouses. Catherine found a disused slaughterhouse (which Cromwell had utilized to be a barracks for his cavalry) in Newport Market at the back of Leicester Square in the old Rookeries of the notorious Seven Dials. Catherine personally raised the £1,200 to make the place habitable. Gladstone offered her a hundred pounds if she could raise nine-hundred. In October 1864, the Refuge was officially opened. The men arrived in the evening and found a hundred iron cots waiting for them, coconut matting on the floor and coffee and bread being served. They were used to sleeping under a railway arch or on the pavement. The Refuge was usually overcrowded and some men had to sleep on the floor. The warden had not the heart to turn them away. Following the luxury of washing themselves, they left early next morning. Seven nights was the maximum time they could stay.

Later in the month, a women's ward was added, presided over by the tough, saintly Sister Zillah of the Clewer Community. Catherine demanded that active efforts be made to find employment for people and became increasingly concerned for the children. She started an Industrial School for the boys where they learned a trade and the elements of reading and writing; fitting up the school alone cost £1,500. Those who showed musical ability were placed in a regimental band. Bandmasters boasted, "You can find at least one of Mrs. Gladstone's boys in my regimental band." In December 1864, Catherine persuaded *The Times* to write an article on the Refuge. It raised £3,473 and she opened a section for girls. Not satisfied with that she raised a further £1,000 from the Sassoons, said to be the wealthiest family in the world. "We shall be happy to be guided in this by Mrs. Gladstone's kind suggestion, her name being an ample assurance for the proper dispositions being taken."

The Homeless Poor Act

Catherine shocked the public. A lady sat on Committees. She did not serve or nurse the poor. Certainly, she did not work amongst them in dreadful conditions. Catherine Gladstone was in a position to influence most of the important people of Victoria's England. She recounted dining with the Duke of Wellington, the Cannings and the Duke and Duchess of Buccleuch. Catherine was placed next to the Duke of Wellington and they talked on the great contrasts of life, the poverty and the misery to be found in London side by side with great affluence. At that time much of the administration of the Poor Law was unjust. It was mostly the poverty-stricken parishes which made adequate provision for society's outcasts, while the richer parishes made none at all. Under the Homeless Poor Act, the guardians in the different parishes were required to provide accommodation for vagrants, while the cost incurred in dealing with these persons was spread over the whole of London, instead of each parish being left to pay its own expenses. One result of this new legislation was that what had been accommodation for scarcely a thousand poor in the London workhouses doubled. At a Conference of Poor Law Authorities, held at St. Martin's Hall, on 30th December 1865, it was stated by Mr. H.B. Farnall, C.B., Commissioner of the Poor Law Board, that owing to the new Act "there was nothing like the misery and distress about the streets of London there used to be".

During the mid-nineteenth century some middle-class activists became 'social explorers', staying overnight in the workhouses to find out for themselves how the poor fared. A journalist, James Greenwood, wrote *A Night in the Workhouse* for the *Pall Mall Gazette*. Its impact was tremendous. Catherine, with her direct knowledge, campaigned for workhouses to provide adequate medical provision. Usually, only elderly, illiterate women inmates cared for the sick, many of whom had a drink problem. The 1864 Metropolitan Houseless Poor Act provided separate infirmaries and fever wards. By the 1880s, trained nurses were employed and the poor could use the facilities, even if they were not inmates.

The Cotton Famine

In 1861, America began tearing itself apart. The slave states of the South, the Union, and the Confederates of the North did not come to terms with each other. In the next four years sixty-two thousand soldiers died and President Abraham Lincoln achieved martyrdom and sainthood. Catherine discussed the situation in Lancashire with the Queen. She said, "I never hear her talk without feeling one ought to be better for it, she is so true." The Queen observed, "I am afraid we are apt to have one law for ourselves and another for other people." Catherine noted, "The way H.M. discusses things always interests me, arguing her own points and listening to the differences of others, all the time with a certain decision of manner."

The North blockaded the Southern ports, stopping cotton arriving in Lancashire. Whilst the looms remained empty, the workers starved. In the House of Commons politicians thundered at each other, "What is the effect the American Civil War is having on our constituencies? Gladstone gave an unfortunate speech, *We know quite well that the people of the Northern States have not yet drunk of the cup and they are still trying it far from their lips — which all the rest of the world can see they nevertheless must drink of. We may have our own opinion about slavery; we may be for or against the South, but there is no doubt that Jefferson Davis and other leaders of the South have made an army; they are making, it appears, a navy; and they have made what is more difficult than either, they have made a nation.* The speech caused uproar. Like many of the upper-class English Gladstone was prejudiced against the 'rough Northern Yankee' and considered the 'Southern planters' to be the nearest America could get to 'gentlemen'. His speech made it seem that Great Britain was about to recognize the Southern Confederacy. Diplomatic relations became so bad that the American Ambassador was forced to consider returning to America and enquired, "Shall I ask for my passport?"

We do not know Catherine's views on her husband's speech but we do know she flew 'into activity'. Her standing rose greatly when in the summer of 1862 she left Gladstone and her family to travel to Lancashire. She wanted to see the problems for herself and the ways in which she could be of use. Catherine told her daughters, "A little roughing it without a lady's maid makes one both handy and independent." Catherine found to her surprise a disciplined people. They were used to the rules of the factory and careful with money. Friendly Societies and middle-class charities gave their support to the folk of the Cotton Towns but, despite every effort being made, starvation beckoned for the working people. Only a few months before they had enjoyed comfortable wages.

Not many had foreseen the catastrophe that awaited them. Now most of the mill owners refused to pay wages or even offered their workforce any help. These often self-made men were not Catherine's kind. They knew nothing of 'noblesse oblige'. As she journeyed through Lancashire, Cheshire and the High Peaks of Derbyshire, Catherine organized relief. As usual she saw the need, invented the plan, found the workers, set the machinery going and moved on to meet another need. One small girl asked her mother, "Ma, who do you think we have had at school? It was the Governor's wife."

It was said that those who were outside the troubled areas gave more generously to the needy than those who lived in them. Unlike most of the wives of the great and the good, Catherine's involvement with the poor gave her a particular understanding of their situation. Fight the cotton workers might but the fear of destitution was a reality. Without the safety net of the Welfare State people depended on the compassion of others.

After visiting a soup kitchen, Catherine wrote to Lucy, *it was a stirring life to behold. In the little parsonage at Trinity imagine a kind of open-house from morning to night, the kitchen with its one-handed 'Peggy' cooking in the midst of poor people waiting, mothers their girls for plans, one in search of something to lie upon, another for something to bury her child, or a distressed tailor or dressmaker, and we all making the little kitchen our headquarters and meeting at our several points of interest. But the chief time was spent at sewing classes, industrial classes and kitchens, and oh, Lucy, the Irish stew was excellent! Think of a thousand people fed daily and think of my delight at seeing the people laden with it, good and hot.*

During her time in the Cotton towns, Catherine opened several soup kitchens and started an industrial school. Mary Drew wrote, *in old magazines there are many reports of her, how she would come, discuss questions, give practicable schemes for help and set each place going on lines neither patronising nor hard.*

When Catherine came across girls living in particularly bad conditions, she swept them off to Hawarden and housed them in the empty Dower House in the Castle yard. The senior servants took control of twelve girls and trained them to become domestic servants and nurses. They were found sound places and came with the recommendation, "trained by Mrs. Gladstone". Whenever a girl left the House others were brought down from Lancashire to fill her place. Gladstone met the costs of feeding them, clothing them and housing them. No record exists of the cost of the project which lasted several years. Gladstone also employed groups of men to cut footpaths and roads to run through and around the park. They earned money and improved the Hawarden estate.

Although Gladstone remained far away in London, he was constantly drawn into his wife's web. At the bottom of one of the numerous notes which Catherine scribbled to her over-busy husband she wrote, *William, Don't forget to collect the marmalade from Fortnum and Mason, remember the sherry.* On another occasion she wrote, *Never mind, don't bother, the factory girls are quite happy.* When Gladstone felt relief that all the girls had either married or settled into a good place, Catherine found another use for the house in the yard. Much to the consternation of her neighbours, thirty scruffy, small boys, orphaned by the London cholera outbreak, came to live there. Catherine said, "It is better to cut them off from their London associations." The coachman's wife took charge. She had boys of her own. They learned their lessons at the village school and were taught a trade. In their free time they roamed through fields, climbed trees and frightened the sheep. Catherine's neighbours did not know that, at the time of the Oak Farm catastrophe, she had told Gladstone, "Make me your Master of Horse . . . I'll earn you money." Catherine Gladstone could break in any horse or any bunch of young hooligans who hollered and bellowed their way across her lands.

By 1865 the American Civil War was over and the Northern States the winners. In England, the cotton workers returned to work but were now less sure of themselves. Colonial labour began providing cheap competition. The world was changing, nobody gave a thought to the middle-classes proudly flushing their new lavatories and unknowingly filling the cess-pits to overflowing. The spirilllum bacteria germ floated into river and gutter alike and cholera lurked in the sewage and waste which fed into the Thames. Drunks coming home in the early hours of the morning stumbled over fewer night-soil men.

As the Metropolis swallowed up more of the countryside, farmers required less manure. London had always smelt vile but, by 1858, it stank. Members of Parliament demanded that their curtains were soaked in chloride of lime and began considering 'sitting' at Hampton Court.

Cholera epidemic, 1866
People talked and muttered about the situation. However, in 1866 a plague of cholera hit Bristol in April and, by May, was stalking Liverpool. It travelled south to London and into the East End. The first case was admitted by Whitechapel's London Hospital on the 19th of July. By the end of the month it had killed 1,253 people and by October a further eight thousand were dead, but 1866 was the last year it would destroy so many. The London Hospital overflowed with the dead and the dying. Fearing infection, people covered their mouths and walked by on the other side of the road. A notice on the hospital gates asked for help with the laundry. Poor women stopped and read it. Its terms offered them 'untold wealth' but they quickly passed on. Many hospital staff were stricken and those left, overworked. Few outsiders volun-

teered to care for the sick. Undertakers ordered a new style of hearse — to carry twelve coffins at a time. Even the Registrar-General was moved to report on 27th July, "The mortality is overwhelming." In Great Prescott Street, a Roman Catholic priest spoke of visiting a cholera-struck family, "the father lay coffined, a dead child lay by his side, another writhed in agony on the floor, the youngest was abandoned by the mother, gone to seek relief for the living and the means of burying her dead". When patients arrived in hospital they were usually just skin and bone.

From Whitechapel Hospital, Mr. Nixon, the secretary, complained, 'the state of the wards is frightful'. Diarrhoea and vomiting are cholera's main symptoms. The patient becomes dehydrated rapidly. The few remaining staff scattered sawdust steeped in carbolic around continually. And underneath every bed there was a large bag of sawdust. Mattresses were made of sacks stuffed with straw. As soon as a patient died the mattress was removed and burned. Into this nightmare came Catherine. Mr. Nixon said, "Mrs. Gladstone faced all difficulties, at a time when people outside seemed panic stricken."

Mary Drew, summing up the situation wrote, *Mrs. Gladstone regardless of infection threw herself into the work in home and hospital. In the latter so great was the pressure that the sick had often to be laid upon the floor till death vacated a bed. Mrs. Gladstone comforted the dying with words of faith and promises of care for the orphans left desolate. It was the children who most concerned her. She would wrap them in a blanket. On more than one occasions she asked Mr. Gladstone, 'Should you mind three clean little children being taken to Carlton House Terrace?' These promises took much time and contrivance to fulfil but they were then fulfilled and it was then she carried off the babies rolled up in blankets. One outcome was an orphanage at Hawarden for the boys, Mrs. Tait, (the Bishop of London's wife) taking the girls — in whom to her life's end she took the warmest personal interest, starting them in life, writing to them and understanding their characters.*

Orphanages

On 2nd August Catherine wrote from 11, Carlton House Terrace to *The Times*: *It has struck me that one of the most effective means at this pressing moment of assisting the excellent London Hospital is to provide a temporary home for the children (many of them orphans) who are recovering from cholera. . . . I cannot speak too highly of the work which is being done in this hospital by the chaplain, the doctors, and the nurses — indeed by all — connected with it.* Lucy commented, "She took over 150 'tinies' straight into her arms. . . . Of those not one died." On 15th August she again wrote to the newspaper. This time she appealed for money for a permanent orphanage.

I am anxious to tender my heartiest thanks to the kind friends who have already subscribed at this moment of great anxiety to the Temporary Home for the children recovering from cholera. Will you again give me your valuable help? I wish to extend the plan. Let us not be content with half a work, but make the home a permanent one, and establish it in good air. I am persuaded I shall meet with a noble response.

Whitehall Hospital

Catherine's appeal received a flow of subscriptions. At one point she was forced to stop her work. On 19th August she wrote to Gladstone: *I don't go into the cholera wards now I am so very tired nursing Harry . . .* When her son returned to health Catherine went back to fighting the epidemic.

The Mansion House Relief Committee met for the last time on 29th October 1866. Its final report pointed out, *the filthy, dilapidated, and overcrowded dwellings in which many are compelled to reside.* The committee had sat almost daily for three months. In addition to supporting orphans they discovered 277 widows needing care. The donation of £250 they gave to Catherine was not increased. She was forced to look elsewhere for funds to carry her schemes *forward on a scale of permanent usefulness.* A great public dinner was organized on behalf of the Hospital. Catherine was asked if Gladstone would preside over the event. She replied, "Mr. Gladstone has made it a rule never to take the chair at a charity dinner but, in view of the special circumstances, I will do my best to induce him to depart from this rule, just for once." Gladstone agreed. The administrator called on Gladstone to give him the most important points about the condition of the hospital and the current difficulties under which they laboured. Gladstone asked sharp questions and concluded the meeting by saying, "Call again a day or two before the dinner, with the view of settling final details." Mr. Nixon observed, "When I called, Mr. Gladstone gave me a full report on what he had learned about the hospital since my visit. In ten days he had come to know more about the London Hospital than I knew and I had been working there for years. Mr. Gladstone even put me in a new light on certain matters which had really not occurred to me before." The dinner was, of course, an enormous success. It has gone down in fund-raising hospital history.

A free convalescent home

In March 1867 Catherine once more engaged the attention of the readers of *The Times*. She appealed for donations to start a completely new project, a *free* convalescent home. The earliest had been set-up in the 1840s, but patients had to pay a few pence a week for their keep. Many could not afford even that. Some convalescent homes were so difficult to get into that they were practically unavailable to the ordinary hospital patient. Those who did recover from a serious illness were often exhausted and not fit to return to their often poverty-stricken homes. The hospital allotted about seventy beds for recovering patients but they became a serious drag on its work. Once again, Catherine wrote to *The Times* on 22nd March 1867, *The clergy of the eastern and north-eastern districts and the principal physicians had unanimously expressed their opinion that such a hospital for that quarter of London was urgently needed. With the view of effecting something towards this end a small house at Snaresbrook has been already taken, capable of containing twenty male patients.* Two days later she wrote again to the newspaper. *I venture to trespass upon your good nature again with the view of bringing to your notice two points in the proposed scheme for the Convalescent Hospital which I think deserves special attention. First, FREE admission of patients. Secondly, there will be no card or other system of canvassing. The Lancet* supported her. *Surely nothing would tend more to what the annual enjoyment of change by well-to-do people than the consciousness that they had done something to send some poor shaken patient to a Convalescent hospital like that contemplated by Mrs. Gladstone.* Catherine received numerous donations including one from the Duke of Bedford.

Snaresbrook

A Mr. and Mrs. Charlesworth lived in Snaresbrook, near Epping Forest, where they ran a convalescent home for recovering patients who made a small weekly payment. When the couple heard that Catherine was looking in the neighbourhood for a convalescent home, they offered her their home, with all its appointments and remainder of the lease, but subject to them playing an active role in the home's management. Catherine agreed to their terms and it became known as 'Mrs. Gladstone's FREE Convalescent Home'. In November 1869 the Home was opened. Through the efforts of Catherine, gradually a convalescent home became 'the invaluable and absolutely essential appendix to the General Hospital'.

A non-committee woman, Catherine preferred direct action to discussion but, on this occasion, she did form a committee consisting of seventeen members which included Catherine, Gladstone, Lucy and Frederick Cavendish, Stephen Gladstone, George Lyttleton and Sir Stephen Glynne. With Lucy Cavendish's help she formed a Ladies Committee. The patients were weak, sick and ill-nourished. Perhaps for the first time in their lives they were treated with respect. In return they were expected to behave well. Catherine received 624 applications. Some she could house in the Home. Others she placed in existing institutions. She asked, "but what am I to do with the children?" As the refugees from the Cotton towns had returned home, Mary Drew recollected, *Mrs. Gladstone once again housed boys in the House in the Yard.* Girls were found 'places'. The old Dower House became a permanent orphanage. When the lease ran out on Snaresbrook, the landlord, under pressure from his neighbours, refused to release the property. The trouble with the landlord made the committee have doubts about the worth of the project. Catherine would have none of it. She said, "The home is doing incalculable good and gives practical proof of the value of such institutions. It is true there are difficulties but in the interests of humanity these must not be considered insurmountable."

Woodford Hall

Situated only two or three miles from Snaresbrook and on the borders of Epping Forest, stood Woodford Hall. A former stately mansion, the house was surrounded by charming lawns. It was offered to Catherine and appealed to her because of the open countryside which lay around it. The Hall was also close to George Lane Station on the Woodford Branch of the Great Eastern Railway, about eight miles from Liverpool Street or Fenchuch Street. Catherine raised the £3,000 needed to purchase the place, saying, "Donations are required quickly, as the patients are needed out NOW."

Catherine again wrote to the press, badgered friends and relatives and even contacted Lord Derby. She asked Lucy, "Fancy my courage?" There was a generous response to this appeal. The Queen herself sent £100, together with an autographed copy of her 'Journal'. Catherine explained. "The Home is meant exclusively for those who, having been ill, are tardily recovering, and require, for complete restoration to health, only a change of air, good food, rest and kindly treatment. Such persons are required to fill up a formal application and obtain a certificate from the medical attendant and a clergyman or minister or a secretary of any branch of the Charity Organisation Society. Afterwards they appeared before the Committee of the Home, which meets every Monday at the London Hospital. If their application is approved they enter the Home as soon as there is a vacancy. They have no expense beyond the payment of sixteen pence for the return fare home. The Home is maintained entirely by voluntary subscriptions. Donors enjoy no 'privileges' whatsoever, and the applicants have only to deal with the Committee of Selection."

In November 1869, much to her surprise, Catherine received a large donation. A man signing himself N.P.T. sent a cheque for £1,000. A similar amount was received in November 1870, 1871, 1872 and 1873. It was largely due to this support that the charity was able to keep going. Charities find it difficult to build up reserves as they have to meet a 'constant' need. Woodford Hall seems to have been typical, never rising beyond the convalescent stage in its own funding. Under the pressure of urgent necessity Catherine sent out another appeal on 21st August 1871, and she continued with these appeals until December 1888. The final appeal stated that *the home was grievously in want of funds.*

Much of the success of Woodford Hall was due to the firm control taken by the Lady Superintendent, the motherly Miss Simmons. She placed portraits of Mr. and Mrs. Gladstone around the home and gained Mr. Gladstone's respect by *doing wonders with the small means at her disposal.* She encouraged Catherine to take a personal interest in each patient and spend as much time as possible at Woodford Hall. Mrs. Gladstone's last visit to the Home was made in February 1894, when she was eighty-two. As she left she said, "I hope to come again very soon." Until the last, Catherine attended the Monday committee meetings at the London Hospital.

Catherine organized parties of nurses to spend a day or two at the homes of her friends in the country but in easy reach of the East End. She asked Miss Simmons over and over again. "Is there any good case we can set on its feet?" No sooner was one discovered than Catherine set to work and usually the man or woman found themselves *well started and had a full and fair opportunity.* She surprised Miss Simmons by presenting the home with a cow, priced £25. "No, not to give fresh milk, animals are first-rate interest for people." Indeed, Catherine's intuition was unusual for a woman 'who had everything'. She spent half a crown on a joyful, little canary for a lonely person, 'tuppence' for seeds for a garden, "people enjoy seeing them come up," and a pianoforte for a musical couple, much to the annoyance of the neighbours!

Lucy delighted her Aunt by discovering a bargain for the home, a stoneware cup and saucer, price 2d. Catherine's understanding was instinctive, not intellectual. Patients said, "We never feel under the slightest restraint in her presence." When she found a piano she would sit down and begin to play a dance or old-fashioned country tune such as Sir Roger de Coverley; even the very old found themselves waltzing around the room.

One day, while Catherine was busy selecting convalescents for her Home, Lucy wandered into the men's ward. Something made her approach a man who looked up from his book, *A Tale of Two Cities*, and glared at her. He snapped, "That's what we want here, a revolution." "But surely," said Lucy, "the cruelties and injustices of those days are past; think of all the loving kindness there is in the world — look at Mrs. Gladstone." His face changed and softened. "Ah! Mrs. Gladstone, she is different." Mary Drew writes, *As he spoke the door opened and she came in and looked round with her radiant smile. The old man muttered, "If only there were more like her."*

Like many women, Catherine loved gossip and like many husbands, Gladstone 'tuned out' while his wife chatted on. One day, Catherine burbled, "Cook from the convalescent home is to marry the Captain." He took no notice. "Oh, stupid of me," she exploded, "to tell you. You are too full of your Homer to care." Shortly afterwards he handed her a piece of paper, "There that's all I can do. You didn't give me much information."

THE COOK AND THE CAPTAIN
The Cook and Captain determined one day,
When worthy Miss Simmons was out of the way
On splicing together a life and a life,
The one as a husband the other as wife
Fol de rol, de rol, fol de rol,

It continues on for another two verses.

Fortunately, Catherine did not live to see the time when Woodford Hall would become 'out-of-fashion'. During the Queen's Golden Jubilee many speculators lost their money, but the London 'artisan classes' enjoyed a golden harvest. A trend began for convalescents to travel to the seaside rather than convalesce in the East End's Woodford Hall, even though it was *free*. Up to 1891, admittances to the home were around a thousand a year. In 1897 they dropped as low as 647 entrants. That year's Annual Report stated, *The Committee wishes it to be known that throughout the winter months they are glad to relax the rules, and to admit respectable people suffering only from want, hunger and cold.* However, since 1867, when Catherine established the Home, it had admitted thirty-three thousand people! After Catherine's death the Home moved to larger premises at Ravensbury House, Mitcham, Surrey.

Another use for the Clapton Houses

In November 1869, the London Sanitary Asylums Board became concerned about the growth of Relapsing Fever, an infection caused by the germ spirochaetes. It lives in the blood and is transmitted through lice from scratch marks in the skin. The houses at Clapton had become unoccupied. As the matter was urgent Catherine offered the properties to the Board. She wrote to the newspapers, *At such a moment when prompt action is everything. I feel sure I shall not appeal to you in vain to the sympathy and generosity of the public.* Funding was received and the houses were used until the outbreak was over. During the smallpox epidemic in February 1871, the Clapton houses were again used. Catherine reserved ten beds for Clapton patients and helped the raise the necessary funding. In 24th April 1871, Magistrate Newton listened to a plea at Worship Street Police Station for "the suppression or the removal of Mrs. Gladstone's smallpox hospital". It was reported that when one young lady saw the patients walking about the grounds, she became frightened she would contract the disease. The neighbours said they intended to leave; some had already done so. The whole neighbourhood was in danger of becoming deserted! The magistrate listened. The house remained! And it was *free*.

Fundraising

Much of Catherine's *genius for charity* depended on her remarkable ability to fundraise. It contrasted with the social skills of 'Mrs. Dizzy' who sat the right people next to each other, eavesdropped and reported back to her husband. Mary Anne's entertaining 'took one into Fairyland'. On the other hand, Gladstone's friends and enemies must have wondered how much each meal would cost them. It was no good saying you had left your cheque book at home. "Never mind dear I have an IOU to hand. Sign here."

Catherine asked Lord Palmerston for a donation for the blind. She told Gladstone, "Pam' sends £20 and seems to like doing it!!!" On another occasion she asked for £1,000. The cheque came back made out for £500. "My Lord, I fear you misunderstood me. I asked for £1,000." Catherine received the £1,000 by return, with a note, "Forgive me, my mistake." She was capable of subtle blackmail, saying to potential donors, "William will see the list of supporters. He has offered to top up the amount needed." Gladstone soon learned not to do that. It became far too costly. Busy as he was with his own affairs, he constantly reminded his wife, "Remember, if it's wanted, I'm good for help." Catherine gratefully responded. "May I just throw in that, when you take up the things I do, it makes my poor, little work doubly telling."

For a woman who, in many areas of her life, was a complete scatter-brain, however, where her 'professional work' was concerned she was completely businesslike. Before applying for funds Catherine insisted on knowing the exact financial position of the charity concerned and that the charity she was dealing with had a fully-trained accountant on its board. Her attitude may have been in response to Gladstone's contempt for charities. He considered them to be inefficient and corrupt. In Gladstone's budget of 1863, he proposed to remove the tax exemption that registered charities enjoyed. This would have brought a quarter of a million pounds into the Treasury coffers. In the end it was not put through. Catherine never allowed donations by subscription, a common custom in Victorian times. It gave supporters the right to nominate candidates. With Catherine's charities, applicants were selected by committee and each case was judged on its merits. Her view on those who offered sympathy was, "I do not think much of their pity, when it does not touch their pockets." Gladstone's patience with his wife was unbelievable. Catherine continued drawing him into her world, *Could you order some toothbrushes and brushes cheap for the orphanage? Have you remembered to peep in on the Miss Ds? Only open the Boudoir door and you will find them. Did you manage the flowers for Mrs. Bagshawe? If you have time please bring down a present for my three year old godchild; there are beautiful bible prints at the Sanctuary, Westminster, and also we want a common easel from the same place, 5s to 8/6d, to hold the big maps for the boys?* At the time, he was Chancellor of the Exchequer.

Mary turns fundraiser

Mary tried fundraising too. During an October night in 1857, Miss Syfret, the governess, discovered Hawarden Church was on fire and the roof collapsing. Flames lit up the sky as the fire engine with bells clanging and hose-pipes at the ready, arrived from Chester. People cheered when Uncle Henry climbed through the windows to save the Parish registers. Villagers carried out the pews and organ and discovered the poor-box had been broken into. Everything was destroyed, except the choir-stalls but the lock on the chest containing the church plate remained untouched. For days the air stank of acrid smoke. Ash carried by the winds lay everywhere and sadly the Gladstones learned that the fire had been started deliberately. Catherine asked, "Why did they do it? Nobody in Hawarden is so poor." Mary, the very next day, following in her Mother's footsteps, began fund-raising. Within the year the Parish Church was restored to its former glory!

Helping others

Politics and business were not Catherine's only concern. She instructed her children's nannies, "The children must never disturb Mama or Papa. Every day they must tell Jesus of some little act of kindness or unselfishness they have performed". Her daughters were taught by Miss Syfret to sew shifts for the poor and make mufflers for their brothers. The girls visited the Rectory saying to Mrs. Peake, the housekeeper, "See our knitting has improved." Catherine thought that all young women should be taught to visit and care for the sick and poor. She pointed out, "One will be better for the experience." Unlike many parents, she followed her own guidance. One Boxing Day she learned that the stable belonging to her neighbours, the Potters, had caught fire during the night. She left the celebrations, rushing through the slush to offer support. If she came across a young, vulnerable prostitute she would put out a helping hand. Catherine recounted to friends, "Yesterday I took a poor young thing to the new house. I picked her up in Windmill Street and left her safe." On another occasion she told Gladstone, "I was travelling by train and became of some use, comforting a hysterical woman."

There is a story that Catherine, when she was over eighty, attended early service, walking both ways to church, nearly a mile away and uphill. On her return, she attended family prayers and waited to be served breakfast. The maid arrived. "Ma'am, I think you want to know, the Queen's Ferry nurse, the one looking after the typhoid patients, has been taken ill. Doctor thinks she's got typhoid." Catherine jumped up from the table, climbed into the pony cart and, drove the two and a half miles to see the nurse. She assessed the situation and rushed back to the Castle. On arrival she told the startled maid her plans and drove back to Queen's Ferry. Catherine whipped the nurse off to Chester. For the rest of the day, the two women went from hospital to hospital trying find a bed. Only when one was found and the nurse safely tucked up, did Catherine remember her breakfast and that she had not eaten all day.

Much of Catherine's success, it is true, depended on her super-human energy. She could lie down on a sofa, as if she had not a duty or care in the world, and fall into a deep sleep for just a few minutes. She would wake up, immediately alert and refreshed. In the words of Steyne, her maid of over twenty years, "Madame would then jump into her clothes and was off . . . " When she was sixty-four Gladstone described his wife as, "having the vigour and freshness of thirty-four".

A tiny home for incurables

Approaching her own old age, Catherine wrote in 1875, *our tiny Incurables Home is begun, a little seed.* In the small house in the yard she started to shelter helpless and homeless old ladies who had seen better days. They had a special place in her heart. In 1874 she wrote to Gladstone, *but I don't shut my eyes to the fact that when one has begun a work of considerable delicacy it is not right to run away.* Visitors to the Castle were packed off to entertain the residents of her new home. Lady guests found themselves sitting by the bedside of an elderly lady reading to her. "It makes a break for them. Consider, one day you may need it." Mr. and Mrs. Gladstone followed the teaching of Christ to the letter. "It is better to give than to receive, even if you or your friends could not afford it."

A home for poor little roughs

In 1882 Catherine was invited to become President of the Notting Dale Ladies Association (now known as Notting Hill, West London). Its work was close to Catherine's heart. The Association ran the 'St. Mary's Training Home for the Protection and Care of Young Girls'. It had two houses in Norland Gardens, Notting Hill, caring for seventeen homeless girls. The founder, Miss Ellice Hopkins, began her campaign in 1879, saying, "It is better to prevent such girls from drifting into evil ways than to contend with endeavours to 'rescue' them afterwards". Her skills established other homes up and down the country. The girls received training for domestic service. In order for them to have practical experience, rooms were set apart for three or four lady boarders. They were waited upon by the girls. 'Failure' was never recognized. The Association kept in touch with the girls and, as long as they remained 'respectable', they would always be welcomed back. Sometimes it took a year before a girl's stubborn temper or self-will was conquered. Even if the girl broke down again or left a situation for some reason, she could return. The Association never 'washed its hands' of a girl and kept in touch, long after it had trained them. A number of beds were reserved for girls who were out of a place so that the Association did not lose sight of them and they knew they always had a home to go to.

Once a year Catherine invited old girls and 'trainees' to spend a day with her at the Woodford Home. Forty of them ate on the lawns, sitting under the branches of the sycamore tree. Catherine said, "I remember the tree when it was just a seedling in a pot. Its father, you know, comes from Hawarden. He is our famous, old sycamore tree." Catherine joined in the games and the dances. Before they left she plucked a flower for each girl. On one occasion she learned a girl was to be married. Catherine searched until she found just the gift that the young couple wanted. When Gladstone was Prime Minister, she took the girls to No. 10 Downing Street and showed them around. *They even had a glimpse of Mr. Gladstone himself. After this experience they took tea in the garden.* When Catherine was no longer involved another committee member wrote, *'In the nature of the case of a home of this sort it cannot be self-supporting, as the poor little 'roughs' have to be got out of slovenly ways, and spoil more than they make. As soon as their work is worth anything they are sent to service, and for this outfits are needed!'*

Ever since their marriage, life had been an upward climb for Gladstone and Catherine. By 1870 Gladstone had been Chancellor of Exchequer and Prime Minister. Catherine, too, had a high profile with her 'genius for Charity'. As the wife of such an important man she continued to have influence. Sir Stafford Northcote wrote to her, on 29th April 1865, *I am very glad to find that there is a prospect of some definite action with regard to the sick in*

workhouses. The recent disclosures are a great reproach to us, and I sincerely
hope you may succeed in getting the reforms you mention adopted.

Hospital Sunday

Tennyson observed, "Mrs. Gladstone wears herself out by all her
hospital work, in addition to all the work of a Prime Minister's
wife." In the early 1870s, Hospital Sunday was established. On this
day the Minister or Vicar gave a suitable sermon and the collection raised went to the local hospital. On 10th June 1888,
Catherine wrote a long, angry letter to the press . . . *Alas! More
money is the pressing cry of all London hospitals.* She attacked her
readers, *A certain prejudice is apt to prevail against hospitals on the score
that they form a kind of happy hunting ground for the training of doctors
and surgeons. Careful and conscientious supervision must be always necessary to prevent rash, or cruel, or otherwise objectionable experiments on poor
afflicted human beings. . . . Neither must we forget that the last thirty
years have created the noble and devoted band of nurses trained in hospitals and bringing to their work of mercy all the light and blessing of a
religious spirit and a loving heart coupled with the skill which comes of
constant and varied experience. Times are hard, it is true, and appeals are
many . . . I implore those who have no superfluity to see what self-denial
can do, what a good harsh push of many shoulders to the wheel can bring
about. And I do not apologise for concluding my few words with a hack-
neyed quotation, in so much as the well-known lines convey so beautifully
their inspiring lesson:*
  The Quality of mercy is not strained;
  It droppeth as the gentle dew from Heaven.
  It is twice blessed;
  It blesseth him that gives and him that takes . . . (sic)
  [Mrs. Gladstone should have written gentle rain.]
Mrs. Gladstone made her point.

A lady of letters

In response to the growing awareness of health issues, an
International Health Exhibition was organized in 1884. The

Executive Council asked the Prime Minister's wife to write the preface to the fifty-page handbook, *Healthy Nurseries and Bedrooms, including the Lying-In room.* Catherine wrote, *The strength of this little handbook lies in suggestions derived from many valuable sources in question, coupled only with some practical observations founded on my own experience.* She thanks a dear niece (Lucy) for her support with, *any little work of mine connected with hospitals, convalescent homes and orphanages.* Her daughters were, often, otherwise occupied!

Four million people visited the site of the Exhibition in South Kensington, where the Science Exhibition and Imperial College now stand. Among the exhibits they saw electrically illuminated fountains, sanitary appliances and a replica of an unsanitary, medieval London Street. The *Illustrated London News* observed, *The mind and eye of the average sightseer, however, does not derive any pleasure from the inspection of models of drain-pipes, sewer-traps, cisterns, pumps, roof-slates, filters and ventilators.*

Gladstone and Catherine, so busy living, never considered how the death of a Prince would change their lives, for ever.

CHAPTER FIVE

A Loving Wife, a Widowed Queen and Preparing for Power

The 1860s

A second Budget

On 10th February 1860,Gladstone presented his Budget. He told Catherine, "This was the most arduous operation I ever undertook in Parliament". He had spoken for fourteen hours with a barking cough. For several weeks Gladstone had suffered a severe bout of bronchitis. The House waited, wondering if and when Mr. Gladstone's throat would ever allow him to stand at the despatch box. Catherine dosed him with her usual concoction of eggs mixed with sherry. *The Times* enquired, *How is Mr. Gladstone's throat?* and like everybody else continued to wait. When Gladstone finally spoke, he slashed duties on items of popular consumption. Like a famous grocer's daughter, a hundred years later, he advocated prudent housekeeping. The Chartist politician, John Bright said, "There is not a man who labours and sweats for his daily bread or a woman living in a cottage who strives to make her home happy for husband and children to whom the words of the Chancellor of the Exchequer have not brought hope." The Budget was seen as a success but was followed by a depth of infighting, which was always wearisome to Gladstone. He had once told Catherine, "There are times when I have a feeling of particular femininity, my brain not taking prolonged pressure." Lord Greville enquired sympathetically, "After such an arduous campaign, pray give some life to the half dead, broken down, and tempest-tossed Gladstone."

The Prince Consort dies

Ten months later, on 14th December 1860, Catherine and Gladstone lost a close friend and ally, Lord Aberdeen, who died in Argyll House, St James's, London. He was succeeded by his eldest son, George, who himself died four years later. The 6th Earl was lost at sea. He decided to sail to Melbourne through a terrible storm. A crashing wave swept him overboard. The ship's captain presumed he had drowned!

The 7th Earl and Countess lived into old age! As can be seen from the Hawarden guest-book, they visited Catherine and Gladstone regularly, becoming close friends and colleagues. The Earl assisted Lord Rosebery with Gladstone's Midlothian Campaign.

Another death occurred which would have serious consequences for Gladstone. On a cold November day in 1861, the Prince Consort sent the nineteen-year old Prince of Wales a letter, *written with a heavy heart upon a subject which has caused me the greatest pain I have yet felt in this life.* His son had behaved in a way that many a young aristocrat did. When Bertie arrived at Cambridge he found himself a lover, a young actress, Nellie Clifden, a girl from the back-streets. She was the first woman to give the Prince any real warmth and affection. Soon the young 'bloods' addressed her as "the Princess of Wales". The Prince Consort was horrified. He exploded, "Oh horrible prospect, which this person has in her power, any day to realize. She could have a child!" The Queen, too, was shocked. "Oh! That boy!" she exclaimed. Prince Albert, weakened by too much work and feeling 'out of sorts', caught a train at half past ten in the morning, on 25th November 1861. He travelled to Madingley 'to sort out his son'. On the Prince's return, at half-past one the next day, he felt 'wretched'. Although becoming increasingly sick he continued with his punishing workload. Disappointed in his son, he told the Queen, "I no longer wish to cling to life." International developments scared him and he became frightened of a new war. His health continued to deteriorate. The Queen said, "Albert has had such nights since that great worry. It makes him sick and tired." She told her ladies-in-waiting, "I do not really know where his illness comes from" and went to her room, as if her heart would break.

Lord Palmerston annoyed the Queen by suggesting a new opinion should be sought. On Monday, 2nd December, the Queen noticed her husband's tongue was 'brown and dry,' sometimes a sign of typhoid fever. Eventually, the Prince told his 'Weibchen' (little wife) "I am so tired" and took to his bed. The doctors all agreed, "The Prince has a low fever." The words froze her heart.

On the evening of 14th December 1861, Prince Albert quietly slipped away into death. Victoria went into a deep, unnatural mourning, turning overnight into the dumpy, little black-clad figure, known to the world as the Widow of Windsor.

Life after Albert

Catherine had known the Queen since they were young girls. On 19th March 1862, Mary Drew wrote, *three months after the death of Prince Albert, Mrs. Gladstone met the Queen. The sight of her was so piteous. She saw I was nervous and, when I kissed her hand, drew me to her and kissed me. 'After all I am but a wretched woman.' She said, 'You, who are such a loving wife, I knew how you would feel for me.'*

On the other hand, Gladstone's view of the Prince was not entirely kindly. *He did not fascinate, or command, or attract me through any medium but that of judgement and conscience. There was, I think, a want of freedom, maturity and movement in his demeanour . . . an inexorable watchfulness over all he did and said, which produced that which was related to stiffness and chilliness, in a manner which was not withstanding, invariably modest, frank and kind . . . I do not think he was a man without prejudices, and this particularly in religion.*

Following Prince Albert's death Gladstone had a private audience with the Queen. He told Catherine, "with one who was at once my sovereign and a widowed fellow-creature", a message reached him. *Of all the ministers, she seemed to feel that Mr. Gladstone had entered most into her sorrows. She dwelt especially on the manner in which he had parted from her.* Gladstone was astonished at the Queen's humility!

The politician Benjamin Disraeli, a man whom Gladstone had once overlooked, moved quickly to fill the void in the Queen's life. He wrote to the Queen eulogizing Albert's many virtues. Disraeli's admiration was genuine. However, the Prince had once exclaimed, "Mr. Disraeli is not quite a gentleman." So Gladstone would find! Disraeli amused the Queen with gossip and 'laid on flattery with a trowel'.

Catherine's advice

Catherine knew the Queen's character well. In October 1862 she wrote to Gladstone, *I like to feel that you can be a comfort to that darling Queen, and I know you can. You will take on that this is nearly the anniversary of our visit when all was still bright. I was looking back to the little notes I made the last time that we were to meet on earth. The Prince Consort happened to be speaking to me about fevers and Lord Aberdeen and Peel, and I tried to remember his conversation with you about the American War. You said to me afterwards you liked to think of it as one of his last.*

Catherine told Gladstone of a conversation she had had with the Queen who said, "I often feel if the Prince had tried to live, if he had had more nervous energy, he might perhaps have recovered!" Understanding the grief and guilt of the other woman, Catherine advised Gladstone, "Do pet her a little and for once believe you can, you dear old thing!" Gladstone tried and failed!

Balmoral

The Queen kept to the routine she had enjoyed with Prince Albert, even to keeping his room, just as he had left it. She continued with the Royal family's habit of going to Balmoral in the late summer and remaining there for the grouse shooting which traditionally began on the 12th of August. A year after the

Prince's death, Gladstone found himself the Minister in Attendance; unlike Disraeli, his Scots' blood felt at home amongst the rains and cold winds of the Highlands. Balmoral was full of the 'remembrance' of Prince Albert. It was his wish that the original castle should be demolished and a 'more family-friendly' version built. In 1856, he showed his wife and family around the new place, enjoying its turrets and tartans. In August 1861, just four months before he died, Prince Albert gloried in his newly equipped model dairy. When Gladstone looked out from Balmoral's mullioned windows, he saw spreading out before him rows and rows of conifers, planted by the Prince Consort, to remind him of his homeland. When Albert donned a kilt a different man emerged. "His nature expanded, became simpler and less haughty". His jokes even made the Court laugh. However, the landed gentry continued to despise the Queen's husband.

As the Prince Consort was a poor shot, he did not stalk deer or shoot the birds as they flew overhead. 'Unlike a gentleman,' he demanded they were driven towards him, to be gunned down without a chance. Gladstone wrote to Catherine telling her that the five feet and one inch Queen weighed eleven stone and eight pounds, *rather much for her height*. He suspected her mourning was becoming an obsession.

While staying at Balmoral, Gladstone discovered the Queen worked all day on her papers and, by the time she came to discuss them in the evening, she was exhausted. After the Prince's death the Queen's daily routine became even more restrictive: Breakfast at 9.30 A.M. Luncheon was taken at 2.00 P.M. During the afternoon the Queen took a drive. Dinner was served at 9.00 P.M. After the meal, the younger ladies-in-waiting entertained the company, by playing the piano and singing. Gladstone must have wished Catherine could have been with him!

1862

When Gladstone was apart from Catherine he wrote endless notes to her. They give a 'peep' into their world:

23rd January, *you seem to have taken great pains about stable affairs and I am quite satisfied.*

Arriving at Hawarden on 24th May, *The house looks cleanliness itself, and altogether being down here in the fresh air, and seeing nature all round me so busy wither work of beneficent and beautiful, makes me very sick of London.* (sic)

22nd October, *tell Harry he is right, Latin is difficult, and it is in great part because it is difficult that it is useful!*

29th December, *the strangest feeling of all in me is rebellion (I know not what else to call it) against growing old.*

1863

With some amazement Gladstone wrote from Balmoral to Catherine on 26th September 1863, *Princess Alice has got a black-boy here who was given to her. . . . The people have never saw anything of the kind and cannot conceive it!* Gladstone tells Catherine that he had enjoyed the Ghillies' Ball, dancing a perpetual jig. The occasion would have been a thank you to the skilled male servants who attended to the hunting and fishing parties. He ends the note saying, *you forgot to tell me for what pious object you picked Lord P's pockets!* And he complains, *I do not know where to send the letter, nor do you distinctly tell me where to address, but as you say three nights I suppose it should be Penmaenmawr.*

8th October, *the Queen has had a most providential escape. The carriage, a sociable, very low and safe, was overturned last night after dark.* Princesses Louisa of Hesse and Helena were with her . . . *not at all hurt. . . . The Queen should give up these drives after dark; it is impossible to guarantee them. But she says she feels the hours from her drive to dinner such weary hours.*

The Sea-King's daughter

The Queen blamed 'Bertie' for his father's death, "I cannot look at him without a shudder." She asked 'Vicky' to find a suitable wife for him. Eventually, Princess Alexandra of Denmark was chosen. She was sixteen years old. Royal though the family was, they were impoverished. At one time the King's income had been less than £800 a year and they lived in rent-free, grace and favour apartments. Hans Christian Andersen called to tell the little Princess fairy stories. She even made her own clothes. Alexandra's main attractions were her great beauty and kindness. She was not a 'clever girl' but it was thought she would steady the Prince of Wales. The King of Belgium, Uncle Leopold, was in favour of the marriage. In September 1862, in his grounds, Edward proposed to Alexandra and was accepted.

Dates were discussed for the marriage. The Queen found objections to most of them until 10th March 1863, was put forward. She agreed. The Archbishop said, weakly, that the ceremony would take place during Lent. The ladies complained that the Court would still be in mourning so they could only wear mauve, grey or lilac. The Queen announced that the wedding would be a public occasion, not a state one, and suggested the wedding should take place in St. George's Chapel, Windsor. There were objections. Distinguished guests would find it difficult to find or get to. The Chapel was small and would be cramped and filled to overflowing. Many people would be insulted by not receiving invitations. It was pointed out to the Queen that the normal place for such ceremonies was St. James's Palace in the centre of London, close to good hotels, for those who required them.

Aristocratic ladies were forced to travel by train early in the morning to Windsor, wearing thousands of pounds-worth of jewellery. When they arrived they found the ceremony was badly organized and some 'small people' sat in the aisles, whilst the great and the good were crammed into the choir stalls. Mrs. Disraeli recounted with glee that "the Duchess of Manchester had near hysterics of mortification, when she saw Dizzy and I sitting comfortably in the aisles". Disraeli found on his return to London that the train was so short of carriages and so crowded he had to sit on his wife's knee, all the way back to Paddington!

Photographs show the Queen dressed in a black silk gown, trimmed with crepe, indicating she was still in mourning for

Albert. A widow wore deep mourning for a year and a day. She then 'slighted' her mourning and her black dress would be heavily trimmed with crepe. After eighteen months of widowhood, the crepe could be omitted. The Queen's husband had died in 1861. She sat gazing into the unseeing eyes of Prince Albert's marble bust. The twenty-one year old Prince and the eighteen-year old Princess looked at each other, apprehensively. However, darling Princess 'Alix' became dear to Catherine. She would arrive unannounced at Carlton House Terrace "to take tea with Mrs. Gladstone".

A Queen still in mourning

The Queen continued to live in deep mourning. Nearly two years after the Prince's death, on 1st October 1863, Catherine wrote to Gladstone, *I wonder whether you will have any opportunity in giving advice to the Queen. Do not forget the engine of what the Prince's wishes would be and how he would see it as follows:*

The enormous consequences to the Prince and Princess of Wales to have her to show them the way.

The bad consequences of not taking a certain share after two years.

The duties need not be what she considers the follies. Again, nothing would tend to keep more in peoples' hearts their affection for the Prince than to see the Queen making exertions.

And least but not last to one like the Queen, because it is her duty to take her part. (Sic)

Catherine knew the Queen was irascible, did not possess elasticity of temperament and, without Albert's guiding hand, lacked discipline. Gladstone took little notice of Catherine's warnings. Year by year her loathing for him grew but, until her death, Catherine remained one of the Queen's favourite people. The Queen and Mrs. Gladstone possessed one unusual quality: Common Sense.

The Queen — a Grandmother at last

On 8th January 1864, Alexander gave birth to her first child,

Albert Victor. Prince George followed and then the Princess Royal and the Princesses Victoria and Maud. The final child, Prince Alexander John, died a few weeks after birth, but by this time Alexandra had suffered from rheumatic fever which left her deaf, with a limp and her 'darling Bertie', playing the field.

The Tyneside campaign

Whatever was happening in the great world or in Gladstone's, he was forever the politician. During his second period as Chancellor of the Exchequer, the 'People's William' became known to working people as 'one of us'. They thought that Gladstone was the only British minister who had ever given them 'a right because they should have it . . . freeing taxes upon knowledge and placing duty on the inheritance of the estates of the rich'. The atheist and writer George Holyoake recalled that when Mr. and Mrs. Gladstone visited the north-east in November 1862, *newspapers told of church bells ringing, guns thundering, bands playing as, the boat conveying the couple, led the procession of twenty-five steamers, which majestically sailed down the Tyne. Ships flew their gayest flags, the river banks were thronged with thousands of workers from forge, furnaces, coal-staiths, chemical works, glass factories, shipyards, all eager to welcome, the 'People's William'. Some sang: Honour gives to sterling worth, Genius better is than birth, So here's success to Gladstone.*

Catherine and Gladstone received a reception fit for a King and Queen. For five days he played to packed halls in Newcastle, Gateshead, Middlesborough, Sunderland and York, where they visited the old Minster. Gladstone had become the MAN who understood the working man and, most importantly, the North of England, thus making way for the success of his Midlothian Campaign of 1879/80. It was also a time when old friends departed.

Richard Cobden

Gladstone remained in office until 1866. Success was enjoyable but in middle-age Catherine and Gladstone found, as many people do, old friends left the scene. On 2nd April 1865, Richard Cobden died. He was a loyal friend who had often stayed at Hawarden. Cobden was one of the men who persuaded Gladstone in 1859 to change from being a Tory into becoming a fully-fledged Liberal. With his colleague, John Bright, Cobden was a free-trader and anti-Corn Law man. He was praised by Sir Robert Peel as "the man above all others in repealing the Corn Laws".

A peaceful, poor farmer's son, he loathed war and spoke against the 'stupidity of the Crimea'. An idealist, Lord Palmerston had once told him, *It would be very delightful if your Utopia could be realized, and if the nations of the earth could think of nothing but peace and commerce, and would give up quarrelling and fighting altogether. But unfortunately man is a fighting and quarrelling animal.*

On 9th April Gladstone attended Cobden's funeral, in the little church of West Lavington, near Chichester, West Sussex. Catherine did not attend — women did not in those days. Later, Gladstone reported to Catherine, "Afterwards I went to his home, which I was anxious to see. Also I saw Mrs. Cobden. The day was lovely, the scenery most beautiful and soothing, the whole sad and impressive. Bright broke down at the grave. Cobden's name is great, it will be greater."

The Duke of Newcastle

A few months before, on 19th October 1864, Catherine and Gladstone lost an even more intimate friend, the 5th Duke of Newcastle. Gladstone, visiting Clumber, told Catherine, "The house is full of memories. Thirty-two years before, I came over from Newark to see, in fear and trembling, the old, terrifying Duke of Newcastle." He had been Sir John's great friend and Gladstone's first patron. When the 5th Duke had been Lord Lincoln, Lady Susan had been his wife, the woman whom Gladstone tried to rescue from 'a fate worse than death!' Gladstone once more found himself enmeshed in financial affairs, trying to sort out the Duke's estate and monies owed to his former wife!

The world for Catherine and Gladstone was certainly changing, even in respect of fashion. In 1850 a Mrs. Bloomer had worn the oddest garment and at the beginning of 1866, a Mrs. Addley Bourne of Piccadilly (London), Family Draper, Jupon and Corset Manufacturer to the Court and Royal Family, advertised, 'A thousand crinolines for sale, at half price.' Women's shape was changing! The bustle was emerging. Now a gentleman wished to appear safe and respectable. They wore dark colours only, with added gravitas being given by tall, shiny, silk, top hats. The style of the flamboyant dandy Count D'Orsay, who had once strutted around, *gay in his colours as a humming bird*, was now a thing of the past.

There were other changes, too. Gladstone announced. "I am unmuzzled!" During the General Election of 1865, he lost his Oxford seat. Catherine told Lucy, "I watched him anxiously as the workings of that dear pale face and the pacing of the room showed the deep emotion, but thank God he has been helped through all and though a few short hours afterwards, he was on his legs facing thousands of people at Manchester and then in Liverpool he seemed almost inspired." A month after his Oxford defeat Gladstone stood as a candidate for South Lancashire where he was elected the third M.P.

Death of Lord Palmerston

At 10.45 A.M. on Wednesday, 18th October 1865, Viscount Palmerston died in Brocket Hall, the Mansion belonging to his wife. Behind fans it was whispered, 'Old Pam' was discovered dead, in a state of undress, on a billiard table with an open-mouthed chamber maid by his side, saying over and over again, "I did nuffink!" The official report stated that, on 16th October, Lord Palmerston took a drive in his carriage, contacted a fever and became ill. Shortly before he died, he took a meal of mutton chops and apple tart and washed it down with a glass of port saying, "What an enjoyable meal it made." During the night he died peacefully in his sleep, at the age of almost eighty-one. The news made Chancellor of the Exchequer Gladstone 'giddy'. He heard it at Clumber where he was a trustee. He immediately wrote to Lord Russell, *I am quite willing to take my chance under your banner, in the exact capacity I now fill.* General Grey was mentioned as the next leader of the House of Commons. Catherine exclaimed, "I cannot for the life of me take in how General Grey could lead; knowing all about him, and his weak physique, too, I consider it would not go!"

Disraeli told Lady Palmerston, "I had a great regard for Lord Palmerston", despite in his youth referring to him as *the Lord Fanny of Diplomacy.* To his friends, Disraeli recalled that, "at a recent dinner party 'Old Pam' was offered snipe, or pheasant. He replied, 'pheasant', thus completing his ninth meat dish of the day." Gladstone considered that Palmerston held genuine Liberal convictions but Palmerston said, "Gladstone is a dangerous man. He never behaved to me as a colleague." Disraeli, observing the new government, noted, "If Johnny Russell is the Man, there will be a Reform Bill."

Preparing for power

Lord Russell had been Palmerston's Foreign Secretary. In 1865, Lord Russell, at seventy-three, became the Prime Minister, even though he was in the House of Lords. Gladstone complained to Catherine, "the greatest difficulty is having almost all the important offices in the Lords". A delicate man, born prematurely, prone to fainting fits, unable to cope with heat, deeply sensitive and only five feet four inches tall, Russell stayed in office until 1867, when party disunity forced him to leave politics. He died in 1878, in the home presented to his family by Queen Victoria, Pembroke Lodge, Richmond Park. His grandson, Bertrand, the philosopher, remembered Russell, as 'a kindly, old man'. A lonely boy, Bertrand wandered around the grounds, becoming *accustomed to its wide horizons and unimpeded views of the sunsets.* Gladstone became leader of the Liberal Party. In 1868, he proposed the Irish Church Resolution for the disestablishment of the Irish church and tried to reunite the Liberal Party for government. Disraeli, watching Gladstone struggle *from behind his mask*, called for a General Election.

Gladstone then stood for South West Lancashire and Greenwich. He won the Greenwich seat. In February 1868, Disraeli became Prime Minister. Gladstone considered his rival to be "a light-weight, a man of letters, achieving success in only two areas, by building-up a party out of nothing and revolutionizing the base of the parliamentary constitution". Catherine had written to Herbert, *Is it not disgusting after all Papa's labour and patriotism and years of work to think of him handing over his nest-egg to that Jew*! Disraeli lasted only a few months. In December 1868, his administration fell and the Liberals swept into power. For the first time the Queen appointed Mr. Gladstone Prime Minister. Lady Palmerston told Catherine, "Mr. Gladstone has had the good fortune to be able to form a Government which gives hope of long continuance." Disraeli, five years older than Gladstone, felt he had come to power too late. Gladstone observed, "This birthday opens my sixtieth year. I descend the hill of life. It would be truer to say I ascend a steepening path with a burden gathering weight. The Almighty seems to sustain and spare me for some purpose of his own, deeply unworthy as I know myself to be. Glory to his name!"

Catherine refused, as had Mrs. Disraeli, to live at No. 10, *too dingy*. She remained at 11, Carlton House Terrace. She also learned that Disraeli had persuaded the Queen to create that *ridiculous old woman* the Viscountess of Beaconsfield. Catherine was never known other than Mrs. Gladstone!

She prayed that Gladstone would remember her advice on how to treat the Queen, "and pet her a little". In 1865, the year of the cattle plague, when dairy farmers watched thirty-per-cent of their stock die, in agony, slowly, Catherine begged her husband, "Do not forget how I suggested three years ago, that it is only right you should take the opportunity of showing to the country, the interest you take in agriculture, as well as manufacturing."

Christmas once again came round. The year 1868 found the Gladstone family gathered together at 11, Carlton Terrace. 'Papa' remained in his office, preparing to become Prime Minister. He wrote in his diary, *I feel like a man with a burden under which he must fall and be crushed if he looks to the right or left or fails from any cause to concentrate mind and muscle upon his progress.* And then cheered himself, *It has been a special joy of this December that our son Stephen is given to the church 'whose shoes laces I am not worthy to unloose'.* He had been ordained curate of St Mary's Church, Lambeth and had taken lodgings in a little terraced house nearby, with a kindly widow. The seventeenth-century gardeners, John Tradescant and his son, lie in the churchyard and the Church is now the Garden Museum.

With Gladstone out of the way, Catherine supervised her women-folk. They baked, sewed red flannel petticoats, wrapped up gifts and toys — all destined for the residents of the House of Charity. The men lolled around, discussing the affairs of the day. Above all the noise and bustle, Mary could be heard calling, "Lavinia, we are going to 'Dizzy's' party next Wednesday. Oh! it will be such fun!"

CHAPTER SIX

Enter Disraeli, Departing Brothers and a Great Political Campaign

The 1870s

RETIREMENT THREATENS

In February 1874, Disraeli took over the reins of power for the second time, with the greatest majority the party had had since the 1840s. The administration began just as the Great Depression of 1874 to 1896 took hold. The Conservatives faced a fall in government revenue, rising unemployment, trade crises and the high cost of maintaining the army which was fighting numerous colonial wars. Disraeli ignored Gladstone's demand to reduce the national debt. His government carried out so many social reforms that the Liberal-Labour Member of Parliament, Alexander Macdonald, commented, "The Conservative party has done more for the working-man in five years than the Liberal party have done in fifty!" In 1875 Disraeli sent his secretary, Montague Corry, to see Nathaniel Rothschild to ask him for funds to buy the Khedive's shares in the Suez Canal. "On what security?" asked Rothschild, "On the security of the British government," Corry replied. With this assurance, Rothschild picked up another grape, nodded and Britain took control of the Suez Canal!

Throughout most of 1874, Gladstone considered resigning and returning to his great love, the study of Homer. The thought dismayed Catherine. For over thirty years she had enjoyed having a husband at the centre of things. Now she faced a life she considered would be as humdrum as most women's. An Earl's daughter, Catherine faced the future as the wife of a 'has been'. Ignoring Gladstone's failing health and eyesight, she felt he had made the wrong decision. It was terrible for her. For the first time in her life Catherine considered her husband's judgement was at fault. Surely Gladstone would always be 'at the top of his game', a man of whom his colleagues joked, "Never play cards with Gladstone, he always has an ace up his sleeve and is convinced God put it there." His resignation would mean that Catherine could never again cajole the great and the good into handing over money easily for her good causes. She asked herself, "Would *The Times* continue to print my letters?" Gladstone had no secretary at Hawarden to help him. He dealt with at least fifty letters a day and, to Catherine's dismay, she found Mary was becoming her father's 'right-hand man'.

The whole of 1874 continued to be difficult for Catherine. Not only was her husband considering throwing away his career but was also contemplating selling their London home, without making plans to buy another. Whilst breakfasting at Grillion's, which had become Gladstone's favourite eating place, he told friends, "Conversation with C on the situation. She is sadly reluctant to my receding into the shade." Gladstone was in a strange mood, he was even civil to Disraeli. A man who always lived within his means, in March Gladstone sold the lease of 11, Carlton House Terrace to Sir Arthur Guinness, for £35,000. A sale of his collection of books, art, porcelain and china, which lasted for four days, realized over £9,000. Gladstone described it as, 'like a little death'. Catherine, too, felt slightly depressed. They took a smaller house nearby as she insisted they still needed a London base. Gladstone took a short lease on 73, Harley Street, where they lived for a few years.

Sir Stephen dies

While Gladstone prayed to God for guidance, in June Sir Stephen Glynne suffered a heart attack. He collapsed in the middle of Shoreditch High Street, searching for antiquities amongst the furnishing emporiums. Passers-by took him into a doctor's surgery where he died. Gladstone said, "My brother-in-law was a man of singular refinement and remarkably modesty. His culture was high and his character of deep interest. His memory was on the whole decidedly of the most remarkable known to me of the generations and country. His life, however, was retired and unobtrusive; but he sat in parliament, I think for about fifteen years . . ."

Gladstone, who believed Sir Stephen's affairs were in order, was shaken to the core to find his will had been made out before the Oak Farm fiasco and bore all the signs of 'Boydell's ravages'. Much of the estate had been sold to pay debts. Once more Gladstone was faced with the task of sorting out the financial affairs of his 'in-laws'. Sir Stephen left Hawarden to Gladstone who possessed *a strong repugnance for either becoming the virtual or actual master of Hawarden.* Sir Stephen remained grateful to his brother-in-law for saving him from a criminal charge, of an act of homosexuality.

'Gayness' was unacceptable to the 'normal' Victorian male. Ahead of his time in so many ways, Gladstone may have considered it was a part of Sir Stephen's nature and the passivity he possessed was a feminine trait. When the Oak Farm saga abated Gladstone probably suspected any 'normal' male would not wish to sit at the head of the table, in his own house, with his sister and brother-in-law placed either side, dominating the conversation and being referred to by him as 'the great people'. Sir Stephen is almost a forgotten figure now. 'His children' are to be found in one hundred and six Victorian notebooks stacked in the strong room in St. Dieniol's Library. Purely for his own interest, 'flying about' on horseback he visited 5,500 churches, sometimes ten a day. Numerous cardboard boxes contain sketches of windows, arches and notes. These are a unique record of churches before the Victorian restorers got to work.

The death of Henry
Two years earlier, in July 1872, Catherine's brother, Henry,

after enjoying an excellent dinner, was struck by lightning as he rode through a violent thunderstorm, returning to the Rectory at Hawarden. There was gossip that some years before he had become enamoured with his daughters' governess and proposed marriage to her. Catherine and Gladstone, fearful of Willy's inheritance and telling each other that the young woman was unsuitable, persuaded her to accept a large sum of money and disappear from Hawarden and out of Henry's life. Cottagers nodded their heads and said unkindly, and with no foundation in fact, "she was no better than she should be". Perhaps somewhere, an elderly lady living in reduced but 'genteel circumstances' dusted a mantelpiece, moved a photograph with a sigh, and muttered, "Perhaps . . . "

Henry's death left Willy firmly heir to Hawarden. Gladstone told him, "You will, I hope, familiarize your mind with this truth, that you can no more become proprietor of such a large body of property, or of the portion of it now accruing, than your brother Stephen could become rector of the parish, without recognizing the serious moral and social responsibilities which belong to it."

The death of her brother left Catherine with no brothers or sister. Catherine was now the only remaining child of the 8th Earl and his wife. Even the baronetcy had died with her elder brother. Catherine, who rarely looked back, remembered Stephen as an incredibly handsome little boy, dressed in lace ruffles and frills, black satin shorts and white silk stockings. Nanny pinned his mama's sapphire and diamond brooch on to his left breast. Catherine and Stephen danced together under crystal chandeliers amongst the gilded splendour of a Parisian ballroom. They whirled around together, long past their bedtime, pretending to be grown-ups.

Uncharacteristically, Catherine wrote a desolate letter to Gladstone. He replied, *How much, how extraordinary much love, you have had in your sister and your brothers, but as in the case of money so in this noble matter of love the more we have the more we desire and we become insatiable. And who can wonder that when the river ceases to flow the land should feel parched and thirsty?* Pushed into coping, she wrote to him,

I did not half consider the extraordinary blessings, the wonderful time we have been allowed to be a happy family, above all in having you . . .

In July 1877, Catherine and Gladstone felt in need of a 'restorative'. A close friend, Sir Donald Currie, ran the Castle Shipping Line from London to India and South Africa. They took a trip in one of his steamers from London to Dartmouth setting out at 10.20 for the docks. *We started in the Dublin Castle at noon. We spent the night at Nore, good weather, kind reception, splendid fare. The Cape deputies came with us as far as Gravesend. Among those deputies was Mr. Kruger.*

Four months later, in October, Catherine and Gladstone paid their only visit to Ireland. They were entertained by the Provost of Trinity, spoke with Cardinal Cullen, and talked to the Duke of Marlborough. Gladstone received the Freedom of the City of Dublin and they both delighted in the beauty of Wicklow.

Willy becomes heir to Hawarden

In September 1874, Gladstone signed the papers making Willy 'the absolute owner in law of the Hawarden Estates'. Immediately Catherine opened the park to the public. Sir Stephen had shown unusual force of character by not allowing her to open up the grounds hitherto. She had begged him, "To me it is quite horrid, the entire solitude and the feeling that scarcely anybody may enjoy the innocent pleasure of the lovely park." She could have added, with the old fortress castle standing on the hill, overlooking the elms, oaks and beeches, streams and waterfalls, which as children they watched splashing down, calling out to each other names like 'Niagara'. Standing in the churchyard, one could look across to the Dee Estuary which Gladstone knew flowed into Liverpool Bay. On a good day, if you stood quite still, a Kingfisher might be seen or a Golden Plover diving overhead and here and there a Redwing might make an appearance.

Despite Catherine's longing, Willy did not inherit his father's brilliance but did inherit his parents' love of music. Catherine was a talented pianist who, as a young woman, had been taught by

Franz Liszt. Willie sang and played the organ. He wrote numerous chants, anthems, introits and organ voluntaries which included: *Gracious and Righteous, Withdraw Not Thou* and the hymn tune used for *Dear Lord and Father of Mankind.*

Willy was not made for the 'big scene'. He did not possess any of his father's ambition or energy. He came nowhere near to achieving Gladstone's parliamentary success. He had, however, become Liberal M.P. for Chester for three years, Whitby for twelve and East Worcestershire for five. He was a Junior Lord of the Treasury, Lord High Sheriff, Justice of the Peace and Deputy Lieutenant for the County of Flint. As a sitting member of Parliament, he played football for Scotland and was a first-class mountaineer.

Willy was happiest at Hawarden, but Chester dominated the region together with the powerful Duke of Westminster, his parents' friend who lived close to Hawarden, in Eaton Hall, near to the old village of Ecclestone, just outside Chester. Once the town had been a prominent, medieval, walled city and with its resources, during the late eighteenth and nineteenth centuries, played a major role in the industrial development of the north-west, helped by the growth of the rail network and the Shropshire Union Canal. Willy would have watched the Duke's architect bringing the medieval town back to life with Jacobean-style architecture and knew, like his father, that the town had been a trading centre for Ireland and was still a place where the Irish did business!

While the Duke developed Chester, Willy became the much loved and good squire of Hawarden. He was never a 'womanizer' in the Prince of Wales' style. Nevertheless, he worried his parents with his roving eye and refusal to settle down. In June, Catherine wrote excitedly to Henry, *Willy gives me the idea of thinking of marriage.* Catherine and Gladstone relaxed. A month later Willy became engaged to Miss Gertrude Stuart, the youngest daughter of the last Master of Blantyre. Queen Victoria told Catherine, "I can easily understand how much pleased you must feel that your future daughter-in-law is the grandchild of the dear Duchess of

Sutherland. I do not know Miss Gertrude Stuart but I have always heard her highly-spoken of." Catherine commented, "She has what Willy needs in a wife — decision."

Willy's marriage and the death of Robertson

Gertrude and Willy married on 30th September 1875, later than anticipated. Seven days before, Robertson had died at his home, Court Hey, Liverpool. Following the death of Mary Ellen, his wife, in 1865, he had gone into a decline, taking Gladstone and Company with him. By the time of his death little was left of the company. His last photograph shows a man 'gone to pieces,' having forgotten how deeply his eight children loved him.

Robertson was a man who had achieved much: Mayor of Liverpool, a respected freemason, and the chief executive of his father's Liverpool interests and partner in his father-in-law's bank, Heywoods. He became the first President of the Liverpool Financial Reform Association, *the most persistent and single-minded free trade body England had ever known*. Like his father he had railway interests. In August 1845, he was made the Deputy Chairman of the Grand Junction Railway and sat on the committee of the Birmingham and Oxford Junction Railway. Unlike Gladstone, Robertson's line did not continue: none of his sons had children.

The family enjoyed the wedding of Willy to his Gertrude but was overshadowed by Robertson's 'failure'. The following year, in February, his extensive property portfolio, which he had inherited from his father and built up, was sold. It included the most prestigious streets in Liverpool and a row of good quality houses in Rodney Street, where Sir John had started family life, together with stables and workshops in other parts of the city. By the time of his death Robertson had already lost around £6,000 of Gladstone's share of the Seaforth Estate.

Amongst themselves the other sons said, "Even in his declining years, the old man would not have been such a fool." Sir John, normally such a shrewd judge of character, had made Robertson his right-hand man. His father had despatched his son to Demerara to inspect the family plantations and conditions of the slaves. What he found shocked Robertson. Immediately, he sacked the man in charge. Before sailing back to Liverpool, he instructed the agent to make profits, 'as large as possible'. The plantation profits continued to be huge but, for the slaves, it may have been 'out of sight out of mind'. Sir John appointed a man called James Wyllie as manager of some of his concerns. The moment Robertson died, Wyllie sacked Henry Neville who was working in India for a subsidiary company, Ogilvy, Gillanders and Co. In 1886, the boy travelled back to England alone and into the arms of an infuriated Catherine.

Whilst Catherine enjoyed the marriage of her eldest son, she mourned Robertson and his kindness. On her honeymoon he had said, "You plan to go shopping, pray take my carriage." She also missed her London home but she was happy that all seemed to be in place for Willy and Gertrude to live long, pleasant and uneventful lives. They moved into Hawarden Castle. The arrangement suited Catherine but not her son and daughter-in-law. Lord Blantyre noticed the young people were wilting under the dominance of Catherine's unconscious but managing ways. He persuaded Willy and Gertrude to build 'The Red House' at the end of the village. They were still close to Catherine but far enough away from "dear Mama" to feel comfortable.

When Gertrude produced her first baby, Willy, like many young men, told his father, "I had no idea how awful birth is." Gladstone replied. "Yes, when you were born, it came as a shock to your mother and I." Gertrude produced two daughters and a son who followed his grandfather into Parliament. This boy, William Glynne Charles Gladstone, showed outstanding promise. Like his Uncle Stephen, he became Lord Lieutenant of Flintshire. He died in the trenches in the Great War and lies buried in the churchyard at Hawarden, brought there by order of George V, in respect to his grandfather's memory. The King had been a pall-bearer at Gladstone's funeral.

Willy dies

On 1st March 1889, Willy had a stroke which caused his left side to become paralyzed. He also lost his speech and a brain tumour was diagnosed. Catherine took over the nursing of her son. But on 4th July 1891, shortly after an operation, Catherine's 'treasure' died in his father-in-law's home in Berkeley Square. Gladstone arrived too late to say goodbye to him. As with Jessy's death, his grief was terrible. He told friends, "It is now forty-six years since we lost a child. I suppose all feel that those deaths which reverse the order of nature have a sharpness of their own." Catherine once again removed all photographs of her child. She told Mary, "You will think me a coward but I cannot bear to look at them." Neither Gladstone nor Catherine could cope easily with the death of one of their children. Lord Morley said that Willy "was a man of many virtues and some admirable gifts. He was an accomplished musician and, I have seen letters of his to his father, marked by a rare delicacy of feeling and true power of feeling."

Gladstone wrote to the new Squire of Hawarden, young William, *Hawarden is a kind of sacred trust. It has been only by much care and labour redeemed from alienation and handed down to you and coming generations with its traditions unbroken.* On William's death, his Uncle Henry Neville, bought the estate. He purchased the succession to the estate, paid off the outstanding mortgage and improved Hawarden. He made it his home in 1921 and Henry Neville became known as the 'Good' Squire Gladstone. He succeeded his nephew as Lord Lieutenant of Flintshire and was raised to the peerage as Baron Gladstone of Hawarden in the County of Flint on 22nd June 1932. There were no children of his marriage to Hon. Maud Rendel. On Henry Neville's death in April 1935 the title became extinct. Willy's death left Catherine coping with an elderly husband and six grown-up children, entering middle age.

The Children Growing-Up

Agnes

It was Agnes who described her mother as *having the genius of charity*. She was a quiet, docile and beautiful daughter and had been old Sir John's favourite granddaughter. Disraeli could never stop himself flirting gently with her. One of Agnes's friends said, "You see when I speak to Mr. Gladstone I know I am talking to the cleverest man in the world but when I talk to Mr. Disraeli, I know I am the cleverest girl in the world."

Catherine was shaken when Agnes announced that she wished to follow in Miss Nightingale's footsteps and train to be a professional nurse. Her mother had applauded the support given by the mamas of girls who wished to train in Miss Nightingale's new nursing school at St. Thomas' Hospital in London. Delicate Agnes was another matter. She sympathized with her daughter's 'pretty thoughts', "but Agnes, at twenty-nine, you are too young and too sheltered to leave home and cope with such an onerous life". Catherine ignored the fact that Agnes followed her mother around from one hospital ward to another.

Gentle and placid Agnes did not fight her mother's decision. Catherine felt happier a little later. She forewarned Gladstone, "One of our pretty birds is likely to fly the nest." He ignored the remark and was shaken when Agnes announced her engagement to the Revd. Edward Charles Wickham. He was the Principal of the Royal and Religious Foundation of the Wellington College, a famous public school, built in memory of the Duke of Wellington. Everybody else was expecting it, even Queen Victoria. She teased Gladstone on his surprise and little knowledge of his future son-in-law but, much to his joy, he discovered the young man was a translator of Horace. Gladstone contacted Catherine saying, "I am concerned this great Aye to be said, without a single word on the subject of the means of support forthcoming!" He quickly drew up an excellent marriage settlement for his daughter, explaining to Catherine, "Your family were not worldly-minded people, but you will remember that before our engagement, Stephen was spirited-up, most properly, to put a question to me about means." He wrote again to Catherine complaining, *Yesterday I was not so much struck at hearing nothing on the subject of any sublunary particular; but lo! Again your letter of today arrives with all about the charms of the orphanage, but not a syllable on beef and mutton, bread and butter, which after all cannot be altogether dispensed with!*

For two weeks before Christmas 1873, the weather was delightful and Catherine and Gladstone prayed it would remain so until the 27th of December, when a large and cheerful party would assemble in the little church at Hawarden to witness Agnes and the Revd. Wickham become man and wife. Catherine complained, "I have yet to learn how to part with a child." The pair received 250 gifts. The poor of the parish, together with the school children, enjoyed a free tea. Catherine and Gladstone were touched by the kindness of all from the Queen down to cottagers and poor folks. Two years later Agnes presented Catherine and Gladstone with their first grandchild — a baby girl. In 1894 the Revd. Wickham became Dean of Lincoln Cathedral.

When Catherine and Gladstone were very old, Agnes became seriously disabled. Catherine commented. "Supposing it had been me, oh what should we all have done?" She, of course, was thinking of her many responsibilities! — All those charities, twenty-five children (six of her own, Mary's twelve and George's three later additions and Henry's four girls) and, of course, her dear, grand, old man — Gladstone.

Stephen

When Catherine's brother Henry died, his sister set out immediately to make sure Stephen became Rector of Hawarden. Ever since the mid-eighteenth century a Glynne had been in charge of the parish. Catherine longed for 'Stephy' to become the parson of the family. Despite finding her five-year old son amusing and calling him a 'comic character' she told Gladstone, "Stephy' treasures things. They sink in and come out after one would think they are forgotten." At a dinner party she had told the pretty, young Lady Peel, "There is much in that child for good or ill."

Stephen made good progress at Eton and steady progress through Oxford and Cuddleston Theological College. Despite having two childhood operations and poor eyesight, Stephen grew into the outdoor type. He was one of his father's 'happy woodcutters' and climbed Snowdon and the Swiss Alps. When he was twenty-four, much to his father's joy, he was ordained into the Anglican Church and became a curate in south London. Catherine arrived occasionally to decorate his church, writing to Gladstone, *Tell the girls, I am trying to decorate Stephy's church and that I have seen a new object making letters in straw and a cross of rice.*

It took a great effort on Catherine's part to persuade Stephen to become the Parson of Hawarden and the surrounding villages. He did so towards the end of 1872, after Uncle Henry's death. His cousin Albert was appointed to be his curate. They had been together at Geddington, the small prep. school, which most of his brothers attended. Albert remembered his aunt looking at him with a strange, wistful, almost hungry look, gazing and gazing into his face, striving to see in him something of his mother. Stephen became Gladstone's confessor. Before he died he told his son, "I have never committed that act which betrays the marriage bed."

An unattractive man, Stephen nevertheless married a great beauty — a Liverpool doctor's daughter, Annie Wilson. Society said, "Miss Wilson is not a suitable partner for the son of a Prime Minister and daughter of an earl." They asked themselves, "Has she not a bevy of sisters? Is the market not over full already?" Gladstone and Catherine ignored the remarks. They did not have an ounce of false pride between them and attended the wedding joyfully in Liverpool. The press, announcing the engagement, stated that, *Mr. Gladstone was enjoying excellent health and continued to chop down trees.* When another of the Wilson girls married, Catherine sent magnificent bouquets of flowers to decorate the church. They arrived too late and the family found themselves scuttling around trying to find suitable alcoves for them. The couple named their eldest son Albert. He became Sir Albert, 5th Baronet, MBE and a director of the Bank of England and, amongst numerous other honours, High Sheriff of the Court of London.

Mary

By 1877, Mary still remained unmarried. As far as her family could see she was unlikely to do so. She grew into a lively, independent, young woman who never asked her mother's permission to entertain her friends. Anyway, Catherine was unlikely to be at home — she was so often away, busy with her charity work. Increasingly, Mary ran the household, becoming the ideal private secretary to her father. She inherited her mother's genes and, like her mother, became expert in running other people's lives. However, unlike Catherine she possessed a passion for politics and, without meaning to be, a threat to her position. The family nicknamed Mary *Von Molke* after Bismark's aide-de-camp. Gladstone commented on his capable daughter, *Mary is all-sufficing in point of society.* To the observer she seemed a happy, fulfilled, single woman with many friends and interests, with no need of a man. As time went on Mary became more and more immersed in her father's political life.

In August 1877, Mary and Helen engaged a lady's maid, a young Hanoverian, Fraulein Auguste Schlüter. She called Mary 'my beloved young lady'. Helen continued to live away from them all, in Cambridge, returning to her family only for the holidays. A deeply religious woman, Schlüter adored Gladstone and treated Catherine with great respect. . . . *We sang Home Sweet Home near her bedroom door.* Like Gladstone, Schlüter kept a diary and wrote endless letters.

On 11th December 1885 Mary approached Catherine, as she had done many years before. Now she was thirty-eight and once more in love. Sometime before, Stephen had invited a handsome young man, Harry Drew, to become his curate. He took the position. The Revd. Drew also became godfather to Stephen's son. Now Mary found herself drawn to the curate, eight years her junior. She told her mother, "I know with him the floodgates are open." On 15th December she wrote to Catherine, *The nightmare which seemed to be wrapping its dark wings closer and closer round me is passing away just as you thought it would.* On Christmas Day, after dinner, in the schoolroom, Mary agreed to marry Harry Drew. Schlüter commented, *When I saw Mr. Drew I felt like a tigress wishing to throw herself upon the enemy.*

Society commented, "It is a very small marriage for such as Miss Gladstone." Catherine said sharply, "Mary, at her age, is unlikely to have more than two children." Lulu Harcourt observed bitchily, *Harry Drew looks very aesthetic. I wonder if he is so in his conduct! If he is I do not think he will satisfy Mary.* Lord Granville wrote to Catherine, *So remarkable a woman as Miss Gladstone is not likely to make a mistake on this point.* Catherine agreed. Mary had said, "He is the most wonderful person for fitting in to all my nooks and crannies and yet all the same keeping his own individuality."

Harry's father, John Drew, was an active Conservative and a land surveyor in a large way of business. He acted as agent to Lord Devon for the Powderham and Moreton Estates. Harry was also well educated. He had studied at Keble College, Oxford, with the object of becoming a barrister. When a close friend nearly died of a serious illness, Harry offered up his own life to God for the sake of his friend's.

On 2nd February 1886 — Candlemas, a day when the Church celebrates Christ's Presentation in the Temple and the Purification of the Virgin Mary — Mary married her Harry at St Margaret's, Westminster. Stephen officiated. Mary requested it was a quiet family affair. The night before her wedding she had taken a large dose of bromide, to calm her nerves. As she walked down the aisle she saw the Prince and Princess of Wales sitting in the congregation.

Despite being a Prime Minister's daughter and granddaughter
of an Earl, she and her bridesmaids wore simple, white muslin
frocks, with material bought from the local Co-operative stores and
carried bunches of snowdrops. Mary explained, "I am marrying a
curate and intend to live within his stipend of £300 a year."
Catherine wore her usual blue.

An ancestor was an unseen presence. Sir John Glynne had
bought Hawarden in 1653, and lay beneath the altar. A supporter
of Cromwell, when the Restoration of the Monarchy occurred, he
bowed the knee to Charles II and became Sir John. Mary and Harry
honeymooned at Lady Sarah Spencer's place in Hertfordshire and
returned to live in the Castle. Gladstone did not lose a secretary
but gained an unofficial chaplain.

Catherine was right. Mary did have two babies. One died
shortly after birth and the other baby, a little girl, Dorothy, lived.
She was a blonde, blue-eyed, dimply, bubbly child. 'Dossie'
became the darling of both grandparents and photographers alike.
Catherine was left now with only her 'Sugar Plums' to find their
place in the world.

The Sugar Plums

Henry Neville was Catherine's seventh son, the eldest of her
pair of 'Sugar Plums'. This was the man who purchased Hawarden
on the death of the young heir in 1915 — but all that was in the
future. When the family business in India failed Henry Neville
returned home in 1886. *The whole family flew to the door and received
him with yells.* He needed their warmth. Twelve years before, the
daughter of a close family friend of the Gladstones, the Hon. Maud
Rendel, had broken off their engagement. Henry inherited his
paternal grandfather's business acumen and did well. In 1881 he
became a junior partner in the family firm, at that time called
Gillanders, Arbuthnot & Company. Gladstone gave him £4,000
to buy a senior partnership. And then the disaster occurred. The
company slid into difficulties and Henry's services were no longer
required.

On Henry's return to Hawarden, Gladstone appointed him as one of his private secretaries. Henry and Maud added to the joy of Gladstone and Catherine's silver jubilee. They married on 30th January 1890, at St George's, Hanover Square, London, the church in which Disraeli married his Mary Anne. That, too, was a very happy marriage. Henry continued with his business interests and did well. He was created a director of the P&O and of the British India Steamship Company.

Henry's father-in-law was also a businessman. He was the manager of the London branch of the Armstrong Gunnery Company and Liberal M.P. for Montgomery. Lord Rendel was nicknamed the 'Member for Wales'. However, he did not purchase an estate in Wales but, in 1888, bought Hatchlands, close to Guildford. On his retirement, he became Baron Rendel of Hatchlands in the county of Surrey. Miss Jekyll redesigned the gardens and his son, Harry Stuart Goodhart Rendel, the famous architect, inherited Hatchlands.

Catherine and Gladstone knew Hatchlands well. Lord Rendel was a close friend of Gladstone's and acted as pall-bearer at his funeral. Gladstone was already familiar with the area as his father's friend, the Duke of Newcastle, lived at Esher. On 3rd September 1841 he wrote in his diary, "This day I went to Claremont to be sworn in . . . I visited Claremont once before, twenty-seven years ago I think, as a child, to see the place, soon after the Princess Charlotte's death. It corresponded pretty much with my impressions."

Only Herbert is left. On 7th April 1872, Catherine wrote to Gladstone who had written of his son, *with all his charm and all his merits, he does not know what strong effort and hard work are.* Catherine replied sharply, "Herbert has always suffered from ill-health." Herbert, much to his father's surprise, obtained a First Class Honours in Modern History at Oxford. He was the only son who obtained any real success, following in Gladstone's footsteps.

As Catherine told her last child, Herbert, who was the baby born in Downing Street, "Never be afraid of asking me for money,

I have such a horror of you not having any." It seemed possible that Herbert would never have any. He dithered on which career to follow. He wondered about becoming a land agent. For a time he lectured at Keble College, Oxford. Eventually Herbert followed his father into politics. He was M.P. for Leeds for thirty years and later Leeds West. He enjoyed several senior appointments in the Treasury and became Home Secretary.

He had two disasters. *The first*: The Hawarden Kite. He leaked his father's intentions to *The Times*. He had not been long in London when he felt the party was drifting towards a split over the Irish question. Under this impression he had a conversation with the chief executive of an important press agency. He held an informal interview with the man — no notes were taken and nothing read from papers. Herbert gave his own opinion on the assumption that they were his father's.

Lord Morley commented, "Unluckily, it would seem to need at least the genius of a Bismark to perform with precision and success the delicate office of inspiring a modern oracle on the journalistic tripod." Herbert then had another conversation with a journalist friend where he over-simplified Gladstone's recommendation of 'a great deal of home rule for the Irish'. No statesman was ever more careful of the golden rule of political strategy than Gladstone, i.e. not to take the second step before you have taken successfully the first. His colleagues were unaware of his thoughts.

The second: Herbert upset King Edward VII. He ineptly handled a protest march of Roman Catholics through the streets of London. Shortly afterwards, he found himself appointed Governor General of South Africa.

In 1910, Herbert became Viscount Gladstone of Lanark. At thirty-eight he married eighteen-year old Dorothy Mary Paget. They moved into the prosperous town of Ware, Hertfordshire, close to Hatfield House which Herbert had enjoyed as a child, listening *to thrilling ghost stories in front of a log fire*. He died in 1934, and his Viscountess in 1953. They had no children. The title died with Dorothy.

And those other children

As well as Catherine's birth children, she also had responsibility for other children. They belonged to George and Mary. They, too, were growing up. She continued looking wistfully into Alfred's face seeking her sister Mary. "Where is she? Sometimes I see her." Almost immediately after her mother's death, the eldest girl, Meriel, married sensibly. Catherine declaimed, "She is so like her paternal grandmother." The second girl, Catherine's dearest 'Locket,' in 1864 married into the great Devonshire family. She too would face sadness.

And tragedy

Before Gladstone fought the Midlothian campaign, which would take him into power again, the whole family network — Spencers, Lytteltons and Gladstones — faced a tragedy. Deep down, in the depths of George's happy nature, lay an inherited instability. He committed the most unforgivable of sins. Gladstone blamed himself. He told Catherine, "If only I had persuaded George to translate Homer into English verse. The mental discipline required may have averted this disaster."

In April 1876 George shoved his manservant aside, rushed to the banisters and threw himself over the side, crashing headfirst onto the marble floors below. He lived for twenty-four hours. Nobody was over-concerned that for some months George had suffered from depression. Outwardly, he enjoyed the marriages of his daughters but, on Easter Day, Lavinia found her father 'fidgety and scared-looking'. A year before, in January 1875, his daughter May contracted typhoid fever. On Palm Sunday she died. Catherine considered herself to be the nurse of the family. She acted as she always did when illness threatened those she loved. She pushed her family on one side, cancelled all her social and political engagements and took charge of the situation.

Lavinia wrote, *I shall never forget what she was to us at Hagley, during the nine weeks of May's almost hopeless illness . . . She encouraged and inspired the nurses, fascinated and impressed the doctors . . . I remember seeing her on the bed for hours . . . helping to keep an ice bag exactly in the right position on the patient.* Arthur Balfour was devastated. He said he was about to propose to 'May' but he had danced around her, just as he had done with Mary, all those years before. May complained, "He dangles about and does nothing'.

It was true that George had money worries, but his second marriage to Sybella Mildmay was a most contented one. Her nature was, as her name implied, a gentle one. Catherine wrote, *I am very much pleased with that arrangement.* Sybella only complained about her husband when he insisted on using the Long Gallery as a cricket pitch. After their father's death, Sybella's three little girls looked at Gladstone, wide-eyed. He boomed at them "Do I see three Liberals sitting before me?" "Uncle William is trying to be kindly, darlings," Catherine explained.

Lucy wrote to her aunt, Oh you are right about the sight of the little children reminding one more consolingly than anything else of the new blessings. She reminded Catherine that she had never forsaken her sister's children, *You have never let the poor old dozen feel quite motherless in all these nineteen years.*

Lucy cried after her father's death, "Oh God what can we all be without him?" Thirteen years before, Lucy had become lady-in-waiting to the Queen. She followed in the steps of the Dowager, Lady Lyttleton. However, shortly after her appointment she married Freddie Cavendish.

Gladstone terrible on the rebound

Gladstone described 1878 as a 'tumultuous year'. The Eastern Question continued to dominate politics. There was trouble in the Balkans, uprisings in Bosnia and Herzegovina and revolution in Bulgaria. Rumours of torture dominated the headlines. Disraeli dismissed them but he was out of the fray, sitting in the House of Lords. In 1876 the Queen had created her favourite minister The Earl of Beaconsfield and Viscount Hughenden. Gladstone declared, "His government is supposed now to stand mainly upon its recent foreign policy: the most selfish and least worthy I have ever known." Gladstone did, however, always give Disraeli credit for his genius. The news of the troubles in Eastern Europe made the London mob uneasy and a bunch of jingoistic rioters broke the windows of 11, Carlton House Terrace. They were only mollified when, at the suggestion of the police, Catherine appeared on the balcony. Throughout the year the Eastern question remained, causing problems.

The Midlothian campaign

A photograph taken in 1879 shows Catherine sitting on the steps of Dalmeny House, the Earl of Rosebery's place. She looks comfortable. Catherine knew the Roseberys, as she stayed with them, at Dalmeny, when she was a girl. Then the house was new, built in the year of Waterloo and the first Scottish mansion to be designed in the Neo-Gothic style. Its Tudor turrets dominated the surrounding countryside. In the background stands Gladstone together with the 5th Earl, the thirty-two year old Primrose Rosebery, President of the Midlothian Liberal Association. A great Jewish family, the Rosebery's involvement in Whig politics stretched way back, into distant time.

On 8th March 1880, while Gladstone was studying Homer, Disraeli in the House of Lords was preparing to fight another election. He declaimed against the Irish, "A portion of its population was endeavouring to sever its constitutional tie that united it to Great Britain in that bond which was favourable to the power and prosperity of both. It is hoped that all men of light and leading will resist this destructive doctrine." Gladstone made the decision not to stand again for Greenwich. In Victoria's England the economy galloped ahead, aiding Scotland's growth. The 'thinking classes' started to discuss the Corn Laws, the Cotton Famine and the growth of heavy industry. Coal and iron were to be found in Scotland in abundance.

The heavy industries, ship-building and engineering flourished, as did the great companies who owned many of the coal-mines and furnaces. With the growth of railways communications improved and the trains of the '60s such as the *Flying Scotsman* brought the country closer to London.

Gladstone's roots were in Scotland. His family had originally been 'borderers'. It may or may not have been one of the factors which influenced Rosebery to ask Gladstone to fight the forth-coming contest as a candidate for the constituency of Edinburghshire. It lies South of Edinburgh, a rural area, which contained a few mining villages. It was the first campaign to promote *the cult of the leader*; in reality, a 'personality cult'. It became known as the Midlothian campaign. In his acceptance speech Gladstone stated, "You have been kind enough to supply me with evidence which entirely satisfies my mind that the invitation expresses the desire of the majority of the constituency." Some 3,620 men were eligible to vote. Gladstone also considered Leeds, with fifty thousand voters, but decided to keep this opportunity for his son, Herbert.

In Midlothian, two rival landowners faced each other: the sitting Tory M.P. Lord Dalkeith, heir to the 5th Duke of Buccleuch and Gladstone's friend, and the 5th Earl of Rosebery, whose support came from the Lowlands. In 1873 Rosebery had visited the Democratic National Convention in New York and became fascinated by 'modern' American electoral techniques. It provided him with a great moral spectacle together with a political lesson. In the American style, Rosebery made forward plans and set up bands of enthusiastic supporters. In a way the Midlothian campaign was something of a political come-back for Gladstone. Rosebery arranged that Catherine and Gladstone should travel in a Pullman car, via the Midland railway. Whenever they stopped at a station, Gladstone would clamber onto the platform at the back of the car and address the crowds. Thousands flocked from neighbouring towns and villages.

Rosebery made certain each 'stop' was well publicized and that crowds of well-wishers were there to see 'the Grand Old Man'. Even at wayside spots hundreds assembled, merely to catch a glimpse of the train as it dashed through. The Liberals gained a seat wherever Gladstone's train stopped. Wherever the engine steamed out from Chester North Station for Liverpool, supporters ran alongside the train until they could run no more.

On 24th November 1879, soon after eight o'clock on a bleak wintry morning, Gladstone, with Catherine and Mary, left Liverpool for Edinburgh. It took them nine hours to travel from Liverpool and they arrived just as night was falling. Catherine was relieved that they had been able to enjoy luncheon in style. Gladstone, overjoyed, said, "The journey was really more like a triumphal procession. Nothing like it had ever been seen before in England." On 25th November he delivered his first electoral address, speaking to 2,500 people in the Edinburgh Assembly Rooms, nicknamed, the 'Music Hall', in George Street. Lord Rosebery had met them at Edinburgh station; hundreds ran dangerously close to their four-horse, open carriage. Gladstone told his audience, "The particular subjects before us who separately are grave enough, all resolve themselves into one comprehensive question, whether this is or is not the way in which the country wishes to be governed . . . Never before were the interests of the country so deeply at stake."

Lord Rosebery turned the event into a theatrical experience. As they left Edinburgh to go to Dalmeny House, fireworks and bonfires lit up the night sky. Cottagers placed candles in their windows to light the way. The party galloped through the park, and saw grasslands which rolled down to the Firth of Forth and out to the North Sea. Seeming to welcome them, smoke bellowed from Dalmeny's twisting, 'Gothic' chimneys. Gladstone turned to Rosebery, "I have never gone through a more extraordinary day."

At Dalmeny House, the party rested, knowing they were on the threshold of great events. Everybody had overlooked Mary's thirty-second birthday on 23rd November. The next day a special train took them to Dalkeith. The weather remained bitterly cold. The hills were covered with snow. Nearly fifty-thousand people had applied for six thousand tickets. In the town's Corn Exchange, Gladstone spoke challengingly to a *perfect storm of applause*. One reason he was so popular in Scotland was that they knew "Mr. Gladstone had moral principle."

Mr. and Mrs. Gladstone, with Mary, went to the Forester's Hall to a Ladies Luncheon, where Catherine received a presentation. On 27th November, Gladstone addressed 3,500 people in the West Calder Assembly Rooms.

He spoke vehemently about the agricultural depression and against Disraeli's foreign affairs policy. On 29th November, in the Edinburgh Corn Exchange, he addressed 4,700 people, saying, "No Chancellor of the Exchequer who is worth his salt should be ready to save what are meant by candle-ends and cheese-parings in the cause of his country." Perhaps Catherine remembered her husband's notes to her about postage stamps and keeping rooms dimly lit.

Escorted by Lord Rosebery, the party went into Old Edinburgh's Waverley Market. Here Gladstone addressed a standing audience of over twenty thousand working men and women. As usual he spoke to his audience's intelligence not to their emotions. Nevertheless people fainted and, Gladstone noted, *were continually handed out over the heads . . . and were as if dead*. He reviewed conditions in Austria, Turkey, Russia and the Balkans. People came from all parts of Scotland on a *pilgrimage of passion* to hear the great actor and even greater orator. The press reported Gladstone's speeches verbatim, covering four to five columns. In 1860 Gladstone had repealed the paper duty, remov-ing the tax on education for the working man which helped to produce cheap books and newspapers. By 1864 the circulation of the provincial press matched that of London's. Morley comments, "There is little doubt that Mr. Gladstone's share in thus fostering the growth of the cheap press was one of the secrets of his rapid rise in popularity."

The Midlothian campaign set the style for electioneering into the television age. Summing it all up, on 1st December 1880, Mary commented, "It has been the same story over and over again. And here it is so much more stirring than in England, because the faces are so intelligent!" But her father had taken care to address his listeners whether they were weavers, farmers, villagers, or artisans just as he would have addressed members of the House of Commons.

On 1st December Gladstone received the freedom of the City of Perth. On 5th December he writes in his diary, *after a breakfast-party, I put my notes in order for the afternoon. At twelve delivered the inaugural address as Lord Rector to the University of Glasgow.* Gladstone spoke for an hour and a half. Disraeli had once addressed the same students saying, "Nothing succeeds like success." Gladstone found such a view cynical in the extreme. He left the University at four o'clock in the afternoon, and by six o'clock, Gladstone was speaking in St Andrew's Hall. The Queen was furious when she learned his speech contained the comment that, "becoming Empress of India was theatrical folly". She told Lady Ely, "Nothing will induce me to accept Mr. Gladstone, as Prime Minister, ever again."

As in modern times, a press-corps travelled with the Gladstones. A stationmaster recalled: "Mr. Gladstone was just about to step onto the train and give his goodbye speech, when Mrs. Gladstone shouted 'William, Stop! Stop! Our special reporter isn't here'. The reporter came into view, puffing along the platform. Mrs. Gladstone waited until pencil and notebook were at the ready, then instructed, 'William start now'."

On 8th December 1879, at a quarter to one in the morning, joyfully singing 'Home, Sweet, Home' with gusto, Catherine, Gladstone and Mary returned to Hawarden. The bitterly cold fortnight was now over. Catherine collapsed and took to her bed. Everywhere Gladstone went she had gone. Appreciative crowds showered her with plaids and rugs, shawls and tablecloths. An old woman walked over ten miles to give a gift of homemade butter and eggs to *dear Mr. Gladstone* and vicars found themselves christening babies Ewart or William or both. From their earliest years together, Catherine saw Gladstone as an Old Testament prophet. The Midlothian campaign strengthened her belief. Catherine sat quietly listening to Gladstone while he spoke for up to five hours and addressed several thousand people. With the spread of literacy and fast transport, his speeches were reported in villages and towns around the country and read by 'all manner of men'. Children ran from schoolrooms, women left their washing and teachers their blackboards. They wanted to tell their grandchildren, "We heard Gladstone!" Men left pits, banks and ploughs to shake the hand of the G.O.M. By putting out her own hand, Catherine saved her husband from numerous handshakes. One journalist reported that the ageing Gladstone "seemed to be literally doubled-up by his exertions and to be too tired to respond to the flattering ovation of the crowd on the platform; but Mrs. Gladstone gratified his admirers by coming to the window and smiling graciously".

Catherine never left her husband's side. Mary tells of one incident which was not reported in the newspapers. Following a particularly strenuous meeting, Mr. and Mrs. Gladstone were invited to take tea with party workers. Catherine sauntered towards Gladstone. She took his cup and concealed it under her cloak. Quietly and swiftly she moved to the window. Unseen by the hostess, she tipped the 'stewed contents' into the gardens below.

At another time, as *the audience went wild with enthusiasm*, Catherine suddenly left her chair and crossing over to Gladstone, began wiping perspiration from his face, neck and ears. Child-like he let her. Engrossed as they were they forgot the audience, who were so touched that *they pulled out their handkerchiefs to wipe away their tears.*

Lady Frederick Cavendish noted when it was all over, that "Uncle William was as fresh as paint." Gladstone recorded in his diary that, *I addressed 86,930 people.* Mary could not forget *the reckless crowding of people, pressing on to the carriage, hanging on to the wheels, such pinched, haggard, eager faces."* Rosebery said simply, "He set fire to the Scottish heather." The Midlothian campaign had cost him £50,000 and enabled Gladstone to escape from his constituency of Greenwich, where he had never felt comfortable and, most importantly, he would beat Disraeli, forcing him out of active politics, for ever. Indirectly, the Midlothian campaign inspired Woodrow Wilson, the American President, to establish, the League of Nations after the Great War. Gladstone's style of address during the Midlothian campaign would influence every orator from then on. Morley said that *the great political speech which for that matter is a sort of drama, is not made by passages for elegant extract or anthologies, but by personality, movement, climax, spectacle, and the action of the time.*

Into power again aged seventy

Because the Tories won a by-election, Disraeli decided he was in a strong position and, on 9th March 1880, dissolved Parliament. Despite six bad harvests in a row, he hoped to win the next election. On 16th March Gladstone left London to begin his second Midlothian campaign. He suggested Mary accompany him, leaving Catherine behind, but she protested very strongly. Mary retorted, "Papa imagined himself *en garçon* in lodging" and she had no intention of giving up her Easter celebrations "for the sake of fidgeting at Dalmeny between Hannah Rosebery and Mama for four days".

When Catherine and Gladstone arrived at King's Cross Station they found two thousand people cheering them. On the journey to Edinburgh, crowds gathered at every major station along the East Coast. On 4th April the Queen wrote to Sir Henry Ponsonby, *she will sooner abdicate than send for or have anything to do with that half-mad fire-brand who would soon ruin everything, and be a Dictator.*

On 6th April Catherine and Gladstone left *this most hospitable of all houses* at 8.30 A.M. They left secretly and caught the 9.25 train, travelling all night. They had only three hours' sleep and were kept awake at Warrington *by unearthly noises.* They went on to Chester and returned home to Hawarden, where they immediately set to work on masses of letters, papers and telegrams. By 7th April it was clear that the Liberals had gained a decisive victory. Gladstone wrote, *the triumph grows and grows; to God be praised*!

The Queen was at Baden-Baden and did not return to

Windsor until 17th April. Disraeli then advised her to send for Lord Hartington. He said, "I have every confidence in Hartington." In the words of the Queen, Disraeli was *turned-out* on 21st April, when he formally resigned. He would never again be Prime Minister. Morley tells the story, "Disraeli received the news alone at Hatfield, Lord Salisbury being abroad. There, hour by hour, day after day, news of the long train of disasters reached him. He faced ruin of his government, the end of his career, and the overwhelming triumph of his antagonist, with unclouded serenity and greatness of mind, worthy of a man who had known high fortunes and filled to the full the measure of his gifts and his ambitions."

On 22nd April the Queen asked Hartington to take office. He suggested that she should send for Gladstone. It was felt that the national interest could only be served by his forming a Government. Gladstone wrote, at 6.50 P.M., 23rd April 1880, *I went to the Queen. Who received me with perfect courtesy, from which she never deviates*. Gladstone always spoke admiringly of the Queen's integrity. They discussed positions and possible candidates. Gladstone told the Queen, "It is my duty to submit myself to Your Majesty's pleasure for the office of Chancellor of the Exchequer together with that of the First Lord of the Treasury."

The Queen said, "I must be frank with you Mr. Gladstone, and must fairly say that there have been some expressions." Gladstone was a little deaf and thought she said, "some little things which have caused me concern or pain".

Gladstone replied "that her Majesty's frankness, so well known, was a main ground of the entire reliance of her ministers upon her . . . that my desire and effort would be to diminish her cares, in any case not to aggravate them; that, however, considering my years, I could only look for a short term of office of active exertion". Gladstone ends his entry in his diary with, *all things considered, I was much pleased. I ended by kissing her Majesty's hand*. The 1880 general election and the Midlothian campaign swept Gladstone and the Liberals into power. It was the only time a non-party leader became Prime Minister. Disraeli never tried again to head an administration.

Gladstone renounced Leeds and Herbert was returned unopposed. He kept the seat until 1910. Gladstone was now seventy years old. On 28th December 1879 Gladstone considered his reaching three-score years and ten and wrote in his diary, *to die in Church appears to be a great euthanasia, but not at a time to disturb worshipers. Such are some of an old man's thoughts, in whom there is still something that consents not to be old.* He still had a little time left and would hold office twice more.

On 9th December 1879 Lord Bryce wrote to Catherine from Norfolk Square, London, *Will you allow me to congratulate you on this wonderful campaign and tell you though you are sure to know it from a thousand sources already, what a feeling it has stirred in the breasts of the workingmen and the hearts of the humblest classes even here in London, where people are supposed to be least sympathetic and excitable.*

Secretary Mary

Catherine found that Mary had become her father's confidante and mainstay. Her daughter would enquire, "Shall I make an appointment for you to see Papa, Mama?" Mary told her brother Harry, "Mama is curiously dependent on excitement. It acts just like a tonic on her." On 25th May she confided to her cousin Lavinia Talbot, *It is rather appalling, finding myself this time so much in the position of a 'political intriguer'. I mean people like Mr. McColl, Lord Rosebery, Lord Reay and Lord Acton write me heaps of letters, suggestions, questions, things to mention if possible to 'the Dictator' as Lord Rosebery calls him, papers, general opinions etc. etc. Just now I was saying to Papa I would retire to another table at breakfast and he answered I was not to as Lord Rosebery would be disappointed. Mama said, 'Oh, no, he only uses her as a pis aller when he can't get our ear.' Papa was amused.*

Catherine had never enjoyed being a political hostess. However, she found she missed entertaining at 11, Carlton House Terrace. She decided a London base was essential. On 16 May 1880 Mr. and Mrs. Gladstone moved into 10, Downing Street. Schlüter noted

. . . 10 Downing Street is a jolly old place. Mary wrote from her tiny office under the stairs, *the place is like a rabbit warren, people in the hall, people in the drawing room, dining room, messengers, ministers to be, touts, friends . . .* Guests found every room full. Lord Granville came across Harry, recently home from India, eating his supper off a tray. "Nowhere else," he explained. The Prince of Wales walked in on Mary sitting on the floor, scribbling notes. "Nowhere else," she said. Wherever the Prince went people looked up, "Nowhere else," they said.

Letters poured out of Gladstone's office, at least 25,000 a year, with no typewriters, photocopiers or e-mail. His staff scurried around. Mary was the only woman amongst a team of five men. It seemed natural for her to become interested in ecclesiastical appointments. When Lord Harcourt visited Hawarden late in 1881, with his son 'Lulu,' the young man commented, "Mrs. G. and Mary are willing to keep you company at any hour. The latter is particularly disagreeable and she seems to have a finger in every pie and can be very rude when she likes (which she does often). Mrs. G. is very good natured, very untidy, very careless and very kind."

Der Alte Jew ist der Mann

Returning to power, Gladstone may have felt he had destroyed Disraeli but his ghost would haunt Gladstone to the end of his life. The European Question remained the problem. The Congress of Berlin, a conference of the Great European powers and the leading statesmen of the Ottoman Empire, was held with the object of rearranging the Balkans. It lasted for a month, from 13 June to 13 July 1878, and became known as the Battle of the Chancellors.

The German Chancellor, Otto Von Bismark, led the proceedings with Disraeli's skills playing a major part in limiting the growing influence of Russia and the full independence of the Balkans. Bismark purred, *"Das alte Jew ist der mann."* The Treaty of Berlin was signed in the Radziwill Palace on Saturday, 13 July 1878. Disraeli had achieved 'Peace with Honour' and Britain's principle objective of keeping the Russian navy out of the Mediterranean. Disraeli returned to the Queen, who offered him a dukedom which he refused. However, he accepted the Garter. On 24th April 1880, Lord Granville told the Queen, "Lord Beaconsfield and Mr. Gladstone are men of extraordinary ability; they dislike each other more than is common among public men."

In 1876, Mary had declared, "It all rushed over me in a moment what blessings we had, and as I looked around all seemed so unbroken and beautiful." How often does it remain so! Now, the 1880s approached. Gladstone braced himself to become once again the Queen's first minister and the person she disliked most in the world!

CHAPTER SEVEN

A Time of Change, the Great Courtesans and a Murder

The 1880s

Prime Minister again

On 23rd April 1880, Gladstone became Prime Minister for the second time. He was three-score years and ten and the only man to combine the roles of Prime minister and Chancellor of the Exchequer. Catherine, too, was approaching seventy. Old age beckoned to them both. Her joints were stiffer. He suffered from the first twinges of lumbago, his teeth hurt and when upset he suffered from diarrhoea. His melodious voice was beginning to fail and they both suffered from bouts of insomnia. Gladstone often remained motionless while Catherine slept like a baby. He wrote to Lord Granville on 2nd January 1883, *it is disagreeable to talk of oneself when there is so much of more importance to think and speak about, but I am sorry to say that the incessant strain and pressure of work, and especially the multiplication of these personal questions, is overdoing me, and for the first time my power of sleep is seriously giving way.*

It was a time of change. They knew their children were leaving them to take up their own lives. Oak Farm had taken its toll. No. 11, Carlton House Terrace had had to be sold. For a few years they retreated to a place in Harley Street. When the lease expired Catherine had no London house to call her own. She must rest her head in rented accommodation or, even worse, No. 10 Downing Street.

Goodbye Helen

At the beginning of 1880 one of Catherine's serious annoyances left her. On 10th January, Helen Gladstone was taken seriously ill in Cologne. Catherine's dislike of her sister-in-law had never abated. However, she felt that as Helen was a member of the family she should go to her but she could not. Catherine, herself was suffering from 'St Anthony's Fire'. Within thirty-eight hours of receiving the news, Gladstone, Sir Thomas and his wife, Louise, sailed on the night-boat to Ostend.

On the evening of 16th January, Helen, attended by her maid of thirty years, died of paralysis of the bowls. *In death she looked half her age* but her constitution had been undermined by morphine and other drugs. It took them three weeks to make the necessary arrangements. During this time Gladstone studied the books in his sister's library. He wrote to Catherine that, by doing so, he had, *in a most curious and interesting examination of her books of devotion*, proved to himself that Helen, towards the end of her life, had, indeed, returned to the Anglican faith. They brought her back to Fasque to be buried according to the rites of the Episcopalian church, whether she wished to be or not.

Goodbye Disraeli

A year after Gladstone came to power, on 19th April 1881, a change of deep significance occurred. Catherine's 'Beast' Disraeli was no more. *A waxen assiduous mummy*, who since the death of his wife *moved from dinner party to dinner party*, died at half past four in the morning at 19, Curzon Street. His beloved Grosvenor Gate had been entailed. A keen supporter of homeopathic practices, Disraeli had fought gout and bronchitis for several years. His death at seventy-seven years of age was brought on by both illnesses and extreme exhaustion.

Catherine knew she would no longer have to put up with Mr. Disraeli bowing low over her hand, gazing deeply into her eyes, muttering "Oh those eyes, Ma'am, those eyes." It worked with Queen Victoria; it did not with Mrs. Gladstone. Now Gladstone was forced to stand up in Parliament and give an address, extolling the virtues of the man he most disliked and feared for his mocking charm. Gladstone thought hard, explaining to Catherine, *"Disraeli held high office by the willing support of Parliament and the nation."* His speech on his rival was one of his greatest. It even pleased the Queen.

Gladstone praised *Disraeli's extraordinary career, his strength of will, his remarkable power of self-government.* The Earl of Beaconsfield was, indeed, *an exceptional man, a great parliamentarian.* He was also a man with profound foresight. On the day when Disraeli left Downing Street for the last time he discussed with a friend the future facing the nation, its difficulties with Austria, Russia, and Turkey and of the confusion in Europe generally. Disraeli looked hard at his friend and muttered, "Most of all, Ireland, Sir."

Gladstone agreed with the Queen that such a man must be buried with all the honours the state could give. Like the Queen, he was amazed to hear that Disraeli wished *to lie in the little church-yard at Hughenden next to his dear wife.* Gladstone did not attend Disraeli's funeral but grumbled to his secretary, Edward Hamilton, *as he lived so he died — all display without reality or genuineness.* Nevertheless, during Disraeli's final illness Gladstone had called frequently at Curzon Street to ask about "Lord Beaconsfield's condition". Catherine's dislike for her husband's rival remained, even when he was dying. She never forgave him his jibe, "Gladstone, Sir, is God's only mistake!"

When Mary Anne, Disraeli's wife, died in 1872, Gladstone wrote to Disraeli, *It has been permitted to both of us to enjoy a priceless boon through a third of a century.* During her last illness Gladstone often called at Grosvenor Gate enquiring after Lady Beaconsfield's health. Disraeli was moved to tears by Gladstone's tribute to his wife in the House of Commons. Both men would have agreed with the obituary in *The Times, Who would have supposed thirty-five years ago, that the coming history of English political life would take direction from the unselfish affection of a woman.*

Freddie Cavendish

In 1882 the family suffered a great tragedy. Gladstone is often quoted as saying, "You cannot fight against the future." In May 1882, Lucy travelled with her Freddie to Holyhead. He had agreed to become Chief-Secretary for Ireland and seemed to have a premonition that all would not be well. As he boarded the boat-train for Dublin, Lucy waved *au revoir* to him, expecting to see her husband again shortly. She never did, alive. Before they retired for the night, Freddie and his Under-Secretary, Thomas Burke, strolled through the tree-lined avenues of Phoenix Park. Hiding behind its high walls, men waited for them. At 7.30 P.M., as Freddie and Burke returned to their night lodgings, men sprang from the bushes, digging surgical knives into their backs. They died immediately.

While the murder was taking place, Lucy sat quietly at her home in Carlton House Terrace. As she prepared to go to bed there was a knock at the door. When the maid opened it she found a policeman standing there. He gave her the news. Catherine was dressed and bejewelled, ready to go to a ball; as she entered the house she heard of the murder. "I must be the first to tell him," she said and immediately rushed to Downing Street.

Society could not believe the news. The Prince and Princess of Wales were devastated. The Queen at Windsor commanded that "Mrs. Gladstone sends me a portrait of Lord Frederick."

Late though the hour was, Gladstone and Catherine went to Lucy. She told them, "I see a vision of Ireland at peace and my darling's life blood accepted as a sacrifice for Christ's sake." All they could do was to smile sympathetically and pray for their favourite niece. The elderly couple did not go home until well into the early hours of the morning. From then on Lucy appeared in the Ladies Gallery at the House of Commons whenever there was a debate on the Irish question. Shortly after the murder, a lady addressed Lucy as Lady Cavendish. Quietly, Catherine admonished her, "Lucy likes to be called Lady Frederick Cavendish, because, you see, she does so love his name." Lucy had no sons to remind her of Freddie but they are not completely forgotten. Lucy

Cavendish College, Cambridge is named after her. As she was a pretty woman, still only in her forties, her friends expected her to marry again. She never did. Instead Lucy fought for the reform of women's education.

When Gladstone rested at Hawarden the couple continued to spend their time as they always had done. They rose early for communion, Catherine opening letters on the way, scattering envelopes hither and thither. She described a Sunday afternoon, *Yesterday we had tea in the garden; the bees humming, the magnolia has taken a fresh start and scents the whole air, the children playing around, bright, good and well.*

Lucy described Sundays in London. "Uncle William has been to the full service in the Chapel Royal, this morning and this afternoon. Then he worked for two and a half hours and read a sermon." During the afternoon, they would find time to read an improving book or a sermon to Catherine's lady's maid and Gladstone's valet. Gladstone once told Catherine, "I have been a learner all my life, a learner I must continue to be."

Talk of retiring, once again

In 1882 Gladstone again considered retirement. The middle of December 1882 marked his political Golden Jubilee. Through these long years he had learned many lessons. He had changed his party, his political horizons were far wider and new social truths had imprinted themselves on his impressionable mind. Gladstone was one of the few people who recognized the new growing social forces. His early habits of hard work, exactness and concentration had become cast-iron, but experience had given him no more insight into men's minds or skill in discriminating amongst them than the young man who had entered Parliament in 1832. He talked to Catherine as if he found the world pretty much as he had expected it. "Man," he would say, "is the least comprehensible of creatures, and of men the most incomprehensible are politicians."

Gladstone may not have understood the motivation of his colleagues, but strengthened by his deep Christian faith he never fell into 'the sin of cynical despair', even when they persuaded him to start the Anglo-Egyptian war, for no clear purpose. Above all, it was Ireland that occupied Gladstone's mind. Disturbances still occurred in its countryside. The 1881 Irish Coercion Act permitted the detention of people for as *long as was thought necessary*.

Ireland may have been written on Gladstone's heart but he became enmeshed in the controversies surrounding the Third Reform Act of 1884. It extended the total number of voters by ten million, giving the counties the same franchise as the boroughs. It also ruled that only one person represented a constituency. Parliamentary reform continued to be debated well into the next year and the Redistribution of Seats Act was passed. This, as far as possible, redistributed the seats in the House of Commons so that each M.P. represented an equal number of people. Throughout his difficulties Gladstone found his Cathie *a priceless boom*. He was fortunate to possess 'a wonderful power of relieving his mind from his heavy responsibilities'. In August 1884, Holman Hunt asked Mr. and Mrs. Gladstone to see his nearly completed painting, *The Triumph of the Holy Innocents*, as "a wholesome and practical relaxation."

However, Ireland never left Gladstone's mind. His conversion to Home Rule in 1885 resulted in the fall of Lord Salisbury's government. The Liberal party had joined with the Irish Nationalists, led by Charles Parnell, to vote against the Tories on a land bill. The Irish Nationalists held the balance of power with eighty-six seats and were supported by Gladstone. To the outsider the government seemed in chaos and it looked as if Gladstone might fall from power. During all this the background of Mr. and Mrs. Gladstone's lives remained the same. Catherine went on with her charity work, meeting needs as and when they arose. Gladstone still prowled the streets of London, armed only with a thick stick given to him by his wife. He longed to retire.

However, Catherine felt he was not ready to do so and she so loved being *in the mainspring of action*. If she was free, whenever Gladstone addressed the House, she would run up the eighty-six steps to the Ladies' Gallery. An old Irish judge recounts, *In the House one day I noticed, looking at the Ladies' Gallery, that a small patch of the dull brass grille shone like burnished gold. I asked an attendant if he could explain it. 'That, he said, is the place where Mrs. Gladstone sits to watch the G.O.M. whenever he speaks — she rests one hand on the grating, and the friction, as you can see, has worn it bright.'*

Even today, they say, whenever a great debate is underway, Mrs. Gladstone is seen in the Ladies Gallery, her gloved hand moving up and down. The House does not see her very often.

A more supportive wife

As they began to age Gladstone and Catherine grew closer. She sensed he was growing older and gave him more support. Once, when Gladstone addressed a political meeting in Glasgow, a member of his audience watched as he looked around him, unsuccessfully, for his eye glass, Catherine jumped up, put her hand around the back of his neck, felt around under his coat for about five minutes and then triumphantly pulled out the eyeglass with aplomb, to loud cheers. At another meeting Catherine was described as *a simply-dressed woman who busies herself in warding off the hands of 'enthusiastics' eager to touch him. This is Mrs. Gladstone, with the soft face, high coloured like a girl's {S-shape}, and tremulous mouth, intent on one thing only — her husband!*

Simply-dressed Catherine might be but it meant wearing a tight corset of whalebone. Her bustle would be made of horsehair tied to the waist but was unlikely to be draped with frills, swags and ribbons. Around her neck she may have worn a lace collar with a brooch fastened in the centre. The toque hat was coming into fashion. Hidden from view, underneath the finery, many older women fought the damp and the cold by wearing woollen combinations. In the evening, a lady wore kid or suede gloves reaching to the shoulder or the elbow. Catherine, be-bustled, must have found it difficult to sit behind Gladstone, handkerchief in hand, ready to jump up and mop her husband's face. Whilst the operation went on, he sat quite still, impassive, as if he were a little boy.

At this time Gladstone is supposed to have said, "If anything should happen to Catherine, then indeed, I should close the volume for ever."

Catherine might be showing more concern for her husband but her entertaining skills remained minimal. The story of the 'Kilbracken' incident was repeated even into her seventies. In the winter of 1874, Gladstone and Catherine invited Lord Kilbracken, a one-time secretary of Gladstone's, and his new, young bride to stay with them at Hawarden. When the couple arrived at an out of the way station early in the evening, amid a snowstorm, there was no-one to meet them. The station master found a hawker's cart. Lord Kilbracken loaded the boxes onto the cart and then led the elderly horse for two miles, through the snowstorm, with his wife and maid clinging to the sides of the swaying boxes.

On their arrival at the Castle, Catherine, shocked, gushed, "I will never, ever be so careless again." Gladstone said, "You will." The family gathered the young couple up and sat them down close to the roaring fire. Catherine called for hot punch. Sir Stephen stood in front of the fire. "I wish it known I had nothing to do whatsoever with the arrangements." Catherine's apologies were genuine then. They remained genuine every time she made a social gaffe, even into her old age.

There is another story told by E. F. Benson in his book *As We Were*. He tells of how his parents were invited to dine with the Gladstones. The invitation arrived on paper marked Dollis Hill. The Archbishop and Mrs. Benson naturally assumed that was where the dinner was taking place. It was not. Mrs. Gladstone had quite forgotten that they would be staying at another address in London. Dinner was held, while Catherine tried to remember whether she had actually sent the Bensons an invitation or not. Gladstone became annoyed and eventually gave his arm to his wife saying, "We must not forget that it is Derby Day. His Grace has evidently been delayed by the congestion!"

Catherine could, however, cope with embarrassing occasions. When 11, Carlton House Terrace had been sold, they were staying in the house they leased in Harley Street, for a day or two, with practically no staff. Catherine had arranged to have their midday meal with their next door neighbour. The bell rang and Lord Granville appeared. He asked, "Could you give me some lunch?" Gladstone began to explain that . . . but Catherine quickly interrupted him, "Of course." Lord Granville was shown into the empty dining room. Shortly, the door opened and footmen entered with trays, the cloth was laid, the table dressed, and the butler brought in the wine. Catherine was like a general and rose to any crisis. She had slipped next door to her neighbour!

Catherine, however, did not quite cope with the embarrassing incident of the Brands. She constantly forgot to send the Speaker of the House of Commons and his wife, Mr. and Mrs. Brand, an invitation to her receptions, even though the couples were on good terms. Gladstone explained, "Sorry, it was one of Catherine's embarrassing oversights." But the Brands did not receive a 'card' for her next reception. They decided to go anyway. As they entered the drawing room the first thing they saw was a paper stuck on the mirror, opposite the door, written in a large, scrawling hand, *Mem: Invite those Brands.* The London wits observed, "Mrs. Gladstone files her invitations under her sofa and forgets to tell the servants to pick them up and deliver them."

It was, however, her charitable works which were Catherine's first concern. Dull people bored her. The guests she invited to her 'little Tuesday drums' were usually personal friends or perceived to be of use to her, and not to Gladstone. Lucy said, "Uncle William kicks at the notion of having regular Parliamentary Squashes. Aunt Pussy's little drums are far pleasanter but, I am afraid, many people have their feelings lacerated." The circle of friends was wide. William Wordsworth arrived, speaking like a Roman senator but looking like a countryman. Before appearing in company he removed his rough, woollen socks, to display a fine pair of legs covered in the best black, silk stockings. Thackeray said that he reeled from dinner party to dinner party, "wallowing in turtle and swimming in Shampang!" At Catherine's little 'drums' he was content to complain about a wild girl he had just met. It was Charlotte Brontë.

Entertaining the difficult couple

For hostesses, Mr. and Mrs. Gladstone remained a difficult couple. Gladstone tended to dominate the conversation, ignoring the ladies. Occasionally, Catherine would snap, "Do be quiet, William, you know nothing at all about the subject." On another occasion she said, "Oh! William, if you were not such a great man you would be the most terrible bore!" At a dinner, a young man was holding forth, enjoying the sound of his own voice. He was handed a note, *Do be quiet dear, the G.O.M. wishes to speak. C.G.* He looked across the table. Mrs. Gladstone nodded and smiled. He said not another word!

Catherine was described as *a fine, fashionable woman*, but as a matron her gown would not have been low cut. Like the Queen she disliked the custom of the hostess gathering eyes and leaving the gentlemen to their port and cigars, and bawdy stories. Catherine disappeared leaving the other ladies to gossip and drink tea. When the gentlemen entered the drawing room to join the ladies, so did Mrs. Gladstone. She hardly hid the fact that women bored her and she, in her turn, annoyed women. At evening parties and balls Catherine would insist on pointing out to her hostess, sometimes forcefully, that, "Your cloak-room attendants are over-tired, or your footmen too weary or your link boys can hardly put one foot in front of the other."

When she arrived and stepped out of her carriage, Catherine was the person who saw the old, blind woman in the crowd, straining to hear the music coming from the grand house. While guests dined off numerous dishes *á la Russe*, if they happened to pause to peer between a candelabra and the magnificent tiered gold epergne of fruit and flowers adorning the dining table, they may have observed a footman approaching Gladstone. He would nod and remove a handkerchief from his sleeve. The evening over, Gladstone would stand on the pavement, beneath the gas-lamps, acknowledging the cheers of the crowds. Catherine shook hands with every person she could find. Then with the exquisite courtesy of the eighteenth century, Gladstone took his wife's hand and showed her into their carriage. Out of the corner of her eye, Catherine would see the footman approaching the old woman, with a morsel wrapped in her husband's handkerchief.

Catherine did not question why people waited for hours to see the great and the good enjoying themselves, or ever wondered why it should be so. Like her class, she knew the 'the poor are forever with us', but it was the duty of the gentry to give them a glimpse of a better life; magnificent jewels, fine clothes, a gleam of light or the sound of far off music gave them strength to carry on with their often brutish and short lives. Gladstone was one of the few people who questioned how long the working man would put up with such things. From childhood Catherine had been taught, 'the rich man in his castle and the poor man at his gate'. She had also learned, 'For I was hungered and ye gave me meat; I was thirsty and ye gave me drink; I was a stranger and ye took me in; I was in prison and ye came unto me." She did exactly that!

Leisure time

Catherine and Gladstone may have moved in the best of circles but they were relatively poor folk. Catherine possessed a genius for persuading the great and the good to part with their money for her charities. Her husband's skills lay in getting rich businessmen to pay for their holidays. This way their spirits would be restored and they could continue the Lord's work. As Catherine and Gladstone aged, they felt even more the debilitating effects of their old enemy, St Anthony's Fire. The Second Baron Wolverton, who served under Gladstone, offered them his villa in Cannes. On 17th January 1883 Catherine and Gladstone said *au revoir* to several friends at Charing Cross Station and then boarded the train to Dover. A few hours later they said goodbye to Lord Granville and the following afternoon found themselves in the Chateau Scott, *nobly situated, admirably planned, and the kindness exceeded even the beauty and the comfort.* Here they fell in with foreign ways, taking a snack early, *dejeuner* at noon, dinner at seven, and bed at ten. Catherine wrote to Lucy, *It would have been too bright for me, too heavenly with sleep and all the loveliness of this place if I had been in full force.*

Later in the year another family friend, Sir Donald Currie, founder of the Union Castle Line, offered Catherine and Gladstone a week's cruise on one of his steamships. On 8th September 1883 Sir Gladstone and Catherine boarded the s.s. *Pembroke Castle (a floating castle, four thousand tons and four hundred and ten feet long)* to the Hebrides.

The party included the younger element, 'Lulu' Harcourt, Mary Gladstone, Hallam Tennyson and lively Laura Tennant, who subsequently married Alfred Lyttleton. The trip was so enjoyable, everybody being in such high spirits, that they steamed on to the Orkneys, Oslo and into Copenhagen Harbour. Here they found members of Europe's royal families. Catherine entertained the Czar and Czarina of Russia, the King and Queen of Greece, the King and Queen of Denmark, the Princess of Wales and her three daughters. She took tea privately with the Queen of Denmark. Tennyson read his poetry and banged time on the Czarina's thigh. His behaviour did not stop him receiving a peerage on his return to England.

Queen Victoria was not amused. Her permission had neither been sought for nor given to alight on foreign soil or fraternize with other royals. Gladstone wrote to the Queen. *On the North Sea, Sept. 15th. Posted at Copenhagen, Sept. 16th, 1883. Mr. Gladstone presents his humble duty to your Majesty, and has to offer his humble apology for not having sought from your Majesty the usual gracious permission before setting foot on a foreign shore.* Gladstone ended the letter by requesting that, *under these circumstances, his omission is excused.* The hint that in the excitement of it all he had forgotten Her Majesty did little to soothe relations.

Gladstone also received criticism from his fellow politicians. Lord Churchill declaimed, *Every act of his, whether it be for the purposes of health, or of recreation, or of religious devotion, is spread before the eyes of every man, woman and child in the United Kingdom, on large glaring placards. For the purposes of an autumn holiday a large transatlantic steamer is specially engaged, the Poet Laureate adorns the suites, and receives a peerage as his reward, and the incidents of the voyage are luncheon with the Emperor of Russia and tea with the Queen of Denmark.*

Fortunately for Lord Churchill, 'Little Dossie' was yet to be born. He may have felt that Gladstone's numerous photographs taken with his blonde, pretty, small granddaughter, sitting on his knee gave him an unfair advantage. Nobody tried to calculate the extra votes they attracted.

After over five years in power, manoeuvring through a mine-field of difficulties, Gladstone's government fell. He was seen as having *trampled upon the flag and tarnished his country's honour.* His failure to rescue General Gordon, everlasting problems with Ireland and the failure of the 1885 budget gave Gladstone no alternative but to resign on 9th June 1885, a particularly hot day. He was seventy-six and younger men were beginning to climb their own greasy poles. Some feared that the Irish leader, Charles Parnell, would become 'King'. On 11th June 1885 Catherine wrote to Lucy . . . *Then in came the dear form all grand though I who know him so well could see the struggle for the fact of that speech of his was to win and the parliamentary division lost was like a clap of thunder.*

Resignation and the offer of an Earldom

Gladstone was out of power. The Queen hoped for good and offered him an earldom which he refused! He told her, "Any service that I can render, if small, will, however, be greater in the House of Commons than in the House of Lords, and it has never formed part of my views to enter that historic chamber." Mary organized the packing and they moved out of 10 Downing Street. Catherine found herself living in temporary accommodation, at 1, Richmond Terrace and Mary complained about the house quivering, from the noise of the underground, thundering beneath it.

WOMEN OF EASY VIRTUE

Meeting Places

It was a known fact that "Mrs. Gladstone is a man's woman." However, women did not bore Mr. Gladstone, especially the great courtesans of the day, several of whom became close friends. How did Catherine view these women? We do not know. In the Haymarket in the early hours crowds emerged from the gin-palaces and oyster shops to taste the wares of the 'soiled doves'. Their raucous behaviour kept respectable folk awake and little children were told the ladies were being taken away by the gentlemen to be given dinner!

In the Haymarket, Gladstone could enter the smart area of the Argyll Rooms for two shillings. Lesser folk went in for a shilling. He would find the once great beauty, Kate Hamilton, presiding over the saloon. Now fat, old, greasy, bejewelled and rich beyond avarice, she would enquire, "What, my dear, is your particular fancy?" In 'Old Glad Eye' or 'Willie Do Nothing's' case it was to look and then fight temptation. Beneath glittering, crystal chandeliers, sat bejewelled, beautiful young women, in silks and velvet, drinking champagne. Their long trains slithered along deep-piled carpeting. In a corner a fifty-piece orchestra played softly. Ensconced on plush sofas they listened patiently to respectable gentlemen who had just left their club, dinner-table, opera or theatre. As 'newish' Big Ben struck the hour, the place plunged into darkness, dancing began in the shadows and couples vanished upstairs; carriages could be heard clattering to Pimlico or St John's Wood.

Nearby, in a heavily curtained house in Little College Street, fat, chubby, balding, 'thirtyish' something Alfred Taylor ran a different sort of establishment. A former fusilier, he haunted such places as the Café Royal, finding boys for the enjoyment of gentlemen such as Mr. Oscar Wilde. There was great demand for virgins of both sexes and as young as possible. Even Victorian society was shocked by Josephine Butler's story of a man called Stead, who procured a thirteen-year old girl and sold her into prostitution; Stead was imprisoned for three months and the legal age for a sex-worker was raised to sixteen.

Avoiding pregnancy

The respectable element of society wondered why prostitutes never seemed to become pregnant. Shrewd women such as 'Skittles' Walters knew how to avoid the full act by 'the use of the thighs'. Country women said the seeds of Queen Anne's lace (wild carrot) made an effective contraception. Other women used pennies or sponges soaked in vinegar to block entry. However, Bernard Shaw thought *the rubber condom was the greatest invention of the nineteenth century!*

Mr. Gladstone's Lady Friends

The Duchess of Sutherland

The great Duchess of Sutherland was the first woman to become a close friend of Gladstone. Catherine approved of the Duchess. On 20th January 1842, dining with Mrs. Grenville, Catherine said of her fellow guests, "I was pleased with the Duke and Duchess — she spoke so nicely and naturally about nursing her babies." On another occasion Catherine was shaken to find that, when she wished to return home, the Duchess of Sutherland accompanied her.

Catherine wrote to her sister Mary in March 1854, *The Duchess of Sutherland insisted on returning home with me to see how William was. Fancy me entering his room with her! I fully expected to find him in his old dressing-gown with one candle, in short 'unearthly.' We seated her upon the stool of repentance, her petticoats tipping over everything. William and Willy, meanwhile, devouring mutton chops.*

Mary Drew calls *Duchess Harriet the devoted friend of Mr. Gladstone.* The Duchess was fifty-four to his fifty. Once a great beauty, a portrait of the time shows an obese woman, well-past her prime, but she was a member of the powerful Howard family, a personal friend of the Queen and Mistress of Robes. When the Duke married Harriet in 1823, he took her into another prominent family and one of the richest landowners in the land. Like the Glynnes, the Sutherlands were Whigs, but during the Queen's Coronation Catherine sat in no significant part of the Abbey. A portrait shows the Duchess in Coronation Robes talking to a pageboy, holding a crown.

Politicians and High Society flocked to the Duchess's glamorous, political salon except Karl Marx, who wrote complaining, *The enemy of British wage slavery has a right to condemn negro slavery,* the *Duchess of Sutherland, the Duke of Atholl* or a *Manchester-Cotton-Lord* — NEVER. The Duchess agitated against slavery but the Sutherlands were among the families responsible for the Clearances. Between 1811 and 1820, the Marquis of Stafford, later the first Duke, moved the tenants, from the glens to the coast, where it was felt they could supplement their income by fishing. No mention was made that sheep farming was more lucrative for the landlord. If tenants said "no" they were moved violently. In one day the Duke forcibly evicted two thousand crofters. Looking at her thin, half-starving tenants his wife commented, "The Scotch people are of a happier constitution and do not fatten like the larger breed of animals." The matter reached the House of Commons where the Duke told the House that between 1811 and 1833 he had spent £60,000 of his own money assisting his tenants.

Climb to the summit of Beinn a'Bhuirdh in Scotland and you will find a hundred-foot monument dominating the landscape. The inscription reads, *erected in 1834, by a mourning and grateful tenantry, to a judicious, kind and liberal landlord who would open his heart and hands to the distress of the widow, the sick and the traveller.* In

Helmsdale you will find another monument known as the 'Emigrant Statue, the flight of the Highlanders'. The 1st Duke is remembered for evicting over fifteen thousand crofters from his million-acre estates. Even to-day the Highlands are home to more sheep than human-beings.

In February 1861, Harriet's husband died and Gladstone started staying overnight in Dunrobin, the Sutherland's stately home on the Dornoch Firth. In May, he spent two weekends with her. This developed into staying at Dunrobin overnight at least twice a month. Gladstone wrote endless letters to the Duchess and often visited her during the day in her London home, Stafford Park (now Lancaster House), in Green Park, or travelling to Trentham, Cleveden or to her house in the little village of Chiswick on the Thames. Throughout the whole of 1866, Gladstone did not go home to Hawarden, even once. The Sutherland/Gladstone friendship lasted for twenty years, until Harriet's death in 1868. Behind fans it was whispered, "Mr. Gladstone is the Duchess's lover." We do not know if this was true. The only person, apart from those two, who did know was Catherine! She made no comment. However, Gladstone did say to the Duchess, "I am glad my wife saw you yesterday, for I hope a little that she may have been bold enough to lecture you about not taking care of yourself. If this sounds rather intrusive, pray put it down to my intense confidence in her as a doctor. She has a kind of divining power springing partly from a habitual gift and partly from experience, and she hardly ever goes wrong." He talks of his children, "Our children are gone and the vacant footfall echoes on the stair." On another occasion he says, "It was so kind of you to see our little fellows on their way through town. I hope they were not troublesome."

On 28th October 1868, Gladstone wrote sadly in his diary, *The post brought me a black-bordered letter which announced the death of the Dowager Duchess of Sutherland. I have lost in her from view the warmest and dearest friend, surely, that ever man had. But I feel, strange as it might sound, ten years older for her death . . . None will fill her place for me, nor for many worthier than I!*

Laura

Mrs. Laura Thistlewayte (sometimes spelt Thistlethwayte), the courtesan and evangelist, would be Gladstone's next deep friendship. Society did not accept this relationship. In 1876, Queen Victoria told Disraeli, "Mr. Gladstone is mad in dining alone with the 'notorious' Mrs. Thistlewayte." One of the most successful courtesans of her day, she married well and found God, announcing herself as a "sinner saved by the Grace of God through faith in the Lamb of God". She organized evangelical tea-parties and gave religious performances. Lady St. Helier spoke of Mrs. Thistlewayte's beautiful voice. "She arranges herself so that all the light comes through the small windows behind her. She wears a black mantilla which covers her mass of golden hair. As she moves around, talking of salvation, magnificent jewels and rings flash." The effect was a stunning theatrical performance, one which Gladstone would have admired and enjoyed.

Mrs. Thistlewayte was christened Laura Eliza Jane Bell. She was born somewhere about 1830, in Newry, County Down, Ireland. She may have been the natural daughter of the Marquis of Hertford. Her 'father' managed his estates in Antrim. Laura was first noted working as a shop assistant in Belfast. Here she developed a sideline in 'being nice to certain gentlemen'. She chose carefully and shrewdly. When she moved to Dublin, Dr. William Wilde, the father of Oscar and a notorious womanizer, became one of her clients. Soon her carriage and pair would be seen driving through Phoenix Park in Dublin. Subsequently, Laura came to London, working in the mourning department of Jay's Emporium in Regent Street. Here she continued her 'sideline'.

Soon Laura became friendly with Gladstone's friend, the Duke of Newcastle, and other gentlemen such as the Earl of Bathurst and the Duke of Wellington. Laura dropped the 'day job'. One of her clients was a fabulously wealthy, young Nepalese Prince. It is said he spent a quarter of a million pounds on her within a few months. Until Laura died, Prince Jung Bahadur remained her friend. Napoleon III was also reputed to be her lover.

In 1852 she married Captain Augustus Frederick Thistlewayte, a foul-tempered man with a house in Grosvenor Square. Later he bought an estate in Dorset. There were no children. Laura took to religion. Her porcelain prettiness, education and quick wit enabled her to become one of London's successful hostesses, if not a respectable one.

In 1864, Gladstone met Laura riding in the Park. She was his junior by twenty years. He began calling on her unannounced. A deep friendship developed which lasted until her death in 1894. It was at its most intense from 1869 to 1875. During this time Catherine often complained, "Dear William returns home so angry ... " Fellow politicians put it down to overwork but, for a youngish couple, they were often apart. He wrote in February 1858, *My own Cathie, What would I give to have you here or come to you this night.*

Catherine became aware of his relationship with Mrs. Thistelwayte through a 'dear friend'. Gladstone questioned, "Do I understand you that Lady J recommended that I should not go often or so often to 15 Grosvenor Square?" Catherine must have been shaken when Gladstone informed her, "I am sitting for Mrs. Thistlewayte, at great inconvenience to myself, for a bust in clay. Mrs. Thistlewayte will present the bust to you and donate the money from casts to your charitable homes. Let me relieve you from your natural misapprehension about Mrs. Thistlewayte." Catherine's comments are not recorded but the bust was destroyed.

However, Gladstone continued visiting Laura. He gushed over her hair, *rippling ringlets to the knee.* Captain Thistlewayte went on sending the Gladstones venison from the estates he leased in Ross-shire. Like Catherine, he made no comment on his wife's friendship with Gladstone. In 1887, at the age of fifty-seven, he was found dying, a pistol at his side. The death certificate read: *Accidental death.*

During the intense period of the Thistlewayte relationship, Gladstone's letters to Catherine begin, *My own Cathie,* or *my dearest Cathie,* or *My own C* and end, *Your affectionate WEG.* Her letters to him begin, *My most precious, My own, My darling,* ending with *Your own wife, Your own CG.* They discuss births, deaths, marriages, family affairs, gossip and politics.

Laura presented Gladstone with a ring engraved with her name, which he wore. She also sent him violets from Paris, *with their odour wonderfully preserved.* In 1869 her autobiography, in twenty-three parts, arrived in Downing Street. Gladstone commented, "A fresh supply of Mrs. T's MS: xi–xiii has arrived. The tale is told with great modesty, and its aspect is truthful but not quite coherent." Thankfully, no trace of the book remains. His numerous letters to Laura begin, *Dearest Spirit.* He talks of religion, discusses her emotional needs and the difficulties she faces in her marriage.

Mary, writing to Herbert in 1880, when he became an M.P., told him, *"Mrs. Thistlewayte had sent you a long letter of congratulations, together with an invitation to dine with her. I thought it not worth forwarding."* Gladstone believed firmly that the stability of society lay in the sanctity of Christian marriage and family life. Algernon West, his private secretary, commented, *after years of intimacy, private and official, I have never felt capable of adequately depicting a hundredth part of his complex character.*

There is a postscript to the Thistlewayte affair. In 1881, Lady Susan Opdebeck, previously Lady Lincoln, called on Gladstone in Downing Street. "After some thirty-two or thirty-three years, I felt something and should say much." Gladstone asked Laura Thistlewayte to advocate Lady Susan's claim on the Newcastle estate!!!"

Towards the end of Laura's life, she lived in straitened circumstances. Occasionally, Gladstone, accompanied by Catherine, took a drive out of town, calling on Mrs. Thistlewayte in her 'Hampstead Cottage'. When she died in 1894, he did not attend the funeral. The whole affair remains a mystery, perhaps not to Catherine, who understood her husband. Gladstone went on to enjoy deep friendships with other high-profile women of easy virtue. A commentator observed, *Gladstone manages to combine his meddling with a keen appreciation of a pretty face.* Catherine's thoughts on the matter still remain a mystery.

'Skittles'

Laura Thistlewayte was used as a role model by the last of the great courtesans, Catherine (Skittles) Walters. She came from Gladstone's home town of Liverpool and was born in 1839, in the poorest area of Toxteth, at 1 Henderson Street. Only twenty years later she is found working near Park Lane, in Chesterfield Street, in a bowling alley and became nicknamed, 'Skittles'.

By the 1860s, 'Skittles' had established herself in Mayfair. Gentlemen appreciated her discretion as well as her huge, violet-coloured eyes and delicate 'English rose complexion'. The little girl from the back streets of Liverpool had grown into, reputedly, the most beautiful woman in Europe.

Her lovers included the Marquis of Hartington (the Prince of Wales's 'Harty-Tarty' and son of the beautiful, gambling Georgina Duchess of Devonshire). He established 'Skittles' in a house in Mayfair and granted her an allowance of £2,000 year. Until the day of her death the Devonshire Estates honoured the arrangement. The Prince of Wales also paid court to her. The poet, Wilfred Blunt, worshipped 'Skittles' until the day he died.

In a world which prided itself on its equestrian skills, Skittles hypnotized Society. Wearing a skin-tight riding habit, she outshone all the other pretty little 'horse breakers' riding in Rotten Row. Society whispered, "She is completely naked underneath." The 'ladies' may have been shocked but they slavishly followed her style. In middle age, semi-retired Miss Walters chose to host tea-parties on Sunday afternoons. Distinguished gentlemen flocked to them. Gladstone called to discuss the prostitute problem of London and was overcome by her charm.

In the St James's Clubs, gentlemen learned with dismay, "Skittles is retiring." She left High Society at fifty-one, a very wealthy woman, owning at least two hotels in France. She died in 1920 leaving £2,764 19s 6d.

Lily

At the suggestion of the Prince of Wales, Mr. and Mrs.

Gladstone became friendly with one of his 'ladies', the 'Pears Soap beauty' Lily Langtry. A professional beauty, she made herself into the first 'celebrity'. Born in 1853, the daughter of the Dean of Jersey, a notorious womanizer, she was christened Emilie le Breton. It is said one of her ancestors was part of the gang which murdered St Thomas à Beckett.

Lily had an unsettled childhood. In 1872 she married a wealthy Irish landowner, Edward Langtry. The couple came to London, renting a house in Belgravia. She entered into High Society dressed simply in a black frock, so delicately cut that it showed off the tightly-corseted body underneath. Highly educated for a woman of her day, the gentlemen enjoyed the wit of Mrs. Langtry. Millais painted the *The Jersey Lily*. Burne-Jones and Frith also painted her portrait. Lily was used by Mr. Pears the soap manufacturer, who paid her by 'her weight', pound for pound. Whenever Gladstone opened a newspaper he was met by Mr. Pears advertizing soap.

In 1877, Mrs. Langtry met the Prince of Wales. He fell in love with her instantly. They enjoyed a passionate affair, regularly escaping to a love nest in Bournemouth. Aware that few houses would receive Mrs. Langtry, the Prince introduced his lover to the Gladstones, who had a real affection for him. Gladstone called on Mrs. Langtry, delivering 'goody books' for her to read. He gave her his private code-signal so she could contact him directly, also suggesting, "When you write to me, use the 'double-envelope' method." His private secretaries would not open the letter, not even Mary. Through the Prince, Lily was presented to Queen Victoria, who responded with remarkable frostiness. As usual, the Prince became bored with this love. He snapped, "I've spent enough on you to sink a battleship." She replied, "You have spent enough in me to float one!"

By 1880 the affair had spent its course, partly because of the arrival of Sarah Bernhardt in London. Now Lily found herself with financial worries. With her great beauty, Oscar Wilde encouraged Lily to go on the stage. Fickle in love, 'Bertie' was loyal to those friends who stood up to him. From then on he spoke highly of 'dear

Mrs. Langtry' and her acting abilities. Of course, she was not anywhere near Bernhardt's league, even when she tried to become Shakespeare's 'Cleopatra'. However, Lily did become a successful race-horse owner and entrepreneur.

In 1880 Mrs. Langtry produced a little girl. Rumours abounded as to who had fathered the child. In 1897, the Langtrys divorced. At forty-six, Lily married again to Hugo de Bathe, a wealthy but much younger man. The marriage was not a success. She turned to her butler's wife for companionship.

In 1882, she went on tour to America, where they loved her. In 1897, she took American citizenship. President Roosevelt spoke of her with admiration. America believed Gladstone was her lover. She denied it, "Never, he was too old." Long before, in 1851, Gladstone had written to Catherine, *How little you know of the evil of mine of which at the last day I shall have a strange tale to tell.* It was said of Gladstone he committed adultery only in the heart. Certainly, he commissioned William Dyce to paint the portrait of the beautiful Mrs. Dale, making no secret of her attraction for him but the 'girls' nicknamed him, *Old Willy Do Nothing.* Catherine must have prayed it was so. Lily Langtry died in Monaco in 1929. She is buried in Jersey. Her ghost is said to haunt Langtry Manor Hotel, Bournemouth, the love nest she shared with the Prince of Wales.

Rumours surrounding Gladstone's motives continued long after his death. In 1927 a journalist, Peter Wright, wrote a book titled *Portraits and Criticisms.* In it he hinted that, "It was Mr. Gladstone's habit in public to speak the highest and strictest principle and in private to pursue and possess every sort of woman." A court case ensued led by Gladstone's sons. Mrs. Langtry sent a telegram exonerating Gladstone, saying he was too old for her anyway! With other evidence his name and reputation were cleared.

It is surprising that with so many enemies, more people did not attack Gladstone. It may have been that many gentlemen had secrets. An up-market, tightly-knit circle, they shielded each other. It is doubtful that any barrister would wish to challenge Gladstone, the greatest debater of his age and, if he did so, there was Disraeli. A fair man, he would jump to his rival's defence. In Disraeli's view, Gladstone was mistaken and naïve but his motives were entirely honourable. If all else failed, there was Catherine, and she would have fought like a lioness protecting her cubs. Catherine Gladstone would certainly have taken no prisoners, especially where William was concerned. The more worldly-wise of Society viewed Gladstone's night-walking with mistrust, asking, "Is he a fool?"

And a very different lady
Angela Burdett-Coutts

Miss Angela Coutts was the friend of Dickens, Disraeli, Gladstone and a personal friend of Catherine's. The Prince of Wales described Miss Coutts as, *after my mother the most remarkable woman in England.* She was certainly the richest woman in the land and received numerous proposals which she ignored. Marriage was not on her agenda except, it was rumoured, she had asked the Duke of Wellington to marry her. He replied "Too old ma'am." Miss Coutts' fortune was worth at least three million pounds.

Angela Burdett was born in 1814, to the M.P. Sir Francis Burdett and his wife, the former Sophie Coutts, daughter of the banker. Through the generosity of her grandfather's second wife, whom he married when he was eighty-four, Angela found herself, at the age of twenty-three, the sole owner of Coutts, the bankers. There was one proviso, she must take the name of Coutts.

From then on Miss Coutts became the benefactor of numerous charitable causes. With Charles Dickens, she supported 'Urania Cottage', *a home for young women who had turned to a life of immorality including theft and prostitution.* She was one of the few people aware of the real destitution, insanity, over-crowding, and sheer poverty which so many of Victoria's 'family' faced.

A keen member of the Church of England, Angela Coutts built several churches, including St. Stephen's at Westminster. She followed in the steps of Peabody with buildings for the poor, converting old burial grounds, such as St Pancras churchyard, into playgrounds for poor children. A sundial commemorates the dead lying there. She never visited Australia but sponsored the Institute for the Improvement of Aborigines. The Baroness, too, possessed *'a genius for charity'*. She was inspired by a meeting of the RSPCA (The Royal Society for the Prevention of Cruelty to Animals) to establish the National Society for the Prevention of Cruelty to Children (NSPCC). Into her old age her interests remained eclectic. In her later years she even became the President of the Bee-Keepers Association.

Baroness Burdett-Coutts insisted that any organization to which she lent her name was well run and respectable, something Catherine would have noted. Like 'Skittles', everybody flocked to her parties but for different reasons. Catherine attended them because Angela was a close friend and a principal source of charitable funding. The Baroness firmly refused to give to political causes and kept herself completely away from that 'minefield'.

In 1871, Queen Victoria created Miss Coutts the Baroness Burdett-Coutts of Highgate and Brookfield in the County of Middlesex. In 1872 she became the first woman to receive the Freedom of the City of London and, two years later, she enjoyed the Freedom of the City of Edinburgh. For over fifty years her 'dear companion' had been a Miss Hannah Brown. She was bereft when she died.

At the age of sixty-seven, the Baroness suddenly married. Society was shocked. Her husband was a penniless, twenty-nine year old American — and even worse, her secretary. Gladstone pronounced her behaviour 'loathsome'. He refused to see her. Catherine agreed to do so but was relieved when Angela failed to make the appointment. Mr. William Lehman Ashmead Bartlett changed his name to Burdett-Coutts. In 1881, he became M.P. for Westminster. With the marriage, Catherine lost a major source of funds from the lady she had so admired. A donor to Catherine's charities had told her on 27th October 1851, "Happy I should be to contribute my mite and follow you in any influence I may have elsewhere. There is a good Angel amongst us whose heart and hand are always open." For William's sake she could never approach the Baroness ever again.

The Baroness Burdett-Coutts died in 1906 and is buried close to the west door of Westminster Abbey. During her lifetime, she gave away over three million pounds. After her death Mr. Burdett-Coutts continued his wife's charitable works. Despite the enormous gap in their ages they were happy, but society never forgave the Baroness for falling in love with a man young enough to be her grandson.

Into power for the third time

Growing old as Catherine and Gladstone were, despite everything else, the correct use of power remained the dominant factor in their lives. As 1886 approached, the atmosphere in London became thick and hot with political passion. Old people declared that "our generation has not seen anything like it", and, much to the Queen's annoyance, Gladstone returned to power for the third time.

CHAPTER EIGHT

Death of a Soldier, Ireland, a Jubilee and Mrs. Gladstone Enters Politics

1886–1892

General Gordon

On 1ˢᵗ February 1886, Gladstone returned to power for the third time. The Queen told her secretary, Sir Henry Ponsonby, "The Queen does not in the least care, but rather wishes it should be known, that she has the greatest disinclination to take this half-crazy and really in many ways ridiculous old man — for the sake of the country."

She had been especially angered by the death of General Gordon, which had happened a year before. A brilliant soldier and something of a 'Boys Own Hero', he arrived in Sudan in February 1884. His orders were to evacuate the Egyptian forces from Khartoum, which were threatened by the Sudanese rebels. The city came under siege. In January 1885 rebels broke into the city, killing General Gordon. They cut off his head, placing it on display to be mocked. The public and the Queen blamed Gladstone for allowing the disaster. When he was given the news, Gladstone was staying with the Duke of Devonshire, in North Lancashire. At once he left for London. Whilst changing trains at Carnford Junction, to catch the London train, the station master handed Gladstone an unciphered telegram. It came from the Queen.

The Queen's rebuke was plain for every Tom, Dick and Harry

to see. *This news from Khartoum is frightful and to think that all this might have been prevented and many precious lives saved by earlier action is frightful.*

On his arrival in London, Catherine gave Gladstone his favourite meal of eggs and mutton chops whilst trying to persuade him not to attend the theatre, at least until the press no longer called him *Gordon's Old Murderer.* He told her he had booked and paid for the tickets. All she could do was to retaliate and say, "I am glad the murder has not caused you sleepless nights."

On 2nd March 1885, John Bright, wrote a note to a friend saying that he had dined with Mrs. Gladstone. After dinner, he sat for half an hour or more with Gladstone. They talked on Egypt. Gladstone said that "the sending of Gordon had been a great mistake. A man totally unsuited for the work he was to undertake. I never saw Gordon. He was appointed by ministers in town and I concurred, but I had never seen him."

Ireland

The seventy-six year old Gladstone must have dreaded his future relations with the sixty-seven year old Queen. Soon after midnight, on 30th January 1886, Sir Henry had delivered the Queen's commission, to Gladstone verbally, but edited. On receiving it, Gladstone began immediately to form his third administration. It was during this time that an old story began to circulate. One afternoon in November 1868, while Gladstone was cutting down a tree, a messenger arrived with a telegraph from the Queen inviting him to form his first premiership. He opened it, muttered 'very significant', and placed it back in its buff envelope. Gladstone looked around him and announced, "My mission is to pacify Ireland." As if it were an omen of bad times ahead with the Queen, the tree crashed down.

Twenty years later, Ireland still remained in turmoil. Now Gladstone was an *old man in a hurry*, with little time to finish his task. Catherine, sympathetic to Ireland, wrote to her husband from Hawarden on 3rd July 1886, their forty-seventh wedding anniversary. As usual she used a quill pen, for she had never bothered with new fangled objects such as fountain pens.

My own own,

We are away from each other but not in spirit. My mind travels back to the forty-seven years of blessed memory with a thankful heart. Thank you for all you have done, for all you are, and for the lovely example you have been to me, in sorrow, or in joy! And Almighty God strengthen and help you more and more, and lift you up continually, so that if further work and further toil and anxiety be yours, the same Hand which has so mercifully sustained you, may still lead you along the earthly path, until it leads to the Heavenly Habitation of rest and bliss, to the shadowless light of a full day.

Darling old thing, I long to give you such a kiss. We are just going to Church, and the best thing of all will be to pray for you, and to thank God for the extraordinary mercies which for forty-seven years have been given to us.

Till tomorrow
Your loving
Wifie.

Gladstone returned not only as Prime Minister but as Lord Privy Seal with the ambition to sort out the 'vexed question' of Ireland. Such was the strength of feeling concerning Home Rule that even the Duke of Westminster took down a Millais portrait of Gladstone hanging in Eaton Hall and flung it into the cellars. Some months later Catherine wrote, "Oh, can you believe it? We hear that the Duke of Westminster has sold father's beautiful picture . . ."

Throughout the controversy Gladstone remembered a conversation he had with Lord John Russell, who observed, "The true key to our Irish debates is this: that it is not properly borne in mind that as England is inhabited by Englishmen and Scotland by Scotchmen, so Ireland is inhabited by Irishmen." Gladstone was to cross swords with a protestant, paranoid, sleep-walking, Irish land-lord called Charles Parnell who could never forget the stories told to him by his American mother about the unrighteous English. He had terrified the Speaker of the House of Commons with his questions and Bright thought he possessed the eye of a madman.

Schlüter's story

Like many a twenty-first century prominent politician, security for Gladstone was a problem. During the Irish troubles so deep were the feelings against him that he received postbags full of threatening letters. The Home Office became concerned and appointed detectives to shadow the Prime Minister. Mary's maid, Schlüter, told the story of the evening when Gladstone, Catherine and Helen were due to be guests at nearby Soughton Hall, an hour or so before they were due to leave, a message arrived from the stables. The coachman had injured his hand badly and could not drive. As no one else could be trusted with the frisky pair of horses, Gladstone ordered the fly. It had been commandeered by the detectives!

Staying at Hawarden were Lord and Lady Aberdeen. His Lordship offered to drive the coach and the difficult horses. Willy said he would give directions and, pretending to be the footman, he jumped up on to the box with Gladstone, Catherine, Helen and Schlüter sitting inside. Gladstone had no idea who the coach man was.

As dusk fell Lord Aberdeen drove the coach and pair through the dusk and breathtaking scenery to Soughton Hall. On their arrival Willy, footman-like, jumped down from the box and placed the luggage inside the front door. Schlüter, overcome at being driven by a Prime Minster with Master's son acting as footman, wrote an account of the drive for Lady Aberdeen and ended, *Alas, the delightful Wonderland came to an end. Had I known I was to write this I would have had pencil and paper in the carriage.*

Your Ladyship's humble, Auguste Schülter.

The party never knew the view of their host, the Rt. Hon. Lord Justice, Sir Eldon Bankes. Perhaps he was amused. His forebear,

Lord William Bankes, was unconventional. Sixty years before, inspired by his travels to the near East with his friend Charles Barry, he had renovated Soughton Hall. In 1836, Barry won the competition to redesign the House of Westminster. To Catherine and Gladstone weddings took place in churches. They would have been shocked to learn that in the twenty-first century the Hall is a venue for fashionable weddings.

Mrs. Gladstone enters politics

A year later, against her better judgement, Catherine, too, entered politics. She was a woman of her class who regarded politics as unfit for ladies to touch, beyond their understanding and certainly dangerous to female morals.

Better health, communication, education, even the advent of the bicycle, made younger women consider themselves independent of men. With the development of the typewriter, a few middle-class women considered earning their own living. Some demanded the vote, which Gladstone thought unwise. On 11th April 1889, he told the M.P. Samuel Smith, "I have too much respect for the difference between the sexes to seek 'to trespass upon the delicacy, the purity, the refinement, the elevation of women's nature."

In 1870, Dr. Pusey, an Oxford don, friend of 'Lewis Carroll' and leader of the Oxford movement, complained of indecency in dress, "inexcusable in the young or middle-aged married woman, because in them it can hardly be to please their husbands! . . . I have known cases when persons without beauty or much sense have been attractive, simply by their freshness and simplicity!" Catherine may have considered Mrs. Pusey, 'quite plain'.

Independent Women

The occasional 'odd' woman considered becoming an M.P. Queen Victoria thought them all 'hussies'. Catherine, unconsciously independent herself, had no sympathy with such views. She was shocked when Mary persuaded her sister, Helen, to pursue an academic career. Feminist Mary might be but, as a Christian, she could not agree to her friends limiting the size of their families. Many of them produced fewer than five children.

As society changed its views on women, politics altered too. In 1883 the Primrose League was formed, with the aim of attracting Tory sympathizers to actively support the Conservative party. By the 'eighties' the Liberal party was no longer dominated by the great Whig families. Many had joined the Tories. Others were no longer interested in the ideals of the Liberal party. Less testosterone-led than the Tory party, the Liberal party attracted women. Up and down the country, women who favoured the principles of the party joined together to form associations. Bristol, York and Darlington saw the first associations. The Liberal Ladies of South Kensington formed themselves into a group, independent of the provincial associations.

The M.P. for Darlington's wife, Mrs. Theodore Fry, considered joining the groups together in order to start a national movement, i.e. the Women's Liberal Association. By 1886 there were fifteen independent associations, with a membership of 6,000 women. Many were in favour of Home Rule for Ireland. Few considered lobbying for the vote. Why should they? They had influence through their husbands.

On 27th May 1886, a Conference was held at 22a Queen Anne's Gate with Mr. and Mrs. Fry in the chair to discuss future progress . . . *This meeting strongly urges that those already existing should be further supported and enlarged with the special object of promoting a more extensive knowledge of Liberal principles amongst women of all classes, such as shall enable them to form sound opinions upon public questions.*

In 1887 a National Federation was formed which brought the groups together. Women's suffrage was not on the agenda. 'Dear Mrs. Gladstone' was invited to become the first President. Catherine, who had little time for women or committees, felt, for William's sake, she must agree. At the same time she was invited to become President of the Liberal Association. She muddled up the invitations and agreed to become President of the Liberal

League which had both male and female members. Confusion followed, causing embarrassment to all and sundry. Eventually, a notice appeared in the newspapers. 'Due to a clerical error, Mrs. Gladstone has agreed to be president of the wrong organisation.'

In February 1887 Catherine presided over the inaugural meeting of the Women's Liberal Association, held at the Hotel Metropole, London, on 25th February 1887. By this time there were forty associations and 9,000 to 10,000 members. Catherine nervously presided over the meeting. She was used to standing *on her hind legs* at mass meetings but not controlling them.

Her silvery, quiet voice could not be heard beyond the front few rows. She told a later meeting, "But, of course, Ireland is the subject that we are thinking of very deeply. Ireland is very near our hearts." The husband of one of the members, Mr. Charles Hancock, commented, "Mrs. Gladstone is no ornamental president," adding, "Of course, what I meant to say, not merely an ornamental president."

Mr. Parnell

Catherine told the members of the Women's Liberal Association "I have just come from the court. You know what court I mean." They did. The Irish landowner and leader of the Irish Parliamentary party, Charles Parnell was suing *The Times*. Gladstone described him as "the most remarkable man I have ever met". The newspaper was anti-Gladstone. It accused Parnell of approval of the murders of Lord Frederick Cavendish and Thomas Burke.

On 18th April 1887 the newspaper printed a letter seemingly signed by Parnell. It was dated 15th May 1882, and read; *To denounce the murders was the only course open to* us . . . *But* . . . *though I regret the accident of Lord Frederick Cavendish's death,*

I cannot refuse to admit that Burke got no more than his desserts. A handwriting expert had agreed it was written by Parnell but in fact the whole thing was a tissue of lies forged by Richard Piggott, an Irish journalist and pornographer. He betrayed himself by spelling certain words, such as hesitancy, inaccurately. Parnell, a well-educated man, would not have done so. Charged with perjury, Piggott fled to Madrid. As the police burst into his hotel room, he shot himself. The costs of the inquiry amounted to £250,000 and were awarded against *The Times*. Catherine attended every one of the court hearings.

The great event for the ladies of the Federation was the soirée held later in the week, on 7th November 1887, at Grosvenor Gallery, with Charles Parnell as guest of honour. Gladstone, probably to his amusement, found himself supporting his wife. He addressed the gathering with, " . . . it is with particular satisfaction that I find myself associated with my wife — the partner of fifty years, and any further years please God may grant to us." The ladies presented Catherine with a cameo of Gladstone as a commemoration *of the wifely devotion and the womanly help she has given to England's greatest statesman.*

The two men shook hands behind Gladstone's opera hat. Catherine thanked her friends, saying, "Women can do a great deal with gentleness, patience and kindness and charity . . . for you must educate your opponents and not quarrel with them — You can do a great deal for the cause you have at heart". Perhaps she was thinking of Ireland.

In December 1889 Parnell arrived at Hawarden at 5.30 in the afternoon. Gladstone had two hours' conversation with him. On 19th December the two men spoke for two hours more on Irish Government plans. Gladstone observed, "He is certainly of the very best people to deal with that I have ever known. I took him to the old castle. He seemed to notice and appreciate everything."

Major Barbara

Catherine struggled on, slightly deaf, smiling, shaking hands, opening functions and addressing meetings. Her presence added prestige to the Women's Liberal Association. On 29th May Eddie Hamilton observed, *that wonderful woman Mrs. Gladstone is frisking to London to attend a charity concert and a political female gathering.* In

February 1892, the woman who had inspired George Bernard Shaw's creation, Major Barbara, gained the majority vote at the general council meeting.

She was the suffragette and feminist, Rosalind, Countess of Carlisle. Her success meant that the Executive Committee promoted the parliamentary enfranchisement of women on the same terms as men.

She was unpopular, and nicknamed the Radical Countess. Her husband, the 9th Earl, supported her campaign for temperance but not enfranchisement. Even he must have been startled when she poured the priceless contents of the Castle Howard Cellar into its Atlas Fountain. Catherine had once spoken up for her, "There is something to like about Rosalind. And probably something to be done about softening her, I think." Catherine was probably the only person who thought so. Like her, the Countess had a large family, six sons and five daughters. That is all the two women possessed in common.

Catherine was expected to resign. She was now eighty, the other woman forty-seven. She stayed until Gladstone became prime minister for the fourth time. Then, and only then, she did not stand for re-election. She wrote to the committee, knowing that they would understand, *I have already enough on my hands, as much as I can do.* Lady Aberdeen assumed the Presidency and Helen joined the Executive Committee. Rosalind continued being involved, splitting the Federation in two. The Countess of Carlisle is remembered for presenting Thomas Gainsborough's unfinished portrait of a housemaid to the Tate.

Out of Power

In 1886 Gladstone joined the Irish Nationalists. The Bill split the Liberal party in two. It was thrown out on the second reading and, much to the relief of Queen Victoria, Gladstone's third term of office came to an end. On 30th July 1886 Gladstone arrived at Osborne in the Isle of Wight to tender his resignation. His place was to be taken by the wise, urbane, cultured and amusing man, Lord Salisbury. He appealed to the Queen, almost, as much as 'dear Mr. Disraeli'. She would have been annoyed to know that the waves of affection and patriotism, unexpectedly released by her Golden Jubilee, had helped to take Gladstone into power for the third time. The main purpose of this administration had been to deliver Ireland a reform which would grant them a developed assembly.

The Gladstones, at this time, were living on a 250-acre estate in Dollis Hill, near Willesden, in North London, lent to them by Lord and Lady Aberdeen. They used Dollis Hill for fifteen years, away from the centre of London where the aristocrats, the Rothschilds and the political world lived. The Duke of Devonshire lived in Park Lane, the Rothschilds around Piccadilly, Disraeli opposite Hyde Park, at No. One Grosvenor Gate, W.H. Smith in Grosvenor Place, Lord Zetland and Lord Salisbury in Arlington Street and Lord Northcote in St James's Place.

Most of the Gentlemen's Clubs were in and around Pall Mall. They were all close enough together to have discreet words. As Disraeli said, "One brief conversation is worth a dozen letters." To celebrate the Queen's forthcoming Jubilee in June 1887, the Gladstones organized a party shortly before the celebrations on 27th May. They invited colonials who were arriving in London for the Golden Jubilee. Unfortunately, Catherine sent out the invitations too late.

The few guests that did arrive sat out on the lawn, in a bracing cold wind, facing a 'mountain' of meat sandwiches. They were astonished to hear Gladstone say that, "In all my life, I have only eaten once in the House of Commons and that was because I was too tired to return here." Even the colonials must have heard of Catherine's housekeeping skills or lack of them. It was said that one evening Gladstone returned home tired, to find the house empty, the servants away and the cupboards bare. Only a sad-looking peach met him.

He could, however, always rely on a cup of tea. He wrote, with some feeling, *If you are cold, tea will warm you. If you are too heated it will cool you. If you are depressed, it will cheer you. If you are excited it will calm you.*

The eccentricities of the Gladstones continued to be legendary. Eddy Hamilton recounted the story of how, late one night, on a mid-winter evening the couple drove through Hyde Park in a 'pea-souper' of a fog. They were going home to Dollis Hill five miles away. No one else was seen abroad, certainly not trying to attempt a five-mile journey. The two of them struggled on until, nearly exhausted, they managed to find shelter and collapsed before a roaring fire.

The Queen's Jubilee

The Queen, wilting under the return of Gladstone, must have been strengthened by the success of her Golden Jubilee in June 1887. She discovered her people still loved her and said with surprise, "Their affection will encourage me on my task, often very difficult task, for the remainder of my life." But this Victoria was different from the slim, lively Princess Alexandrina Victoria, who called out to the 'Two Pussies', "Are you coming to the ball?" Catherine had remained slim and beautiful. The Queen, on the other hand, had grown into a little, stout, widow woman, dressed all in black.

For her Jubilee she refused to wear the Imperial State Crown. "Too heavy", she said. Instead, she removed the white widow's cap with its long streams, to wear a tiny crown, made to fit on top of her mourning veil. Her black, silk dress was trimmed with white *point d'Alençon*. Rows of pearls hung around her neck. Covered in Orders on that June morning, the Queen stepped into her carriage to take part in the procession from Buckingham Palace to Westminster Abbey. It *stretched the limit of sight in both directions* in heat which was very great.

Queen Victoria drove through crowds so huge that the like of which had never been seen before. Flags flew from everywhere. The little lady, in the centre of things, showed no sign of wilting. Catherine noticed that as the party processed along the aisle, all eyes were on the little woman who walked alone and then, before the High Altar, sat on Edward the Confessor's chair — alone. It was Her Majesty who possessed the greatest presence. The Queen returned to the Palace amongst immense crowds and almost deafening cheering. A child asked her, "Oh, Grandma, does not this make you very proud?" "No, my dear child, humble, very humble."

However, for Catherine, the joy of Victoria's Jubilee was marred. When they were young, Gladstone always refused to attend grand, formal occasions. Now, as an old woman, she found herself still going alone to the numerous banquets, organized to celebrate the Queen's fifty years on the throne.

Another Jubilee

Two years later, on 25th July 1889, the Gladstones held a celebration of their own. It was their golden wedding anniversary. On 29th December, Gladstone would celebrate his eightieth birthday. Letters arrived and telegrams came from all over the world. Cardinal Manning wrote to Catherine, *There are few who keep such a Jubilee as yours: and how few of our friends and companions now survive. We have had a long climb up these eighty steps*. The King of the Belgians conveyed his warmest greetings.

People of all sorts sent presents. The Prince and Princess of Wales gave a large silver-gilt inkstand. Lord Rosebery sent a gold-topped walking stick for *the old parliamentary hand*. So many gifts arrived that some, to this day, remain stacked in the cellars of Hawarden. Queen Victoria sent a chilly telegram of congratulation, and refused Catherine's invitation to stay at Hawarden while she was undertaking a tour of North Wales. Instead, the Queen preferred to stay with the biographer of the Prince Consort, Sir Theodore Martin, near Llangollen. Catherine felt hurt. She thought they were friends.

As Parliament was still in session, Lord and Lady Aberdeen arranged for the wedding breakfast to be held at Dollis Hill. They supervised the meal, checking that sprigs of orange blossom adorned each guest's gold and white plate. Milllais's portrait of Gladstone with his grandson, Will, was unveiled, commissioned by the Liberal Women of Great Britain. In the evening, a reception was held at the National Liberal Club. A guest complained, "Mrs. G. got another hundred out of me."

A year before, one hundred and sixteen colleagues and friends presented the couple with a portrait of Gladstone by Frank Holl and a portrait of Catherine by Hubert von Herkromer, three massive silver cups and a signed address. Gladstone replied, "It is difficult for me to give any adequate idea of the domestic happiness I have enjoyed during the fifty years of my married life".

On 3rd August Gladstone and Catherine returned to Hawarden. Mary described the arrival of her parents as *most touching and overwhelming*. The village was decked with flags and arches of flowers. People processed and bands played. Feelings were so deep that, at about six o'clock in the evening, the villagers pulled the carriage to the Castle. As dusk fell, a firework display lit up the scene. In the flickering lights Catherine looked around her proudly. All her children were there, grown into good people, all happily married except Helen. She was so very clever. So was Catherine, but she did not go round advertising the fact, especially to dear William. She looked at him. He was no longer her Peter Pan but a slightly dishevelled old man. She wondered what would have become of his beloved Jessy. Probably, the girl would be the prettiest and cleverest of the lot. Catherine again looked around her, looking into the shadows, searching and searching. She was not there. Mary was not there. But why should she be? Wasn't she always with her?

As the old couple walked into the Castle, through the stone porch, a present from their family which replaced the wooden edifice, nicknamed the bathing machine, Petz, the Pomeranian, barked a welcome. Catherine took Gladstone's arm. He was frailer now but he could still walk twenty miles, chop down trees and address the House for over three hours. Loyal, sensible Schülter stood in the doorway to greet them. Modern villagers of Hawarden still recall the Golden Wedding of 'the great people'. As they entered the Glynne Arms, a fountain — a memorial of the occasion — faced them.

Dossie

On the 11th of March 1890, Mary gave birth to Dorothy. She grew into a pink, bubbly, curly-haired blonde toddler, who loved to sit on 'grand-pa's' knee. She was a photographer's dream. Up and down the country, photographs of the two of them appeared on kitchen mantles or grand sideboards. Recently invented, postcards of the two hurtled around the country. 'Dossie' was a great comfort to them both, especially as a year later, in July 1891, their beloved Willy died. In the following year, while Catherine and Gladstone enjoyed Biarritz, the childless Cardinal Manning died. Gladstone described him as a man 'where the flesh was extinct'. In his youth he had married but had remained celibate ever since his wife's death. They found around his neck a chain with a locket. In it was a miniature, of his wife!

The death of Parnell

It was the same year as Charles Parnell was named as a co-respondent. Captain O'Shea divorced his aristocratic English wife who had a long-time liaison with Parnell and three of her children were his. It is not known why O'Shea decided to divorce his wife. The air was filled with recriminations between those for Parnell and those against him. Contemptuously, many rougher men called his mistress, Mrs. Katherine O'Shea, 'Kitty', a nineteenth-century term for a low-level prostitute or an immoral woman. The couple married on the 25th of June 1891. Four months later Parnell had a heart attack and died in his wife's arms. He was forty-five. Some of the Irish vilified Gladstone because he had deposed Parnell. A Parnell supporter, Pierce Mahony told Catherine, "In the course of the last ten days expressions have been used, in moments of great excitement and passion, regarding Mr. Gladstone, which have given me great pain."

Catherine was in the Ladies Gallery when Parnell appeared; she

spoke about, "his sickening appearance, the astounding revela-
tions, the mixture of ability and folly, the contradictions in that
unfortunate man, the terrible throwing away of extraordinary gifts
. . . ". Gladstone was shaken when Parnell assured him, "I never
read Irish history."

A short rest

Fifty years before, on 6th January 1842, Catherine had declared
"I am thirty today — terrible thought!" At a dinner party on 5th
January 1892, friends looked at her, "Mrs. Gladstone eighty today.
What a marvel . . . !" That evening Gladstone was extraordinarily
gay. He gave his wife a present of silver. She tried to guess the price
and after the manner of wives, put the figure provokingly low.
Gladstone then put on the deprecating air of a tradesman with
wounded feelings. It was all great fun. When the laughter subsided
he returned to playing backgammon with his host. He never forgot
his 'Cathie' was a woman but sadly only ever saw the Queen in
terms of being head of state. A few months later, in August 1892,
Her Majesty was once more dismayed. Gladstone formed his fourth
and last administration. She continued to lament, "People are apt
to forget that the Queen is a woman — who has far more on her
hands and far more to try to mind and body than is good for any
one of her sex and age." Unlike Gladstone, Catherine's 'beast'
Disraeli never did forget.

This final administration was a minority Liberal government
promising Home Rule for Ireland. Gladstone was now eighty-two
years of age. He had spent the previous six years from 1886 to 1892
in opposition, finding time to happily study Homer in his refuge,
his Temple of Peace and sort out his 27,000 books. Catherine was
delighted. From the moment of their first meeting she had known
Gladstone was special. She feared his retirement, both for him and
for herself.

Once, she had written to Sir Henry Ponsonby, "I never can
make him think he is a great man." She never would, until an Irish
Parliament stood on Dublin's College Green. But Ireland

continued to be *squalid, dismal, sullen, dull, expectant, sunk deep in hostile intent!*

CHAPTER NINE

Winds of Change and Departure

1892–1896

The Fourth Premiership

On 15th August 1892, Gladstone returned to power. Appointed at eighty-two, he was the oldest person ever to serve as Prime Minister. He took on a job which was comparable to being a twenty-first century President of the United States. The Queen again expressed dismay. "It is like a bad joke", she said.

However, she did enquire sympathetically about Gladstone's encounter with a Welsh cow. Late in the afternoon of 29th August, Gladstone was attacked by a wild heifer wandering, like him, alone in Hawarden Park. Catherine wrote to the Queen, *Dear Madam, I hasten to thank you for the kind enquiries after my husband — it has been a miraculous escape and he has quite recovered from the effects of the accident. A Welsh cow which had escaped into the woods — actually rushed at him throwing him upon his back and then stood over him but he never for a moment lost his presence of mind. The cow has been shot.*

The Queen was not amused.

The cow's head is displayed in the Glynne Arms. Shortly after the animal's death, a wreath arrived at the Castle. It read, *To the memory of the patriotic cow which sacrificed its life in an attempt to save Ireland from Home Rule.*

Catherine was not amused.

In 1892 the villagers of Hawarden were entertained when the train companies ran thirty-two 'specials'. Over six-thousand people poured into Hawarden Park. They were all coming to the Summer Fête. The weather was sunny and warm. Mary laid out the

Golden Wedding Anniversary presents for all to see. Gladstone wandered around the flower gardens, *meek as a lamb.* All in all, it was a wonderful day. £1,200 was raised to rebuild Hawarden's Mechanics' Institute. The visitors spent well. Wooden chips from trees, cut down by the G.O.M., sold well. Then the multitude tumbled into the Glynne Arms, drinking the health of the 'Old Couple'. While the tills rang, the landlord raised his glass to wish "Mr. Gladstone and his lovely, lady wife, a long life."

The visitors to Hawarden may have sensed that 'the wind of change' was blowing throughout the land; certainly the Queen felt it, as did Gladstone. He understood that the trains which brought the visitors into Hawarden were a major reason for the profound change enveloping Britain, together with the competition from the developing industries of Europe and *the growth of that dreadful military spirit.* Gladstone and the Queen had one thing in common, they had both come to power as the Industrial Revolution came into its own and now they faced a world, not entirely to their liking.

It was with some trepidation that on 15th August 1892 Gladstone arrived in Osborne to kiss the Queen's hand. The two old people leant on their sticks as they exchanged pleasantries. Gladstone told Catherine, "The meeting with the Queen was rather like an interview between Marie Antoinette and her executioner." Gladstone could not sleep that night. He was kept awake by a maid of honour who strummed a piano, in the next bedroom, into the early hours.

Gladstone said, he "found the Queen slower in mind and her judgement unreliable." She thought him much older. *His face shrunken, deadly pale, with a weird look in his eyes, a feeble expression about the mouth, and the voice altered.* The Queen would have been dismayed if she had heard that Gladstone's physician, Dr. Clarke, believed, "He could live to be a hundred." *(The doctor died at sixty-seven, Gladstone at eighty-eight.)* The Queen was more complimentary about Catherine. In November 1892 she had written to one of her daughters, *She is wonderful — 80 and looks like 65!*

Changes

As the great world changed so did the private lives of Gladstone and Catherine. The birth of Mary's 'Dossie' had made Schülter lose face. She was a superior servant, well-mannered, neat, stylish, refined and knowing her place. Her duties consisted of looking after Madam's bedroom and dressing-room. As well as caring for her clothes, styling her hair, helping to bathe her and generally look after her lady's person, a lady's maid's expertise must include: dress-making, mending/repairs, delicate laundry-work, ironing and packing. The elegant dresses of the nineteenth century would need to be wrapped in tissue paper and packed carefully in massive, tin trunks. Instead, Schülter now found herself helping with the housekeeping and, at the same time, coping with new staff. She wrote in her diary, a *nanny looks after the wee baby who is very good. Cook seems nice, but the butler, I do not approve of. Our Castle is full of company, mostly family — Lytteltons, Talbots and Wickhams.* After a great deal of thought, in October 1898 Schülter left her beloved lady. Her last letter to Mary was dated 20th March 1917, nearly twenty years later.

They all missed Schülter. For twenty-two years she had been 'part of the family'. Mary was now occupied with her baby and had less time for her father. Agnes, the busy wife of the headmaster of Wellington College, had little time to spare, especially for a demanding 'Mama and Papa'. This left only Helen free. She had turned down the opportunity of becoming the Head of London's Holloway College, saying "I am not of immense use to my mother, at any time, but at least I am available." Mary decided not to ask the daughters-in-law for help.

As she said, "It takes a lifetime to learn how to live with her and it is really impossible for daughters-in-law, unless they utterly give up their own wills, which is impossible and would not be right."

Meanwhile, Stephen, as Rector of Hawarden, was becoming unsettled and Mary's husband, Harry, wished to move on. For six months Stephen struggled with a nervous breakdown and then

returned to his post. Harry, on the other hand, was offered a position for six months with the Anglican Church in South Africa. On
13ᵗʰ January 1894 he boarded a ship in Southampton and left
behind him Mary and his baby. Whilst Catherine and Gladstone
coped with these problems, Zadok Outrem, Gladstone's valet,
went missing. He had been with the family for twenty-five years,
promoted from being a footman. Gladstone and Catherine were
distraught. They blamed themselves for Outrem becoming an
alcoholic and having been forced to 'sack him for drunkenness'.
Ten days later, on 14th December, his body was fished out of the
Thames. Like Schülter he had been considered indispensable to the
smooth running of the household.

Catherine and Gladstone had lost the two rocks on which their
domestic lives were built. Nevertheless, the couple continued to
struggle on without them. In November 1892, when Gladstone
had been Prime Minister for three months, Mary needed him and
searched the West End of London for her father. Eventually she
found him at the Lyceum Theatre in the Strand. Mary looked up
into the flies. Amazed, she saw her father perched high up in them.
It would be a difficult climb for anybody but an incredible feat for
an eighty-two year old man with bad eyesight. The management
explained, "Mr. Gladstone had been offered his usual seat in the
wings but said he preferred to look down on the proceedings."

Gladstone's theatre

In 1892 the theatre's actor/manager, Sir Henry Irving, one of
Gladstone's greatest friends, ordered that Gladstone's special chair
was taken to the opposite side of the stage and re-upholstered.
Velvet curtains were placed around it to protect G.O.M. from any
draughts. Nicknamed 'the Governor', Irving oversaw every detail
of the Lyceum's management including sets, lighting, design and
casting. He even instructed a stage-hand to "make sure that the
roller curtain does not come crashing down and kill the Prime
Minister!" Like many theatre-goers Gladstone complained that
"acting is not what it was in my youth". Irving thundered to his

cast, "I want actors not dolls." Unusually for the nineteenth century he was accepted by society as a divorced man. The great Ellen Terry became his business partner and leading lady, playing opposite to his Hamlet as Ophelia, Lady Macbeth to his Macbeth and is especially remembered for her 'Quality of Mercy" speech in *The Merchant of Venice*. The audience never knew whether they were lovers or not! Gladstone campaigned for his friend to be granted a knighthood. In 1895 Irving became the first actor to be addressed as 'Sir Henry'.

A new lease of life

In February 1893 Gladstone introduced the Second Home Rule Bill. The battle gave Gladstone a new lease of life. Randolph Churchill considered that "the G.O.M. would probably reach his real prime about the middle of the next century". The Bill was passed in the House of Commons in September and rejected by 419 votes to 41 by the *dead batch of Peers* sitting in the House of Lords. Many Members of Parliament felt that the House of Lords was a comfortable club for the aristocracy and distinguished folk who no longer took an active part in life. Despite what the Queen considered Gladstone's eccentricities, Catherine's relationship with her remained warm. She received a letter from Windsor Castle, 7th May 1893. *Accept my best thanks for your kind letter and congratulations on the betrothal of my dear grandson George, with Princess Victoria Mary of Teck.* The Queen finished her letter, *It is, indeed, a very long time that I have known you. At York, in '35, I saw the two very beautiful Miss Glynnes and have not forgotten it. How much of weal and woe has happened since that time.*

The Princess grew into the formidable, toque wearing, much loved Queen Mary. George called her 'his darling little May'. Her family described her as "high-spirited, full of fun and up to any prank which we might suggest". When she died, Princess Marie Louise wrote in *My Memories of Six Reigns*, "We have lost the rock in our family." Previously, Mary of Teck had been engaged to Prince Albert Victor, Duke of Clarence and Avondale (Prince Eddy), the second in-line to the throne. They planned to marry late in 1891. On 15th January 1892, Catherine exclaimed, "I need not tell you the pang which last evening brought. I heard the tragic intelligence of Prince Eddy's death." He was not a physically strong man and died in the influenza pandemic of 1891/2.

Princess Mary sent a bouquet of orange blossom, to be placed on Eddy's coffin. A charming, gentle, attractive and non-intellectual man, he was considered by many to be mentally retarded. Queen Victoria, privately, referred to her grandson as 'dissolute'. There were rumours of a homosexual scandal which took place in a Cleveland Street brothel. Later, rumours abounded that Prince Eddy was Jack the Ripper, but no evidence has been found to support the claim. The Prince doted on his mother, Princess Alexandra. He wrote to her, *Darling Mother, I smelt some scent which you always use, and it made me so sad.* Gladstone considered the Prince's death 'a great loss to our party'. The 'great and the good' were considering making the young man Viceroy of Ireland.

Another letter from the Queen, dated May 1894, is especially poignant. *Thank you a thousand times for your kind letter of congratulation on the engagement of my charming nephew, the Cesarevitch, to Alix of Hesse, dear Alice's youngest daughter-they both seem very happy and I do hope that this union will be for their mutual blessing and for the welfare of our country.* Princess Marie Louis recalls saying to Alix, "You always play at being sorrowful: one day the Almighty will send you some real crushing sorrows and then what are you going to do?" In 1917, together with their children, the couple were shot during the Russian Revolution. George V had refused to grant his cousin asylum.

On each occasion that the Queen saw Gladstone he appeared frailer to her. He had told a member of his secretariat, "You have attached yourself to a corpse." Catherine too thought her Grand Old Man was day by day growing a little weaker, blinder and deafer. A cataract was forming in Gladstone's left eye but he refused to be deterred and had written to Catherine, *Your affectionate anxiety as to my eye may be fully allayed. It is I think admitted to be hardly if at all distinguishable from the other eye.* Age and ill-health caused him to be increasingly out-of-step with his colleagues.

In this his last administration Gladstone felt attacked on all sides. He unsuccessfully fought against the increase of expenditure on the Navy. Even Herbert opposed his father on this issue. On New Year's Day 1892, Catherine told Lord Morley, "I am pleased you have not scrupled to put unpleasant points to him, as he must not be shielded or sheltered as some great people are." At this time Catherine must have decided, "William needs me." In 1893 she wrote to Gladstone, *You never saw such a day, brilliant sunshine, clear views but I am longing to get back to somebody, Who can that be?*

Gladstone may have become more dependent on his wife and family but Catherine and her daughters were out of favour with his colleagues. For some time complaints were made against them: *Mrs. G and Helen waylay everybody, scheming this and scheming that, intercepting letters and almost listening at keyholes.* Herbert was now an M.P. and strode along the 'corridors of power'. Catherine relied on him to give support to his father. She wrote to Herbert, *each day I expect a letter for you from you for father, be very firm in it, for I do want you to be about his path and about his bed.*

But despite Morley's comments, none of Gladstone's colleagues dared to tell the Grand Old Man, "Sir it is time for you to retire." Catherine continued in her belief that, even as a wearied old man, her husband still possessed the greatest intellect of the age. There is a family story that a theological question was being discussed. An elderly lady remarked, "What a comfort it is that there is ONE above who will be able to tell us." Catherine smiled, "Yes, it is. William will be down in a minute."

On 14 December 1893 a colleague of Gladstone's, Sir Algernon West, complained, "Mr. G. is becoming more and more a mere tool in Mrs. G's hands, and she is less and less scrupulous about plans. If she wants Mr. G. to go away, he goes, regardless of public calls; and there is more and more spongeing on Armistead. It was Armistead to do this, and Armistead to do that, without appar-

ently any thought of the expense to which this good-natured creature was exposed." Dossie called Armistead *Mr. Pins*. An exotic
man, he was the son of an English jute manufacturer, living in
Latvia.

He was educated in Wiesbaden and Heidelberg. A wealthy
man, in 1843 he established the George Armistead Shipping Line.
As a close friend of Catherine and Gladstone, he accompanied them
on many occasions and offered the couple cruises on his ships. He
always footed the bill! Armistead had been the Liberal M.P. for
Dundee. He refused a baronetcy from Gladstone but accepted one
from Balfour.

On 18th December 1893, and this time with the Queen's
approval, Catherine, Gladstone and Helen accepted Mr.
Armistead's invitation to spend Christmas, Gladstone's eighty-
third birthday and New Year's Day with him in Biarritz. The two
men discussed many subjects including the possibility of a channel
tunnel. They dismissed the thought as impractical! During
January the party returned to England, very much refreshed.

On 9th January 1894 John Morley wrote to a friend, *I told her
the reign was over. And the only question was whether the abdication
should be now or in February. The poor lady was not in the least prepared.*
"In the background we could hear Mr. Gladstone playing
backgammon with Armistead."

On 27th February 1894 Gladstone sent his resignation to the
Queen. He gave as his reasons his great age, his deafness and blindness. Catherine thought he was forced to resign on a lie. When he
met the Queen she asked him to sit down. She did not offer him a
peerage and told him she would have done so, *but she knows he would
not accept it.* In June 1885, the Queen had written to Gladstone
saying that she wished to offer him an Earldom, as a mark of her
recognition of his long and distinguished services . . . *and she believes
and thinks he will thereby be enabled still to render great service to his
sovereign and country — which if he retired, as he repeatedly told her of
late he intended to do shortly — he could not . . . the Queen believes it
would be beneficial to his health . . . Only the other day — without refer-*

ence to the present events — the Queen mentioned to Mrs. Gladstone at Windsor the advantage to Mr. Gladstone's health of a removal from one House to the other, in which she seemed to agree. Gladstone told Catherine, "I was dismissed as if I were a tradesman."

Three days later, for the last time, Catherine and Gladstone visited Windsor. After breakfast on 3rd March, the Queen saw Catherine alone and wrote in her journal, *She was very much upset poor thing, and asked to be allowed to speak, as her husband, could not speak.* According to the Queen, with tears in her eyes, Catherine told her, "Whatever errors he might have committed his devotion to your Majesty and to the Crown was very great. She repeated it, begging me to believe her." The Queen said she did and *I kissed her when she left.* She wrote in her journal that *I was convinced it was the case, although at moments, his actions had made it difficult to believe.*

When Gladstone came into power for the fourth and last time, he said, "One fight more, the best and the last." Nobody else dominated the House as he had done for over half a century. On 1st March, the members knew that when the G.O.M. rose to address them this would be for the final time — an era was over. The House remained in respectful silence whilst Gladstone spoke on the Government of Ireland bill. He talked for over two and a half hours!

Dossie, brought by her mother to watch the great occasion, thought that "Grandpapa was doing his *nastics.*" In the afternoon Gladstone chaired his last Cabinet. He closed it by saying, "God bless you all" and left the room. His colleagues said goodbye to him with tears in their eyes. He referred to it as *the blubbering cabinet.* Gladstone had chaired five hundred and fifty-six cabinets. He would never do so again. On 12th March 1894 Mr. and Mrs. Gladstone left 10 Downing Street for the final time. Their carriage stood waiting at the door. Dossie wandered from room to room, singing 'Alleluia' over and over again.

In May, Gladstone had an operation for his cataract and a further operation was necessary in September. Catherine wrote, *When father has mounted his four pairs of spectacles, he will see by their aid the smallest print, distant views, and the human face divine!* But, like the Queen, in order to read the words he needed them to be written in very thick black ink. He was not forgotten; visitors came to Hawarden and Catherine and Gladstone paid visits. They called on the Prince and Princess of Wales and played with David, their baby grandson. He was the little boy destined to become the King that never was, Edward VIII.

The next year, much to Catherine's disappointment, Gladstone gave up his seat in the House of Commons. Mary had said of her mother she so loved *being inside the mainspring of history, and all the stir and stress and throb of the machine are life and breathe to her*. From then on Catherine became increasingly frail. Gladstone started to look 'wild' and both began to look untidy. The Queen asked Lord Rosebery to become Prime Minister. Gladstone and Catherine hoped she would choose Lord Spencer. She did not ask Gladstone for his advice.

In 1894, as Gladstone was being sworn in to be a Privy Councillor, he looked up. A portrait of Disraeli looked down on him. He knew he had beaten his rival's record. He had been Prime Minister four times and an elected Member of Parliament twenty-six times. The Queen had offered him a peerage, which he had refused, but he could never forget she had offered Disraeli a Dukedom and the Garter.

The tragedy of the Archbishop

In October 1896 a couple of old friends, the Archbishop of Canterbury with his wife, needed to recover from crossing the Irish Channel and invited themselves to Hawarden. They arrived on a Saturday evening, planning to attend Church in the morning. A Classicist, the Archbishop, Edward White Benson, had much in common with Gladstone, who thought Mrs. Benson the cleverest woman in Europe. The two men may have discussed the disestablishment of the Irish, Welsh and English churches, which Gladstone advocated and Benson opposed. On the other hand, they may have talked about the latest ecclesiastical appointment, where they usually agreed. On the morning after the Bensons' arrival, the two couples attended morning service. While they knelt to recite the confession the Archbishop collapsed from a heart attack and immediately died. Society was shocked both by the suddenness of the death and Mrs. Benson's subsequent behaviour. She enjoyed a close friendship with a former Archbishop's daughter, Lucy Tait. Despite Mrs. Benson having produced five 'unpermissibly gifted' children, the two women moved in together and shared a bed. The press of the day made no comment and the view of her family remains unknown. However, her two daughters became gay. One went mad and tried to murder her mother. A son had numerous breakdowns and another became a Roman Catholic! The youngest, Fred, E.F. Benson, created the 'Mapp' and 'Lucia' series about their exploits in the imaginary town of Tilling. Fred lived in Henry James' old home, 'Lamb House' in Rye, Sussex, where, it is thought, the tales are based. None of the children ever produced a family of their own.

On the following Tuesday, three days after his arrival, Catherine and Gladstone saw the Archbishop's body leave Hawarden Station to return to Canterbury, for burial. As the 'old couple' entered the Castle, 'its arms' seemed to close around them. Outside, the evening shadows lengthened. Mr. and Mrs. Gladstone clutched each other, for they knew, too, they did not have much longer to be together. Earlier in the year, on 8th January 1896, Gladstone had said to a friend, "I am not so much afraid of democracy or of science as of the love of money. This seems to me to be a growing evil. Also, there is a danger from the growth of that dreadful military spirit." Neither Catherine nor Gladstone could ever have foreseen the horrors of the Great War or how it would kill young William, their beloved grandson and heir.

CHAPTER TEN

Goodbye to Catherine
1897–1900

Final resignation

On the day after his resignation Gladstone left Windsor, and the Queen, to return to London. He travelled by the 'Council' train, the Privy Council having met in the Castle in the morning. In the afternoon he finished his translation of the *Odes* of Horace, dined with Lord Kimberley and began his new life. On 26th March 1897, Gladstone met the Queen for the final time. She was resting in Cannes prior to her Diamond Jubilee celebrations. Gladstone hoped that when they were all over she would abdicate. Princess Louise, Duchess of Argyll, the Queen's sixth child, was staying in the same hotel as the Gladstones. She invited them to take tea with her. After the meal the Queen, who was also in the hotel, sent for Mr. and Mrs. Gladstone. She shook hands with him, *which had never happened with me during all my life* . . . The Queen kissed Catherine and invited Mary to bring Dossie to visit her at Windsor.

On 6th May, Dossie met the Queen at Windsor Castle. A lady-in-waiting asked the six-year old, "Have you ever seen the Queen?" "Oh, yes, but she has never seen me." The Gladstones, who were deeply hurt by the Queen's refusal to visit them at Hawarden, were secretly elated when, on 10th May, the Prince and Princess of Wales invited themselves to lunch. As always, Catherine found the Princess of Wales as "dear as she is lovely". The couple brought with them the Duke of Westminster, his main topic of conversation being his newly-redesigned country home, close by Eaton Hall.

It is considered a masterpiece, one of Alfred Waterhouse's best. It cost over £800,000. Even for somebody as rich as the Duke, it was a staggering amount at the time.

As Catherine's mind was too vague to allow her to organize such a prestigious event, her children took over. Gladstone blamed his wife's condition on the bromides which she took for neuralgia. In the afternoon they started to climb up the hill to the old fortress-castle. Catherine walked with the Prince and Princess. Gladstone bounded on ahead, frisky as a three-year old. On reaching the bridge over the moat, Gladstone called out, "Shall we go to the top?" The Princess sprang forward, but gave a glance at Catherine for approval. She gave an almost imperceptible wink. Quick as lightning, the Princess replied, "Oh Mr. Gladstone you quite forget my poor leg." When the royal couple left, Mary wrote, *the bands played and the sun peeped forth and the orphans cheered and the old women waved, and they all went off in a general flourish.*

Gladstone made his last public speech on 2nd August 1897, to the Hawarden Horticultural Society. During that year, Harry obtained a parish. Mary, Harry and Dossie moved to Buckley, the next village — a rough, poor place in which even the vicarage needed modernizing. It had, however, a major advantage. It was close enough for Mary to jump on her bicycle and pedal over to see her parents. Some afternoons she brought Dossie with her to ride with Grandpa and Grandmama, who she called Dan-Dan in their Victoria carriage. Dossie recalled, as an old lady, that "when it rained the hood and the apron were drawn-up, we watched the puddles forming on the apron and waited to see which would be the first to absorb the others".

On New Year's Day a telephone line was installed, linking the castle to Buckley Vicarage. Catherine found it difficult to hear whether it was a man or a woman speaking. She still asked Mary, "What should I give Father for breakfast? He is so poorly," even though Helen was now in charge. As the only single daughter, she had left Cambridge to care for her parents. Gladstone continued to complain about an uncomfortable feeling in his left cheek-bone.

Eventually, cancer was diagnosed. The pain grew so intense that not even copious doses of morphine could ease it. However, he still took his daily drive and, if possible, worked at his desk throughout the hours of daylight and, before dark, took a short walk. But he could no longer get out of bed in time to attend early morning service. It was changed to compline.

Dan-Dan and Grandpa

Each day saw Catherine growing frailer. She still loved her thirteen grandchildren who so enjoyed being with 'Dan-Dan'. They remembered the faint smell of verbena clinging to her, her dresses belonging to a world long gone, a shawl draped around her shoulders and a lace cap sat on top of her head. But only Grandpa could recite, 'Fee-Fi-Fo-Fum, I smell the blood of an Englishman, Be he alive, or be he dead, I'll have his bones to grind my bread,' with blood-curling relish. She might have become somewhat vague in manner, but Mrs. Gladstone could still chivvy her guests to walk across the Castle courtyard and visit her ladies in the old House in the Yard. It was an unused property and had housed orphans and all manner of people. Now it provided a home for vulnerable, elderly ladies and Catherine said, "They become so lonely if nobody speaks to them."

Knowing he was dying, Gladstone wrote his will. He endowed St. Deiniol's Library with £30,000, and £10,000 to build a permanent structure. Harry, as Warden, received a salary for the first six months of £200. Gladstone allocated £10,000 to each son and his daughters were to receive £5,000 each. He wished a small monetary gift to be given to each of his grandchildren. Catherine would be left relatively comfortably-off. Mainly through the efforts of Gladstone, the Hawarden Estates had been restored to seven thousand acres, with an income of £10,000 to £12,000 a year, and able to support two hundred and fifty people.

His affairs in order, Gladstone agreed to Lord Rendel's recommendation to stay in the warmer climate of Cannes, which his friend felt would ease his pain. On 26th November 1897,

Gladstone travelled to Cannes to stay with Lord Rendel. On 29th December he celebrated his eighty-eighth birthday at Cannes. In February 1898 Gladstone and Catherine did not return to Hawarden but went to Bournemouth instead. It was in Bournemouth, on 18th March, Gladstone learned that he had not long to live. They were joined by Mary, Helen, Herbert, Henry and Lucy Cavendish. All of them were worried about Catherine's condition as much as by Gladstone's illness. Mary tried relieving her father's suffering by playing the piano to him softly for two or three hours at a time. On 20th March 1898, Gladstone returned to Hawarden to die. On 28th March Stephen wrote to Lady Aberdeen, *My Mother does not fully know yet. We dread the shock for her, and want her to understand gradually.* As he entered the train to return to Hawarden, Gladstone turned round and said to those who were seeing him off, "God bless you, and this place and the land you love." It was like a blessing.

The acute pain in Gladstone's cheek became worse daily and Catherine's mind continued to mist over. Gladstone prayed to God, *Lord be merciful and let me die.* On Sunday, 15th May, Mary told her father, "We are all going to church." He said, "To Church! How nice! How charming! Pray for me, Mary dear, and for all my fellow Christians, and all unhappy, miserable people."

Death of Gladstone

Four days later, on Ascension Day, in the early hours of the morning, Gladstone died. Stephen prayed for his soul and placed his missing forefinger in his left hand. Catherine had not left his room for two days and nights, and was with him when he died. Immediately, when the House of Commons heard the news, it adjourned. On 20th May, in the House of Lords, Lord Rosebery, speaking about Catherine, concluded, " . . . by her tender vigilance, I firmly believe, sustained and prolonged his years . . . I think that the occasion ought not to pass without letting Mrs. Gladstone know that she is in our thoughts today." Lord Salisbury proposed and Arthur Balfour in the Commons requested that the G.O.M.

should have a State funeral. Many years before, the philosopher Jeremy Bentham advised, "If you would gain mankind the best way is to appear to love them and the best way of appearing to love them is to love them in reality" which Mr. Gladstone had done and Catherine followed his example. Summing up his life Gladstone observed, *Swimming for his life, a man does not see much of the country through which the river winds, and I probably know little of those years through which I busily worked and lived.*

The family discussed the matter and agreed, "A State Funeral please, but simple." But who was to tell the Queen? Unlike Disraeli's death, Gladstone's death was not mentioned in the Court Circular. The Queen wrote in her diary, *I am sorry for Mrs. G.: as for him I never liked him, and I will say nothing about him.* She did, however, send a representative to his funeral.

She felt she was right to do so but wrote to her daughter, Vicky, *He was a clever man, full of talent but he never tried to keep up the honour & prestige of Gr. Britain. He gave away the Transvaal & he abandoned Gordon, he destroyed the Irish Church & he tried to separate England from Ireland & and he set class against class. The harm he did cannot easily be undone.* She concluded, *but he was a good & very religious man*

When the Queen heard that the Prince of Wales was to be a pall-bearer, she telegraphed him asking, "What precedence have you followed, whose advice have you taken?"

Whilst the country tried to adjust to a world without Gladstone, Catherine learned of a mining accident on the Hawarden estates. She ordered the carriage, slipped out of the Castle and insisted Mary drove her to see a young miner's wife, widowed the day before. Catherine was an old woman now, used to the sadness of life but the young were not!!! In the Bible did it not say, *the dead should bury the dead?* Gladstone would understand that a young, ignorant, poorly equipped girl, with her life before her, needed comfort. The living were more important than the dead!

On 25th May, tenants and villagers pulled a hand-bier. It was to take Gladstone's coffin from the castle to the church. At the railway station thousands stood bare-headed to say "good-bye". Many came from Manchester and Liverpool, and other manufacturing towns. Gladstone's body was taken by rail to London. He lay in State in Westminster Hall. On his body was placed a jewelled Armenian cross, a gift from the Irish. They would never, ever forget him. The final part of the journey was taken via Westminster Underground.

It would have amused him. Dossie, in her old age, remembered the ride through the City in the dark. "It was frightening for a child of eight, to see pavements crammed tight with thousands of people, all remaining eerily silent. Everywhere I looked I saw policemen on foot or horseback."

The funeral of William Ewart Gladstone took place on Saturday, 28th May 1898, at eleven o'clock. The mists in Catherine's mind cleared and she remembered she was an Earl's daughter, the widow of a Prime Minister and the greatest man of his age. She walked behind his coffin with grace and dignity. When it was all over, she asked, "May I shake hands with the Pall Bearers?" The Prince of Wales walked over to where she sat, raised her hand to his lips and kissed it. Lord Rendel, George Armistead, the Earl of Rosebery, the Earl of Kimberley, the Marquis of Salisbury, the Duke of Rutland and the Duke of York, later George V, followed suit. Gladstone was mourned world-wide: France, America, Russia, Italy, Greece, Norway, Denmark and the Balkan Provinces — all the nations that had struggled or were struggling to be free. Lord Morley states in his biography of Gladstone, *No other statesman on our famous roll has touched the imagination of so wide a world.* He concludes with an extract from a speech Gladstone made on 19th September 1877, to a group of schoolboys. *Be inspired with the belief that life is a great and noble calling; not a mean and grovelling thing.*

When Catherine left the Abbey her children took her back to Hawarden. By that evening she was once again in the castle. She stood quite still, listening. No footsteps came hurrying along the passage. The door did not swing open to show him standing there with arms wide open, waiting to hug her. Catherine had written to the Queen, *How I am to live without him, I can only leave that to God*. The clouds in her mind returned.

The Queen, remembering her own great sorrow, remained concerned about Mrs. Gladstone's welfare. On the day of the funeral she sent a telegram to Catherine. She concluded, *I shall ever gratefully remember his devotion and zeal in all that concerned my personal welfare, and that of my family*. On the death of Prince Albert the Queen had opened her heart to Catherine who replied, "*I always feel the desire to go to your Majesty whether in sorrow or in joy.*"

Nearly three years later, in 1901, during a bitter January night, the Queen died. The age of Victoria was over. Towards the end she had complained to an archbishop, "As I get older I cannot understand the world. I cannot comprehend its littleness. When I look at the frivolities and littleness, it seems to me as if they were all a little mad."

Catherine — alone

Towards the end of May, Catherine was strong enough to go to Hawarden Church to attend the dedication of the window designed by Edward Burne-Jones. Its blues and greens illuminated the scene of the Nativity of Christ, a present to Catherine and Gladstone from their children. A year later, Burne-Jones died. He had once told Mary that "London society is insignificant. It has its good side too, it is always wrong." When she told her mother, Catherine did not laugh.

For the remaining months of Catherine's life her children loved and protected her. In July 1898, Mary wrote to Eddy Hamilton to tell him her mother was bearing up *with wonderful fortitude, that her health was good and she was still full of interest in things . . . we go . . . near Felixstowe in August as she pines for the bracing air*. In the autumn of 1899, Catherine rented a house at her beloved Penmaenmawr, the place where they had spent so many family holidays.

During her stay she visited Penrhyn Castle for the last time. On 4th October, she cut the first sod for St. Deiniol's Library. The following day she watched as the Duke of Westminster laid the foundation stone. It was part of the nation's memorial to Gladstone. A few weeks later the Duke died.

In April 1898, while Gladstone lay dying, Catherine received a letter, at Hawarden, requesting for a young girl to go into the Woodford Home. Under stress, she put the letter on one side and forgot about it. She suddenly came across it again and sent it immediately to Miss Simmons who told a friend, "It seemed as if she could hardly reproach herself sufficiently for having overlooked the matter, and as if she would never be able to forgive herself if the girl should become worse because of the delay. I wrote on Saturday. *Today is Monday and she is here.* Even at such a time, I know Mrs. Gladstone will be delighted to learn that the girl has been admitted to the Home."

Catherine, fading fast, spent most of her time in the past. People read to her, over and over again, political biographies by Justice McCarthy and Sir T. Wemyss Reid, and sermons by Gladstone, the Revd. Wickham and the Revd. Harry Drew.

Catherine never left the Castle again. In May 1900 she caught a cold which developed into pneumonia. She drifted into unconsciousness for about seventy-two hours and then during the evening of 14th June 1900, at 5.40 P.M., she died. On 18th June the funeral took place of Catherine Gladstone, *being as private a character as possible*, in Westminster Abbey. By courtesy of the Dean of Westminster she was buried next to Gladstone, as he had requested. Mourners included friends from Woodford Convalescent Home, London Hospital, Newport Market Refuge, Hawarden Orphanage and the Women's Liberal Federation. The Prince and Princess of Wales were unable to attend. They sent a wreath to 'Dear Mrs. Gladstone'.

Her plaque reads: *Here are buried William Ewart Gladstone and his wife Catherine. The daughter of Sir Stephen Glynne, Eighth Baronet of Hawarden Castle.* No mention is made of her *genius for charity*. Neither does it say that she was offered a peerage in her own right, or that the College of Heralds said she was entitled to the Baronies of Percy and Poyning. Catherine preferred to be known, simply, as Mrs. Gladstone.

Eddy Hamilton summed-up Catherine's life. *She was unquestionably a remarkable woman, and very few persons have spent a more unselfish life than she did, in actually striving to do good to others in the kindest possible way. Her first consideration was her husband — how to spare him and how to advise him to spare himself. Her second consideration was the poor and the sick; and her third consideration her friends. She had considerable capacities. People were apt to make a joke of her but she always attained her end. . . . I remember Mr. G. once saying, 'My wife has a tidiness and order of her own.' He meant that if she had lost a letter she generally knew where she had lost it . . . She would say exactly the right thing when it was wanted to be said. From no one did I receive greater or more uniform kindness.*

Following her mother's death, Mary helped organize a memorial fund. In August, she dictated a letter to Dossie to send to the Queen. The ten-year old wrote, *Dorothy Drew's humble duty to Your Majesty: it would be a very great honour and privilege to receive a subscription towards the memorial: it is a Free Convalescent Home which Dan-Dan founded in 1866 and which has received since then between thirty and forty thousand pounds and people who loved Dan-Dan want to help the Home to go on. Dorothy will never forget her visit to Your Majesty at Windsor Castle and Your Majesty's loving kindness to her, and she feels very sorry now to think of the Queen's great sorrow and is her devoted subject, Dorothy Drew.*

Dossie received the same reply as her grandmother. "Her Majesty never gives to individual memorials." Dorothy did not pursue a similar career to her grandmother. She upset her mother when she was twenty-one by marrying "a rather common-place sort of man". Catherine would not have been so judgemental. She would have asked, "Is she happy? That then is all that is important. Life is not a fairy-tale. A Prince Charming rarely comes along."

However, for Catherine, in some ways her life was a fairy-tale. She was lucky. She found a Prince among men but, as Eddy Hamilton wrote to Mary, *without her the world has become a much duller place now.* We agree with him, don't we? We long to hear her calling out, "William, a need to be met. Come Locket. My Own, don't forget my diamond earrings." And we see her donning her bonnet, praying, setting forth: 'doing a Mrs. Gladstone.'

We miss her — don't you?

Bibliography

Atterbury, Paul and Fagence Cooper, Suzanne. *Victorians at Home and Abroad*. London: V & A Publications, 2001.

Battiscombe, Georgina. *Mrs.Gladstone, the Portrait of a Marriage*. London: Constable, 1956.

Benson, E.F. *As We Were, a Victorian peep-show*. London: The Hogarth Press, 1930.

Biagini, Eugenio F. *Gladstone (British History in Perspective)*. London: Macmillan Press, 2000.

Cassin-Scott, Jack. *The Illustrated Encyclopaedia of Costume and Fashion from 1066 to the Present*. London: Studio Vista (a Cassell Imprint), 1994.

Dawes, Frank. *Not in front of the servants, a Portrait of Upstairs, Downstairs Life*. London: Century (Imprint of Hutchinson), in association with the National Trust, 1989.

Drew, Mary. *Mrs. Gladstone, by her daughter*. New York and London: G.P. Putnam's Sons, 1920.

Fagence Cooper, Suzanne. *The Victorian Woman*. London: V&A Publications, 2001.

Fisher, Trevor. *Prostitution and the Victorians*. Gloucestershire (UK): Sutton Publishing, 2001.

Gooddie, Sheila. *Mary Gladstone, A Gentle Rebel*. Chichester (UK): John Wiley & Sons Ltd, 2003.

Hughes, Kristine, *The Writers Guide to Everyday life in Regency and Victorian England from 1811–1901*. Ohio, USA: Writers Digest Books, 1998.

Jenkins, Roy. *Gladstone*. London: Macmillan, 1995.

Magnus, Philip. *Gladstone, A biography*. London: John Murray, 1954.

Margetson, Sheila. *Victorian High Society*. London: B.T. Batsford, 1980.

Marlow, Joyce. *The Oak And The Ivy. An intimate biography of William and Catherine Gladstone*. New York: Doubleday, 1977.

Morley, John. *The Life of William Ewart Gladstone*. 3 Volumes, London: Macmillan & Co. 1903.

Pratt, Edwin. A. *Catherine Gladstone. Life,Good Works, and Political Efforts.* London: Sampson Lowe, Marston, 1898.

Princess Marie Louis. *My Memories of Six Reigns, Queen Victoria's grand-daughter looks back over eighty year of rich experience.* London: Evans Brothers, 1956.

Woodham-Smith, Cecil. *Queen Victoria. Her Life and Times, Volume One. 1819–1861.* London: Hamish Hamilton, 1972.

Index

CG = Catherine Gladstone, WEG = William Ewart Gladstone